Looking back, looking ahead

– land, agriculture and society in East Africa
A Festschrift for Kjell Havnevik

Edited by Michael Ståhl

Nordiska Afrikainstitutet
The Nordic Africa Institute

ISBN 978-91-7106-774-6

Cover photo: Stuart Freedman/Panos
Photo of Kjell Havnevik: Elnaz Alizadeh

Production: Byrå4
Print on demand, Lightning Source UK Ltd.

Contents

Introduction

Michael Ståhl

This Festschrift is dedicated to Kjell Havnevik and his research.

Professor Kjell Havnevik is retiring from the Nordic Africa Institute (NAI) in 2015. For four decades, he has carried out research, taught and supervised students as well as participated in policy debates on different aspects of agriculture, the environment and African and international development policies. His output has been voluminous and is internationally recognised. His academic record includes research and teaching positions at universities and research institutes in Tanzania, Norway and Sweden as well as shorter assignments in several other countries[1]. Yet his intellectual home has over the last three decades been at the Nordic Africa Institute in Uppsala.

NAI has therefore taken this opportunity to publish a book mainly centred on development issues in Tanzania in the context of rural development in Africa – a theme that Kjell has pursued throughout his career. The book brings together research issues with which Kjell himself has been actively involved.

It is my hope that this will be more than a traditional Festschrift, inasmuch as it includes reflections on the academic and wider intellectual debate on development issues from the 1970s until today.

The book includes the following contributions.

Deborah Bryceson sketches the evolution of politics in Tanzania from the *Ujamaa* days to the present. Her focus is on the agrarian situation and she argues that the peasantry in Tanzania is unravelling and, indeed, that a process of "de-peasantisation" is under way. She starts by considering the agrarian idealism of the original developmental vision and then traces the subsequent trajectory of change, relying heavily on Kjell's and her own research findings. In so doing, she poses the question of how and why the original agrarian development aims were side-lined. Moreover, she considers how the economic and social coherence of the Tanzanian peasantry has been eroded over the past 40 years.

Stig Holmqvist provides an exposé of the eviction of the Barabaig people from their homeland. In the struggle for land, the losers are the pastoralists who insist

---

1. Kjell conducted his research at the Chr. Michelsen Institute (Bergen) 1975–1985; at the Bureau of Resource Assessment and Land Use Planning, currently IRA, (University of Dar es Salaam (1978–1980); and at the University of Bergen (1987–1988). He has been adjunct professor at Agder University (Kristiansand) since 2005. He was senior researcher at the Nordic Africa Institute Uppsala (1985–1987, 1988–1992 and 2005–2015 and professor of rural development at the Swedish University of Agricultural Sciences, SLU Uppsala (1996–2005).

on maintaining their way of life, grazing their herds over vast areas. As minority groups, they are marginalised and lack political influence. Both small farmers and large investors cast their eyes at this land. Stig follows some Barabaig families on their trek from the high plains of central Tanzania to various parts of the country and eventually all the way to the Indian Ocean coast.

Andrew Coulson contrasts the farming systems of small-scale farmers and large mechanised estates. He summarises the history of large and small scale farming in Tanzania, looking especially at the myths and misunderstandings that have been used by proponents of large-scale farming in Tanzania to suggest that small scale has little potential. His chapter concludes by reviewing the present position. The evidence suggests that many Tanzanians will continue to be small farmers for at least the next 20 years, and that they can produce surpluses of many crops.

Bertil Odén reflects on the relations between the government of Tanzania and the aid community during the period 2005–15. He provides a brief historical overview of aid relations from independence until 2005 before turning to the ensuing years, when the Paris Declaration principles to improve aid effectiveness were implemented. During this period development cooperation relations moved from euphoria to disappointment. His analysis emphasises the role of mutual trust in all sustainable development cooperation.

Aida Isinika and **Anna Kikwa** review to what extent land policies in Tanzania have been gender sensitive. They argue that individual titling is considered a way to strengthen land rights. However, implementation of land policies has mainly been gender-blind and failed to address the multifaceted relations between women and men, as if the society and households were undifferentiated. Land laws are interpreted against the background of customary law and religious practice, which include provisions that undermine women's rights. Advocacy for recognition of the rights of women in actual land deals is weak, since the women's movement in Tanzania has an inherently urban bias, and is therefore slow to react to rural concerns.

Rune Skarstein reviews the phenomenon of large-scale land acquisitions in Africa, often referred to as "land grabbing," which he places in the broader historical perspective of capitalist development by applying Marx's notion of "primitive accumulation." The process of land grabbing is discussed, with particular emphasis on its consequences for agricultural smallholders. He argues that the process of land grabbing in contemporary Africa is a form of primitive accumulation that will lead to injustices as well as explosive social conflicts.

Mats Hårsmar reviews how the ideological debates of the 1980s and 1990s over the primacy of economic growth or social development have today developed into a discussion about how economic growth should be framed in order to lead to social development. Linkages between the character of growth and social development are now more strongly pronounced. He reviews macroeconomic studies examining the character of current growth in sub-Saharan African countries and poses the question whether it is sustainable and can lead to structural change.

Opira Otto and **Michael Ståhl** discuss land tenure as a factor in agricultural development in the densely settled regions of East Africa. They review various tenure regimes and attempts to reform land policies as part of modernisation strategies. How can land-tenure reform help smallholders secure property rights and how can it boost agricultural productivity? Should one aim at full privatisation of land, including individual title deeds, or should one strengthen individual rights through customary arrangements?

Herman Musahara analyses Land Use Consolidation (LUC) in Rwanda in relation to its potential to achieve food security and agricultural transformation. The scheme has been instrumental in dramatically raising the yield of major food crops and in improving food security. Musahara analyses the LUC's prospects for achieving inclusive and sustainable development and what the scheme can learn from other schemes tried elsewhere, specifically in Tanzania.

Atakilte Beyene explores why large-scale land and water acquisitions in Tanzania and Ethiopia face similar challenges when implemented, despite the marked differences in governance systems. What common and/or differentiating attributes can be identified to explain the challenges in the current large-scale investment deals? The focus is on investment patterns and the rights and powers of local communities.

Terje Oestigaard analyses the concomitant spread of Christianity and of witchcraft and ritual killings in Sukumaland, Tanzania. Chieftainship has been abolished, the role of the ancestors has diminished and tradition is no longer important in culture and cosmology. Instead Christian churches flourish – as does witchcraft. The author analyses whether the declining role of ancestors is enabling the spread of both Christianity and witchcraft? How and why are witchcraft and Christianity as religious practices seemingly working perfectly well together?

Tekeste Negash's chapter stresses that education in Ethiopia is not contributing to the development of the country, because it is given in a language (English) that is hardly understood by teachers or students. Moreover, massification of education irrespective of quality and relevance continues to affect the development of the education sector. Education is important to development, but is not the only variable. The rule of law and protection of property are equally important. The author argues that Ethiopia will only get the added value of education if it changes the medium of instruction to Amharic and Oromiffa, the two major local languages.

Prosper Matondi traces the research by Kjell Havnevik in light of the current realities in Africa. Western television images show a continent plagued by drought and poverty. Yet, there is a need to understand Africa better, and Kjell has contributed enormously to this through his research on agriculture and smallholder farmers. It is necessary to focus on the role of agriculture and rural production in averting poverty and promoting economic growth. Matondi surveys the many challenges that African smallholders and rural producers face, challenges that Kjell Havnevik and his colleagues and students have long sought to research, understand and critique.

Michael Ståhl
Editor

Reflections on the unravelling of the Tanzanian Peasantry, 1975–2015 *

Deborah Fahy Bryceson

Introduction

Looking back to the 1970s, the decade when both Kjell and I arrived in Tanzania for the first time, one can't help being nostalgic for the optimism and vibrancy of academic debate and analysis that prevailed then, against the backdrop of a national government that was actively pursuing visionary policies and plans. At the time, the Tanzanian nation-state, having achieved its independence in 1961, was flourishing both economically and politically. Julius Nyerere, as father of the nation and president, set the country on an egalitarian development path aimed at eliminating ignorance, poverty and disease. While virtually all newly independent African states embarked on modernisation, there were a handful that embraced socialist objectives. Tanzania's "African socialism" combined traditional familial values with the objective of building a modern economy and polity (Nyerere 1968; Bryceson 1988a).

The story of Tanzania's political and economic rise (Cliffe and Saul 1973; Shivji 1975; Pratt 1978), then economic descent (Bevan, Bigsten, Collier and Gunning 1987; Msambichaka, Kilindo and Mjema 1995) has been documented in great detail and heatedly debated. The country's recovery is less well known and, indeed, some would question if there has been a real recovery (Edwards 2012). This article refers to Tanzania's undulating progression towards a very different society from what prevailed 40 years ago. And because this is a Festschrift chapter written in honour of Kjell Havnevik, who has dedicated much of his career to the analysis of Tanzania, I want to try to convey this Tanzanian story through the eyes of two researchers who lived and worked in Tanzania in the 1970s, namely Kjell and myself. We have shared the same starting point, witnessing a country whose economic foundations rested on a cash-crop producing and subsistence peasantry. Since then, both of us have contributed to the literature on the changing nature of Tanzania's rural economy, but from different thematic vantage points. Kjell has documented aspects of the peasants' use of natural resources, land access and environmental sustainability, whereas I have focused on their food security, agricultural marketing, the social dynamics of rural households and labour transformation. We have both researched

---

*   I am grateful to Kjell Havnevik and Chambi Chachage for their critical comments on an earlier draft, but the views expressed and interpretations of cited evidence in this chapter are solely those of the author.

aspects of non-agricultural income diversification and collaborated closely on dissecting the impact of Tanzania's and, indeed, Africa's neoliberal agricultural policy regime.

My aim in this chapter is threefold: first, to consider the agrarian idealism of the original developmental vision; second, to trace the subsequent trajectory of change, relying heavily on Kjell's and my research findings, posing the question of how and why the original agrarian development aims were side-lined; and third, to consider how the economic and social coherence of the Tanzanian peasantry has eroded over the past 40 years.

Based on Shanin's (1976) work, I define peasants in terms of four key criteria, namely: 1) *farming*, involving the pursuit of an agricultural livelihood that encompasses both subsistence and commodity products; 2) *family* labour and social organisation serving as the unit of production, consumption, reproduction, socialisation, welfare and risk-spreading; 3) *class* coherence, given external subordination to state authorities and regional-cum-international markets through which surplus is extracted; and 4) *community*, in terms of local village residence and adherence to a traditional conformist collective attitude (Bryceson 2000a). In the following, I schematically trace when, how and why the Tanzanian peasantry began to unravel. However, in view of the fact that the Tanzanian nation-state was originally founded on and designed with peasants' political, economic and social aspirations in mind, this topic warrants far more detailed analysis beyond the scope of this chapter.

Peasant Agrarian Foundations and Nyerere's African Socialist Vision, 1960s–1970s

When Tanganyika[2] achieved national independence in 1961 with the handover of power to Nyerere and his Tanganyika African Nationalist Union (TANU), it was an overwhelmingly agrarian country (Iliffe 1979; Coulson 2013). Ninety-three per cent of the population lived in the rural areas and produced their livelihoods in smallholder household units (Bryceson 1982, 1988b). Tanzania's main exports were coffee, cotton, tea and sisal. The first three were peasant-produced.

Tanzania began nationhood with a large youthful population. Nyerere's (1967) African socialist development strategy was informed by familial sentiments that linked localised tribal identities with a unified national identity. Nyerere's interpretation of socialism was Fabian and modernist in content rather than Marxist, stressing egalitarian values. Anticipating a proliferating occupational division of labour as the educational level of the citizenry improved, his aim was to set a precedent for keeping income and property ownership dispari-

---

2.   Renamed Tanzania upon the union of Tanzania and Zanzibar in 1964.

ties in check, as reflected in his Ujamaa[3] philosophy. Nyerere implemented a villagisation programme in 1973–74 with the modernising objectives of nuclearising peasant household settlement in villages where schools, health dispensaries and agricultural inputs and productive infrastructure for farmers would be on hand to boost peasant farmers' agricultural productivity (Boesen, Madsen and Moody 1977). The villagisation programme's coverage was not extended to the most densely populated highland areas of Tanzania, notably Kilimanjaro, where such services already existed. In some areas, over-zealous TANU party leaders were involved in the removal of households from one locality to another by force. The programme was disliked in some areas for that reason.

The corollary of this programme was follow-up delivery of these services by national, regional and local government. In the aftermath, a number of ambitious government development programmes were devised, which depended on state delivery by an efficient and disciplined bureaucracy. These included: the Universal Primary Education Programme, whereby all children were to be given free primary school education; the expansion of health dispensaries throughout the country; and a World Bank-funded National Maize Project (NMP). This programme was introduced in 1975 and raised peasant maize yields remarkably in Tanzania's poorest regions, Ruvuma and Rukwa (Bryceson 1993). Those regions, along with Iringa and Mbeya, became known as the "Big Four" surplus maize-producing regions of the country.

For academics at the University of Dar es Salaam (UDSM), the 1970s were years of intense debate about the nature of Tanzanian socialism, the state, party and national economic development (Coulson 2013). Marxists at "the Hill," as UDSM was called, felt that Tanzanian socialism lacked clarity and direction and failed to serve the interests of the poor relative to the ruling class (Shivji 1975). Others from the opposite end of the spectrum, less willing to publicise their views, complained that the Tanzanian state was too interventionist, particularly when its material interests were at stake. Some working in government were not enthusiastic about Nyerere's insistence on a Leadership Code. Nationalisation of urban rental properties, a policy that Nyerere conceded to appease the segment of the population keen on hastening Africanisation of the economy, was deeply resented by the urban Asian population, catalysing the exodus of 40,000 of their number (Aminzade 2013).

But above all, it was Nyerere's villagisation and agricultural "modernisation" policies that ignited debate at the university. Both Kjell and I were involved in gathering empirical data to ascertain what trends were emerging in peasant production and welfare. Although these were early days, the indications were that peasants were being provided with more services and infrastructure and

---

3. Translated as "familyhood."

the trajectory was one of improvement. Nonetheless, there were premonitions of difficult times ahead. The first oil crisis hit in 1973–74 amidst drought and the implementation of villagisation. Famine in the countryside was averted, but Dar es Salaam, increasingly dependent on staple food imports, faced food shortages. Fortunately, good coffee and food harvests between 1976 and 1978 allowed the country to bounce back, but this recovery did not prevail for long (Bryceson 1990, 1993).

Nationally and internationally, 1979 was a crippling year for Tanzania. The then president of Uganda, Idi Amin, attacked Tanzania, prompting Nyerere's retaliation. The Tanzanian army moved to the northwest front, commandeering lorry transport right at the time when the maize harvest was under way, causing a seeming "harvest failure" that year. Of equal seriousness and more long-lasting effect, 1979 marked a second oil crisis, causing non-oil-producing countries like Tanzania, with vast distances between its scattered peasant agricultural production units and Dar es Salaam port, to experience a serious rise in the cost of transporting their bulky peasant-produced export crops to port (Bryceson 1990).

Dashed Dreams: Global Market Realignment and the Dictates of Debt, 1980s–1990s

In the wake of the second global oil crisis, Tanzania's terms of trade declined precipitously. Foreign exchange earnings from farmers' export crops fell drastically while import requirements could not be easily pared back with the growing population and efforts to maintain production in the country's fledging factories. Financial loan assistance was sought from the International Monetary Fund (IMF) and the World Bank, but such help was only forthcoming with heavy conditionality (Havnevik 1987; Toye 1994).[4] Kjell Havnevik (1987) published the book, *The IMF and the World Bank in Africa*, one of the first analyses of the international financial institution's Structural Adjustment Policies (SAP). SAP served to deepen the economic crisis and paralyse African formal sectors in one country after another.[5] Despite the fact that most non-oil-producing, agrarian-based African countries faced the same economic fate vis-à-vis the vagaries of the world market, the World Bank and IMF blamed much of Tanzania's problems on its state-led development programme that encompassed ambitious state-subsidised crop inputs for peasant farmers and a large parastatal industrial sector (Wangwe 1987; Campbell and Stein 1992). It was the era of "Reagonom-

---

4.   Tanzania sought IMF assistance in 1979.
5.   By contrast, when the global financial crisis of 2008 occurred, Western governments generally reacted with inflationary "quantitative easing" policies and low interest rather than the deflationary, stringent cost-cutting approach of structural adjustment policies.

ics" and "Thatcherism," when economic thinking was dominated by Milton Friedman's and Friedrich Hayek's market-led theories of neoliberalism.

The World Bank, and especially the IMF, imposed SAP conditionality on one African country after another characterised by: 1) devaluation of the exchange rate, 2) severe cutbacks in state funding of social and productive services, 3) the reduction of the parastatal sector. Nyerere resisted acceptance of the World Bank's SAP with his famous 1980 New Year's speech in which he challenged the power of international financial institutions to interfere in the policy-making agenda of a sovereign state. For six years thereafter, lack of agreement on loan conditionality continued.[6] Nyerere considered the IMF's conditions economically punitive and politically unacceptable. The government implemented its own structural adjustment policy with the National Economic Survival Programme (NESP), which included devaluation, stringent government cutbacks and disbandment of poorly performing parastatals and the replacement of crop authorities with marketing boards (Bryceson 1993). But without supportive external finance from the IMF or from Western donors, who took their cues from the IMF, Tanzania's peasant production of agricultural exports plummeted.

Productive and marketing infrastructure eroded and peasant export-crop output became uncompetitive in the global market due to high transport costs to Dar es Salaam port and the removal of crop input subsidy programmes such as the NMP. Operations of the crop parastatals declined and many were gradually abolished, causing a reduction in the provision of productive infrastructure and services as well as crop-standards control. Smallholder agriculture increasingly lost its commodity production component and was characterised primarily by subsistence food-crop production. Meanwhile, agrarian communities experienced the decline of their health and educational services (Lugalla 1995). These trends marked the beginning of an abrupt unravelling of the peasantry.

The downward spiral was an outcome of a reinforcing negative chain of events and policies, beginning with the 1979 oil crisis. The implementation of SAP during the 1980s, in effect, precluded peasant recovery from that crisis (Gibbon, Havnevik and Hermele 1993). By removing peasant subsidies, cutting back drastically on parastatal marketing budgets, closing down crop marketing boards and crop grading facilities, Tanzania's key export crops – coffee, cotton, tea and cashew – stagnated or declined, notably coffee in Kilimanjaro and Bukoba, cotton in Sukumaland, cashew in southern and coastal Tanzania and tea in the southern highlands.

A similar chain of demoralising experiences took place with regard to staple grain crops, especially maize. The NMP had increased yields by 50 per cent in

---

6.   See also Odén, in this volume.

the years in which it operated (Bryceson 1990). It bore similarity to the Asian Green Revolution, which had succeeded in raising wheat and rice yields significantly, reducing the incidence of famine and creating grain-exporting nations. But these achievements resulted from sustained investment in crop yield improvement over several years (Havnevik, Bryceson, Birgegaard, Matondi and Beyene 2007). Tanzania's NMP was much more short-lived, though it had nonetheless succeeded in boosting the regional economy of the "Big Four" the seven years in which the subsidies were available.

After the retirement of Nyerere from the presidency, the new president, Ali Hassan Mwinyi, acceded to IMF conditionality in 1986 thereby releasing loan support, which provided some degree of relief to the beleaguered agrarian economy. Nonetheless, pressure from the IMF and World Bank continued to be exerted on the Tanzanian government to liberalise the border trade and for the country to adopt an open economy. Many other African governments were being directed to do the same during the 1990s, far in excess of countries in most other regions of the world. Neoliberal advocates argued that price deregulation and free market competition would result in the "right" input prices and higher producer prices for farmers, spurring them to increase efficiency, produce more and make investments to raise land and labour productivity.

Market liberalisation opened the floodgates to the expansion of the informal economy in rural and urban areas, which provided livelihoods, albeit on generally uncertain, low-pay terms. Staple food buying was liberalised and controls on retail trade were eased (Bryceson 1993; Bryceson, Seppälä and Tapio-Biström 1999). In view of the strong disincentives to agricultural production, vast numbers in the countryside took to trade and service provisioning to earn cash (Bryceson 1999, 2004). Often this involved all economically active members of the household. Male heads of household, who had experienced the erosion of their income from export crop production, searched for alternative income sources. Rural women and youth, who had hitherto been largely outside the cash economy, joined the scramble to help provide sufficient income for the households' basic purchases (Bryceson 2002a and b). In addition to trade and services, farmers started digging for gold and precious stones in mineral-rich parts of the country (Fisher, Mwaipopo, Mutagwaba, Nyange and Yaron 2009; Jønsson and Bryceson 2009; Bryceson and Jønsson 2010).

These spontaneous economic initiatives by rural household members were part and parcel of a process of deagrarianisation and declining coherence of the peasant household unit, which became socially fragmented and sometimes economically decentralised, as various household members took up individual cash-generating activities. Most households performed a varied portfolio of non-agricultural activities in addition to continuing to engage in basic subsistence agriculture (Havnevik 1993; Havnevik and Hårsmar 1999; Bryceson 2002a,

2002b). A family's spread of income-generating activities and constant experimentation with income diversification by individual members yielded income and security, much as farmers had previously varied what crops they planted and when in order to ensure they had some output regardless of weather and price volatility. Experienced traders or miners were the most likely to be able to accumulate wealth (Bryceson and Jønsson 2010). The widening of economic differentiation fragmented the social fabric of the community and eroded the peasantry as an identifiable class with common political and economic interests.

Paradoxically, these internal changes in the peasantry during the 1980s and 1990s were not generally emphasised in the social science literature.[7] The 1970s debates about the nature of the Tanzanian peasantry were largely forgotten. Most of the literature dealt with coping strategies under SAP cutbacks, with income diversification being the most prominent.[8]

What was clear was that Tanzania was forced to deviate from the political, economic and social foundations of the country's original agrarian base, forsaking Nyerere's visionary planning (Havnevik and Isinika 2010; Bryceson 2010) and was to follow rather than lead the way in development policy, accepting the international financial institution blanket policies of SAP and neoliberalism. National development policy was replaced with government stringency and anti-poverty projects, as people struggled to cope with their straightened circumstances, the deteriorating prospects for their age-old agrarian practices, and lack of access to improved agricultural production methods with the abandonment of government agricultural support.

Foreign Direct Investment and Mineralisation: Golden Future for a Few in the 21st Century?

In the new millennium, policy pressure from the World Bank and IMF has been directed at extending commodification to capitalist ownership – as opposed to customary tenure or state control – through "LIMP" (liberalise, marketise and

---

7. Forster and Maghimbi's (1992, 1995) edited collections provided a number of interesting rural case studies without contesting the meaning and applicability of the term "peasantry" to Tanzania's post-SAP rural farmers, amidst the proliferation of casualised labour in Tanzania's neoliberal economy of the 1990s. As Giblin's (1998:206) book review notes: "farmers across the country have seen their hold on land weakened and the departure of their young, who, despairing of making a living on the farm, flee to the urban informal sector."

8. Havnevik (1980) was one of the first researchers to identify the importance of income diversification for Tanzanian peasantries. In the late 1970s, he found peasants in the Rufiji river valley and delta resorting to non-agricultural income diversification in craft production, fishery and forestry. This could be explained by the historical uncertainty of flooding cycles in the delta, proximity to Dar es Salaam as a market for craft production, and for work migration and, above all, the environmental displacement Rufiji peasants experienced after villagisation in their new settlements on higher ground in the Rufiji valley away from the flood plain they were accustomed to.

privatise). They have exhorted the Tanzanian government to maximise foreign capital investment in the country with a specific focus on land and natural resource markets. Certainly, foreign direct investment has been on an upward trajectory, almost all targeted at the extractive industry in response to the rising price of gold and other valuable metals and precious stones. The Land Policy of 1995 and new Mining Act of 2010 have both served to encourage foreign investment. But has this period intensified the unravelling of the peasantry? This section explores the tendencies towards concentration of control of natural resources and land and their effects on rural farmers.

Rush for Mineral Resources

Mineralisation of the Tanzanian economy has been very pronounced from a base of almost no mineral production in 1990 to mineral export dominance a mere 20 years later. The early stages of mineralisation provided opportunities for people, mostly men, to enter artisanal mining. Artisanal mining sites now dot most regions of the country, but a preponderant majority have been gold sites located along the contours of the East African Rift Valley in what we refer to as Tanzania's "ring of gold" (Bryceson, Jønsson, Kinabo and Shand 2012).

In the late 1990s, new mining legislation was passed seemingly giving scope to the artisanal mining sector, but at the same time clearing the way for substantial foreign mining investment (Butler 2004). This catalysed mineral exports from large-scale gold mining companies, which rose from less than 1 per cent of export revenues in the late 1990s to 50 per cent in 2005 (World Bank 2006). However, the legislation weakened the artisanal miners' position, leaving them to compete with international mining companies for access to minerals (Bourgouin 2014; Lange 2008).

Heavy criticism of the government's administration of the country's natural resource base ensued. The main issues were unjust resettlement schemes for farmers, coercion directed at artisanal miners and limited national benefits from large-scale mining. Exploration and mining companies working in mineral-rich areas, where artisanal miners had already been mining for decades, were seen to be displacing artisanal miners. Lange (2006) estimated their numbers to have declined to 170,000 in 2006, whereas the government maintained that artisanal miner numbers were above one million (Hayes 2008).

Currently, the Tanzanian mining sector encompasses one medium-scale and six large-scale gold mines, with a number of proposed gold mining projects in the pipeline. Tanzania also has one of the world's most advanced gemstone mines extracting tanzanite. Williamson Diamond Mine, operating since the 1940s, was taken over by De Beers and then sold to Petra Diamonds in 2008, and is still producing. Moreover, there are in the pipeline nine preparation projects targeting uranium, coal and nickel. Mining "juniors," small and medium-sized exploration companies with a high skills base and professionalised management structure often abroad, are present in Tanzania. However, by far the largest proportion of miners is artisanal.

Artisanal mining's impact on the peasantry since 2000 is largely one of deflecting labour away from peasant household agricultural production. Such mining is far more remunerative, and has attracted ambitious and generally young men into the mining settlements, to which young women quickly follow. The inter-census period between 1978 and 1988 revealed that Mwanza's, Shinyanga's and Mbeya's small towns witnessed higher rates of urbanisation as people flocked to these urban settlements, whose rapid growth was catalysed by mineral discovery (Bryceson 2010, 2011, Bryceson, Jønsson, Kinabo and Shand 2012). Most, but not all, of Tanzania's artisanal miners originated in the rural areas.

Second, a minority of Tanzanian artisanal miners managed to save and accumulate on the basis of their involvement in mineral extraction, especially in the gold sector. Many of them invested in transport, hotels and various businesses in nearby regional towns, rather than returning to their rural areas to retire. They represent a broadening of the urban capitalist middle class beyond the capital city Dar es Salaam.

Other miners returned home to their rural areas, especially those who failed to make a living in mining. Their return to agriculture, often involving embarrassment and regret that they had not succeeded, points to the central significance of smallholder agriculture as a subsistence fall-back for those who have failed to maintain a non-agricultural livelihood and for older people and others who prefer not to risk seeking work beyond the natal household context. This must be borne in mind with respect to the issue of land commodification.

Land Commodification: Towards Marginalising and Dispossessing Peasants

Tanzania's land area amounts to 885,800 square kilometres of which an estimated 340,000 is agricultural land with 90,000 square kilometres considered arable (World Bank 2015). According to the Land Policy of 1995, only 10 per cent of Tanzania land was under cultivation, with 93 per cent being cultivated by smallholders, and only 7 per cent under large-scale farming. Vast tracts are under state control, with 233,300 square kilometres of wildlife-protected land. The game parks alone cover 42,000 square kilometres (Ministry of Natural Resources 2015). Tanzania's approximately 12,000 village councils manage about 70 per cent of the nation's land on behalf of the state (the Commissioner for Land). The remaining 30 per cent consists of about 2 per cent general land and 28 per cent forestry reserves, wildlife areas and game reserves.

It is useful to explore the background to the changing legal status of land in order to discern how land commodification is impacting farmers. Nyerere

(1958) very early on, in his paper Mali ya Taifa, signalled the need to restructure rural land tenure for the modernisation of peasant agriculture, with his sights set on replacing Tanzania's customary land law with government leasehold rather than freehold land (Sundet 2006). This suggests that Nyerere supported the formalisation of land tenure and assumed that the government would carry this out gradually through efficient and impartial bureaucratic procedures.

After independence, land tenure remained as it was cast during the British colonial period, retaining the distinction between statutory land law, which applied primarily to urban areas and non-Africans, as opposed to customary land law, applicable to rural Africans. The 1975 Village Act reframed this legal dichotomy with respect to rural areas. It established the village as the basic unit of local government with an elected village chairman, council and village assembly. The national government vested village land titles in the hands of the village council, which then issued sub-leases to villagers, granting them user rights, but without permission to sell land.[9] Villagers' land rights derived from the village government, which had extensive powers. Most of village land allocation during villagisation was extra-legal and this continued to be a tendency in the post-villagisation 1980s. Village chairmen and councils were apt to arrange land deals without consultation with or the compliance of villagers.

In the early 1990s, with rising confusion and resentment over peasant land rights, the government set up a nation-wide investigative Land Commission headed by Professor Shivji of the University of Dar es Salaam (Tanzania 1994a and b; Havnevik 1995). The Commission's findings revealed that rural people's land was vulnerable to state confiscation, justified in the interest of the public, as well as being affected by arbitrary and sometimes self-interested local-level interference by village chairmen and councils. The Commission advocated moving away from top-down colonial-style land management and national executive power over customary land matters. It recommended the creation of a Board of Land Commissioners and afforded the village assemblies a key role, whereby the village adult population was to be called together to vote on land allocation matters. The national government rejected these recommendations on the basis that land control had to remain in the hands of the national government for development purposes, and the Ministry of Lands rather than the prime ministers' office was vested with decision-making power (Sundet 2006: 8).

The ensuing Village Land Act of 1999 made some concessions to villagers, authorising village councils to issue certificates of customary rights of occupancy as a step in formalising property rights for farmers, which were to be registered at

---

9.   Stein and Askew (2013) document a move on the part of local rural people starting in Mbeya region in 2004 to formalise their property rights rather than remaining with customary rights, which were considered inferior to statutory rights and subject to reallocation by village officialdom.

a district land registry rather than at village level (Sundet 2005). The village as-sembly was accorded a consultative role with the stipulation that land allocations of the village council of under 250 hectares had to be submitted to the village as-sembly for a popular vote, whereas land transactions of over 250 hectares were to be approved by the Minister of Land (Chachage and Baha 2009).[10]

The Land Act of 1999 makes clear that foreigners are not allowed to own land in Tanzania, hence they access land through various types of leaseholds. The Act tries to avert a foreign land grab by stipulating that non-Tanzanian land holdings must be for investment purposes on the basis of leasehold "derivative rights," which will revert to the Tanzania Investment Centre at the end of the leasehold's duration. However, as Chachage and Baha (2009:10) stress, most land for allocation to foreign investors is land previously subject to custom-ary rights of occupancy and therefore constitutes "village transfer land," and they see the transfer of land from villager to external investors as a process of "divestment-cum-investment."

The major area of contention since the promulgation of the Village Land Act has been the government's interest in identifying unoccupied and unutilised village land that could be made available to investors (Stein and Askew 2009; Stein 2013a). During villagisation in the mid-1970s, in the absence of detailed surveys, village boundaries were contiguously drawn regardless of whether the land was settled or farmed, such that there was and continues to be reserves of land within Tanzanian village boundaries. But how much land is unused and unallocated is unknown and cannot be ascertained until detailed land surveys and land titling takes place. After more than a decade since the passage of the Village Land Act of 1999 had elapsed, the then Minister of Lands, Anna Tibai-juka, announced in 2011 that the government aimed to launch a land survey of the country's 12,000 villages. Her stated rationale was that such a survey would identify villages with extra land, with a view to ascertaining available land for investment, estimating that as much as 18 per cent of village land could be used for this purpose (Stein 2013; 2014). The aim was to recategorise unused village land as "general land" for external investment. Tellingly, security of land tenure for Tanzanian farmers was not mentioned, despite farmers' qualms about this issue. This situation invites comparison with the Enclosure Acts in England that Marx (1867) wrote about 150 years ago, involving large-scale privatisation and formalisation of rural land tenure and the dispossession of smallholder peasants of their common land. Marx identified this as a process of primitive accumula-tion centred on confiscation of the commons[11].

––––––––––––––––

10. Sundet (2006: 10) describes the outcome of the Tanzania's Village Land Act of 1999 as "tokenistic devolution of partial authority to village level" that he links to the devaluation of the customary traditional sector as opposed to the modern statutory sector.

11. See also Skarstein in this volume.

In fact, confiscation of land from the peasantry is not new. Under Nyerere, existing peasant farmland was acquired by the state for the creation of state farms as well as the reallocation of farmland under the villagisation project, all in the name of the public interest and national economic development. The emotive term "land grab" refers to the seizure of customary tenure or state-held land for transfer into private or corporate ownership on the part of foreigners or nationals (Chachage 2013). Early attempts at this were contested and labelled corruption.[12]

More recently, as the price of oil climbed in the first decade of the new millennium, affluent Western, Middle Eastern and Asian countries launched a worldwide search for farmland to produce biofuels (Matondi, Havnevik and Beyene 2011). The Tanzanian government, pressured to attract foreign direct investment,[13] secured a number of investor applications for leasehold land, prompting it to try to identify leasable land under the jurisdiction of village governments. Chachage and Baha (2009) and Abdallah, Engström, Havnevik and Salomonsson (2014) compiled lists of biofuel projects under discussion or under way, and provide valuable comparative information on biofuel investment over the last 10 years (see Appendix I and II below).[14] By 2009, out of 23 biofuel projects documented, approximately 617 square kilometres had been requested but less than half of that was allocated (283 square kilometres) and far less still, only ten per cent, became actual planted area (24 square kilometres). Five years later, in 2014, the project listing had increased to 33, which accounted for roughly the same amount of land requests (666 square kilometres), of which only 20 per cent became allocated land, and again less than 10 per cent was actually planted. Appendices I and II list these figures and the reasons the land was not allocated or used. In most cases, the potential investor abandoned the land requested due to hitches with the allocation procedure or because it was subsequently realised that the farming conditions (soils, rainfall, supporting infrastructure) were not conducive to a feasible investment.

By way of illustration, Havnevik and Haaland (2011) documented the case of Swedish SEKAB, a reputed energy company, which incurred a loss of 170 million Swedish Kronor, over 70 per cent coming from Swedish taxpayers' pockets, during the firm's Sida-backed attempt to produce biofuels from sugarcane in

---

12. This is exemplified by the Loliondo land case, which reached a point of intense contestation in the early 2000s (Igoe 2003; Ojalammi 2006; Nordlund 2013).

13. In 2012, the Tanzanian government, among other African governments, signed a cooperation agreement framework with the G8 and was supported by the African Union's Comprehensive Africa Agriculture Development Program (CAADP) to facilitate the acquisition by private investors of agricultural land for large-scale agro-industrial farming (Stein 2014).

14. It should be noted that there is no central registry where these applications can be scrutinised.

Tanzania. By 2009, 422,500 hectares had been requested and 22,500 actually granted. The SEKAB application for a derivative right of occupancy[15] had run into various hitches in the leasehold application system. Havnevik and Haaland (2011: 35) interviewed the SEKAB manager, who expressed his perspective on the land-leasing process thus:

> … the difficult nature of the process had by late 2008 led to the fact that "very few foreign investors have so far been given such derivative rights" … to access village land, the foreign investor and its local subsidiary … were urged … to visit Rufiji district and village authorities in order to identify and discuss the availability of suitable land. For a village to allow foreign investors to lease village land under derivative rights, the Village Assembly, constituted of all villagers above 18 years of age, has to give its consent. Discussions at village level, however, provide ample ground for misunderstanding due to language problems, cultural barriers and insufficient knowledge and information about local rights.

Above all, SEKAB encountered a number of agronomic and technical difficulties arising from its unfamiliarity with the agricultural conditions in the Rufiji district, where they were attempting to lease 400,000 hectares for the production of sugarcane. The volume of irrigation water needed from the river proved technically unrealistic, and the climate and woodland character of the land were unsuitable. In some places, the proposed lease land overlapped with villagers' targeted food production areas.[16] In effect, this investment was threatening to become a repeat of the infamous Groundnut Scheme of the late 1940s, when a large-scale British food production investment proved to be a short-lived fiasco given a miscalculation of the average rainfall in Nachingwea (Hogendorn and Scott 1981).

What the above evidence suggests is that villagers are not in imminent and widespread danger of being dispossessed of their customary landholdings by foreign investors. Many foreign investors are potentially interested to be sure, but the complicated nature of existing land legislation combined with the lack of surveyed land greatly reduces the possibility of investors being allocated leasehold land in secure ways. Even where they are, realisation of the harsh nature of the physical environment and the lack of infrastructure in Tanzanian rural areas leads many investors to abandon their plans to avoid heavy losses. Much of the unused land in Tanzania is in semi-arid areas where human habitation

---

15. A foreign company cannot own land in Tanzania, but can be given a user right or lease through the Tanzania Investment Centre, which manages leaseholds on behalf of the Commissioner of Land. On the basis of a leasehold system, a foreign company is given a derivative right of occupancy for a specified period and must pay an annual fee for the land.

16. The Swedish EcoEnergy took over from SEKAB and had further crippling operational and financial problems http://www.actionaid.se/en/tags/251/375 (accessed 31 May 2015). EcoEnergy is discussed by Holmqvist in this volume.

has historically been sparse and agriculture unpromising due to the inhospitable conditions.[17]

But the above does not imply that Tanzania has no land grab and that the rural commons are safe. Clauses of the Village Land Act provide opportunities for corruption on the part of government bureaucrats, who can acquire well-resourced village land (Section 4) and pass it on to private companies (Chachage and Baha 2009: 14). Tanzanian peasant land rights have yet to be made legally secure in most places, so land grabs by village officials are likely to continue.

Tanzanian land law is a potpourri of democratic sentiments, mixed with the legacy of an autocratic colonial and villagisation legacy carried out in the name of the public good, and unrealistic legal stipulations that cannot be met, given bureaucratic inefficiency and inordinate delays in surveying the country's village land. The vast majority of villagers do not have land certificates that provide them security of tenure and the gap between the country's land law and actual practice is wide, exacerbated by government administrators' lack of training, haphazard record keeping, procedural carelessness, including not bothering with third party validation and signatures on agreements, allocation bias on the part of the bureaucratic agents and lack of judicial oversight. All this creates a lack of transparency and a smokescreen for irregularities and corruption. Fortunately, the Land Rights Research and Resources Institute (Haki Ardhi), founded in 1994, and other NGOs advising villagers on their land rights, have mounted effective advocacy campaigns on behalf of Tanzanian farmers vis-à-vis the government for fairer land allocations where land is in dispute, but they too face the problem of bureaucratic opacity.

Unpredictable Pathways: Tanzania's Disintegrating Peasantry and the Nyerere Legacy

Primitive accumulation in Tanzania in the late 20th and early 21st centuries is distinct from the processes that Marx described for England in the 18th and 19th centuries as the industrial revolution coalesced. Marx (1867) defined primitive accumulation as a process through which the embryonic capitalist mode of production arises and extends itself while dissolving precapitalist production. In the process, peasants are dispossessed of their means of subsistence and means of production and land is concentrated in the hands of capitalist non-producers. It would be simplistic to think that the form this took in England necessarily repeats itself in other parts of the world through time (Bryceson 1980). In Eng-

---

17.   Gillman (1936) noted in the 1930s that two-thirds of the country's population was concentrated in only one-tenth of its land surface, primarily in the highlands, while over 60 per cent of the land was virtually uninhabited. One-third of the population eked out an agrarian livelihood in the country's central savannah land and coastal hinterlands.

land, people were dispossessed of their jointly held "common land" and individual holdings, causing many to migrate to find paid employment. Classically, land dispossession engendered labour displacement in England.

In Tanzania, a reverse process has taken place. Large-scale labour displacement has preceded land dispossession. Since 2000, the latter has been erratically taking place behind the smokescreen of the haphazard implementation of the 1999 Village Land Act. Prior to the Act, Tanzania's peasantry had experienced intense erosion under the stress of the international oil crises of the 1970s, SAPs during the 1980s and the neoliberal policies of the 1990s. As global terms of trade turned against agricultural commodity producers after the oil crises, Nyerere's plans for modernising agriculture and raising agricultural productivity following the villagisation programme's concentration of rural settlements had no chance of succeeding. The global capitalist economy struck a heavy blow to the viability of the peasantry at that point.

The peasantry faced disintegrative forces in several respects. To try to ensure continued access to their basic purchased needs, peasant households had to quickly diversify their income away from farming. In so doing, peasant households became far less coherent production units. Male heads of household faced a loss of livelihood as well as a lowering of their patriarchal position as they lost salience as cash earners within their households. Their wives and youthful offspring became income earners in their own right.

In the scramble for non-agricultural cash earnings, some individuals and households were far more successful than others. This was particularly the case for some artisanal miners who were able to accumulate and eventually to invest in non-mining assets, usually in the district and regional towns in the mining regions. Small town urbanisation accelerated remarkably (Bryceson et al. 2012). Using the definition of urban areas as populations of 10,000 people,[18] the size of population invariably entails a division of labour that extends far beyond agricultural production to embrace an array of trade activities, services and professions, and a multi-ethnic population where peasant and tribal customary ways of life and sense of community are out of place.

This period marks state attempts to woo foreign investors in terms of the country's mineral and land resources. Tanzania's "commons," the unutilised lands between the villages' contiguous boundaries, are now being contested.

---

18. The 2012 national census records the urban population at 30 per cent of the national total, but this understates the proportion of people living in urban areas due to the existing bureaucratic specification of urban populations as official townships and municipalities. This finding shows a strong bias against the acceptance of rural areas which have grown rapidly and transformed into densely populated urbanised agglomerations that are of township size. District officials are reluctant to relinquish such locations from their district jurisdiction, given that they constitute nodes of economic activity that have a richer tax base than the surrounding rural countryside.

While foreign land investment has yet to take off to any marked degree, it is often rumoured that officials in high places are benefiting from the mining boom and efforts to identify suitable land for investment.[19] Nyerere's vision of a democratic and egalitarian nation in which the poor masses benefited has become elusive. Most disappointingly, perhaps for Nyerere – if he were alive to witness it – is the fact that the government bureaucracy has long put aside its adherence to the Leadership Code.

Meanwhile, standards of state delivery of bureaucratic functions and services have deteriorated steadily since the economic crisis years of the late 1970s and 1980s, when the government became extremely under-resourced. Rumours suggest that private land ownership and natural resource investments by elite Tanzanians, notably those with strong connections with government, are widespread. National wealth is expanding, but is being disproportionally distributed to the private as opposed to the public sector. Artisanal mining has boosted class differentiation as miners with money gravitate to urban areas to build high-rise buildings for rental accommodation and expansion of urban business interests.

Where does all this leave the people who are living and farming in Tanzania's rural areas? First, further detailed analysis of the Tanzanian national census results for the rural population who are living in settlements of less than 10,000 people will probably show that the countryside is ageing, as youth migrate and leave older people behind to farm. Second, Tanzania's Labour Force Survey statistics are misleadingly being used to assume that most people in rural areas are still farming, whereas income diversification in rural as well as urban areas has progressed significantly (Bryceson 1999, 2002a, 2002b; Wuyts and Kilama 2014).[20] Most households have more than one non-agricultural income stream. Third, smallholders' agricultural work is primarily for basic subsistence needs. The drastic decline in export cash crop production per capita is a strong indicator of this.[21]

---

19. During Kikwete's presidency, a number of corruption scandals have resulted in cabinet reshuffles. The most recent has been the Escrow scandal in December 2014, which led to the dismissal of the Minister for Lands and Housing and the resignation of the Minister for Energy and Minerals, representing the key ministries with custodial care of Tanzania's privatisation of the country's commons.

20. The Tanzania Labour Survey only reveals people's stated primary and secondary occupations, which rarely reflects the actual allocation of their labour time across an assortment of work activities. People's default occupational identity is "farmer," but they are often engaged in several activities that are not agricultural but are difficult to convey, so the expedient is to simply state "farming" when asked.

21. Large-scale agricultural outgrower schemes are starting to boost export crop production, for example of cotton, but they do not constitute peasant production and are an outcome of large-scale capitalist investment of foreign or domestic origin. Unfortunately, Tanzanian agricultural production statistics do not distinguish between smallholder and corporate outgrower production.

The issue of subsistence brings us back to the significance of the land grab and the destruction of Tanzania's rural commons. I have argued that peasants' loss of village land is not a catalyst for a labour exodus, precisely because that has already happened. Tanzania's urban areas are bulging with youth and people of peak economically active age who are trying to eke out an existence primarily in the urban informal sector. Nonetheless, elite Tanzanians' or foreigners' encroachment on the village commons raises the possibility of obstruction to farmers' subsistence production. Clearly, agriculture continues to be the means of survival for the ageing rural population, but it has possible knock-on effects for people further afield. Vast numbers of people have migrated from their rural home areas but retain ties with their upcountry families that they are likely to draw on when they face hard times in the city or encounter a livelihood crisis wherever they may be. In the absence of a national public welfare system, reliance on a subsistence fall-back through extended household ties is their insurance against destitution. In other words, even though the land incursion may not affect their access to the means of production directly, it could indirectly jeopardise their means of subsistence.

What would Nyerere think now, and could it have been otherwise? The blow to the peasantry over the last two decades of the 20th century was profound. Global market forces have been steering Tanzanian peasants along a pathway towards oblivion. As with any unpredictable event, there are detrimental as well as beneficial effects. Certainly the scramble for non-agricultural income unleashed a great deal of creative energy as people sought new lifestyles and new occupations in the informal sector that offset some of the anxiety and uncertainty associated with the livelihood crisis of two decades of decline in peasant farming (Bryceson 2002a and b). For some, it led to improved standards of living and fulfilment of economic aspirations beyond their hopes, but for many others it has led to impoverishment and degradation that would have greatly disappointed Nyerere as an African socialist.

But Nyerere was, above all, a pragmatist who sought to bring modernity to his citizenry, and was credited with saying "we must run while others walk" towards that goal. He would have acknowledged that plans are bound to deliver unintended consequences. Though the country has strayed from his vision, if he were alive he would probably be pleased that despite all the setbacks and a population that had more than quadrupled since national independence, there has been remarkable progress in the health, education and welfare of the people. Overall, the benefits of modernity have been very unequally distributed. So "running" has succeeded in pushing the nation forward but, most importantly, the population that started the race in 1961 was radically different from that reaching the 2015 mark. There are still farmers to be sure, but not peasants in the classic meaning of that term. The crucial point, often overlooked, is that most Tanzanians are happy to be something other than peasants. A peasant is seen as someone with a traditionally ascribed occupation and lifestyle based on hard work and lacking in the comforts and opportunity afforded by piped water, good healthcare and schools. Nyerere's villagisation programme sought to go a considerable way in rectifying that. However, there continues to be a gulf between rural and urban infrastructure, convenience and lifestyle choices, as is generally the case in most African countries. Hence Tanzanians' quest for modernity is usually urban-bound. In effect, Nyerere's modernist vision and plans for the peasantry have ironically led towards the self-liquidation of that peasantry. In no small measure this has been spurred on by the policy interventions of the international financial institutions.[22]

As for the future, Tanzania's recently discovered enormous natural gas deposits are likely, when developed, to take the country ever further from Nyerere's quest for equality. By the time that transpires, the peasantry will be becoming a distant memory. But the peasantry should not be forgotten. The importance of Tanzanian scholars narrating the trials and tribulations of the country's thwarted plans, unexpected opportunities and its unfolding evolutionary and revolutionary paths towards a diverse, post-agrarian society cannot be over-emphasised. As for Nyerere's vision, it will inevitably fade over time, but his egalitarian, modernising aspirations as the country's founding father and the willingness of millions of peasants to embark on modern nationhood with him at the helm will remain an undeniable historical fact.

References

Abdallah, J., L. Engström, K. Havnevik and L. Salomonsson (2014) "Large Scale Land Acquisitions in Tanzania." In Kaag, M. and A. Zoomers, *Land Grabbing – beyond the hype*. London and New York: ZED Books, pp. 36–54.

Aminzade, R. (2013) "The Dialectic of Nation Building." *Sociological Quarterly* 54: 335-66.

Bevan, D., A. Bigsten, P. Collier and J.W. Gunning (1987) *East African Lessons on Economic Liberalization*. London: Gower.

Boesen, J., B. Storgaard Madsen and T. Moody (1977) *Ujamaa – Socialism from Above*. Uppsala: Scandinavian Institute of African Studies.

Bourgouin, F. (2014) "The politics of mining: foreign direct investment, the state and artisanal mining in Tanzania." In Bryceson, D.F., J.B. Jønsson, E. Fisher and R. Mwaipopo (eds) *Mining and Social Transformation in Africa: Tracing Mineralizing and Democratizing Trends in Artisanal Production*. London: Routledge, 148–60.

22. The eminent historian Eric Hobsbawm (1995: 355) has noted this tendency globally: "The case for maintaining a large peasantry in being was and is non-economic, since in the history of the modern world the enormous rise in agrarian output has gone together with an equally spectacular decline in the number and proportion of agriculturalists: most dramatically so since the Second World War."

Bryceson, D.F. (1980) "Primitive accumulation and imperialism in relation to the reproduction of third world peasantries." *Utafiti* 5(1): 95–128.

Bryceson, D.F. (1982) "Peasant Commodity Production in Post-Colonial Tanzania." *African Affairs* 81(325): 547–67.

Bryceson, D.F. (1988a) "Household, Hoe and Nation: Development Policies of the Nyerere Era." In M. Hodd (ed.) *Tanzania after Nyerere*, London: Frances Pinter, 35–48.

Bryceson, D.F. (1988b) "Peasant Cash Cropping versus Food Self-Sufficiency in Tanzania: A Historical Perspective." *IDS Bulletin* 19(2), 37–46.

Bryceson, D.F. (1990) *Food Insecurity and the Social Division of Labour, 1919–1985.* London: Macmillan.

Bryceson, D.F. (1993) *Liberalizing Tanzania's Food Supply: Public and Private Faces of Urban Marketing Policy.* Oxford: James Currey.

Bryceson, D.F. (1999) "African rural labour, income diversification and livelihood approaches: A long-term development perspective." *Review of African Political Economy* 80: 171–89.

Bryceson, D.F. (2000a) "Peasant theories and smallholder policies: Past and present." In Bryceson, D.F., C. Kay and J. Mooij (eds) *Disappearing Peasantries? Rural Labour in Africa, Asia and Latin America,* London: Intermediate Technology Publications, 1–36.

Bryceson, D.F. (2000b) "Disappearing peasantries? Rural labour redundancy in the neo-liberal era and beyond." In Bryceson, D.F., C. Kay and J. Mooij (eds) *Disappearing Peasantries? Rural Labour in Africa, Asia and Latin America,* London: Intermediate Technology Publications, 299–326.

Bryceson, D.F. (2002a) "The scramble in Africa: Reorienting rural livelihoods." *World Development* 30 (5): 725–39.

Bryceson, D.F. (2002b) "Multiplex livelihoods in rural Africa: Recasting the terms and conditions of gainful employment." *Journal of Modern African Studies* 40(1): 1–28.

Bryceson, D.F. (2004) "Agrarian vista or vortex? African rural livelihoods policy." *Review of African Political Economy* 102: 617–29.

Bryceson, D.F. (2010) "Agrarian fundamentalism or foresight? Revisiting Nyerere"s vision for rural Tanzania." in Havnevik, K. and A. Isinika (eds) 2010. *Tanzania in Transition: From Nyerere to Mkapa,* Dar es Salaam: Mkuki na Nyota Publishers, 71–98.

Bryceson, D.F. (2011) "Birth of a market town in Tanzania: Towards narrative studies of urban Africa." *Journal of Eastern Africa Studies* 5(2): 274–93.

Bryceson, D.F. (2012) "Unearthing treasure and trouble: Mining as an impetus to urbanisation in Tanzania." *Journal of Contemporary African Studies* 30(4): 631–49.

Bryceson, D.F. and J.B. Jønsson (2010) "Gold digging careers in rural Africa: Small-scale miners' livelihood choices." *World Development* 38(3): 379–92.

Bryceson, D.F., J.B. Jønsson, E. Fisher and R. Mwaipopo (eds) (2014) *Mining and Social Transformation in Africa: Tracing Mineralizing and Democratizing Trends in Artisanal Production*. London: Routledge.

Bryceson, D.F., J.B. Jønsson, C. Kinabo & M. Shand (2012) "Unearthing treasure and trouble: Mining as an impetus to urbanisation in Tanzania". *Journal of Contemporary African Studies* 30(4): 631–49.

Bryceson, D.F., P. Seppälä and M-L. Tapio-Biström (1999) "Maize marketing policies in Tanzania, 1939–98: From basic needs to market basics." In Dijkstra, T., L. van der Laan and A. van Tilberg (eds) *Agricultural Marketing in Tropical Africa*. Aldershot: Ashgate, 19–42.

Butler, P. (2004) "Tanzania: Liberalisation of investment and the mining sector analysis of the content and certain implications of the Tanzanian 1998 Mining Act." In Campbell, B. (ed.) *Regulating Mining in Africa: For Whose Benefits?* Uppsala: Nordic Africa Institute.

Campbell, H. and H. Stein (eds) (1992) *Tanzania and the IMF: The Dynamics of Liberalization*. Boulder: Westview Press.

Chachage, C. (2010) *Land Acquisition and Accumulation in Tanzania: The Case of Morogoro, Iringa and Pwani Regions*. Research commissioned by PELUM, Tanzania. Available at www.commercialpressuresonland.org/sites/default/file110406_Land_Acquisition_Tanzania.pdf (accessed 15 May 2015).

Chachage, C. and B. Baha (2010) *Accumulation by Land Dispossession and Labour Devaluation in Tanzania: The Case of Biofuel and Forestry Investments in Kilwa and Kilolo*. Exploratory study. Dar es Salaam: Land Rights Research and Resources Institute, Haki Ardhi and Oxfam's Pan Africa Economic Justice desk in Tanzania. Available at http://www.commercialpressuresonland.org/research-papers/accumulation-land-dispossession-and-labour-devaluation-tanzania (accessed 15 May 2015).

Cliffe, L. and J.S. Saul (eds) (1973) *Socialism in Tanzania*. Dar es Salaam: East African Publishing House.

Coulson, A. (2013) *Tanzania: A Political Economy*. 2nd edition. Oxford: Oxford University Press.

Edwards, S. (2012) "Is Tanzania a Success Story? A Long Term Analysis." National Bureau of Economic Research Africa Project. Available at http://www.nber.org/chapters/c13448.pdf (accessed 31 May 2015).

Fisher, E., R. Mwaipopo, W. Mutagwaba, D. Nyange and G. Yaron (2009) "'The ladder that sends us wealth: Artisanal mining and poverty reduction in Tanzania." *Resources Policy* 34(1–2): 3–38.

Forster, P.G. and S. Maghimbi (1992) *The Tanzanian Peasantry: Economy in Crisis*. Avebury: Aldershot.

Forster, P.G. and S. Maghimbi (1995) *The Tanzanian Peasantry: Further Studies*. Avebury: Aldershot.

Gibbon, P., K. Havnevik and K. Hermele (1993) *A Blighted Harvest: The World Bank and African Agriculture in the 1980s*. Oxford: James Currey and Africa World Press.

Giblin, J.L. (1998) Book review of *The Tanzanian peasantry: Further studies. African Economic History* (26): 296–308.

Gillman, C. (1936) "A population map of Tanganyika." *Geographical Review* 26(3); 370–2.

Gordon-Maclean, A., J. Laizer, P. Harrison and R. Shemdoe (2008) "Biofuel industry study, Tanzania: An assessment of the current situation." Report for the World Wide Fund for Nature. Available at http://files.theecologist.org/resources/E-INFO-WWF-TPO_Biofuel_Industry_Study_Tanzania.pdf (accessed 16 May 2015).

Havnevik, K. (1980) *Economy and organization in Rufiji district: The case of crafts and extractive activities.* Bureau of Resource Assessment and Land Use Planning, Research Paper No. 65, University of Dar es Salaam.

Havnevik, K. (ed.) (1987) *The IMF and the World Bank in Africa: Conditionality, Impact and Alternatives.* Uppsala: Scandinavian Institute of African Studies.

Havnevik, K. (1993) *Tanzania: The Limits to Development from Below.* Uppsala and Dar es Salaam: Nordic Africa Institute and Mkuki na Nyota Publishers.

Havnevik, K. (1995) "Pressing land tenure issues in Tanzania in light of experiences from other sub-Saharan African countries." *Forum for Development Studies.* No. 2. Oslo: Norwegian Institute of International Affairs, 267–85.

Havnevik, K., D.F. Bryceson, L-E. Birgegård, P. Matondi and A. Beyene (2007) *African Agriculture and the World Bank: Development or Impoverishment?* Policy Dialogue No. 1. Uppsala: Nordic Africa Institute. October. nai.diva-portal.org/smash/get/diva2:275867/ FULLTEXT01 (accessed 10 May 2015).

Havnevik, K. and H.S. Haaland (2011) "Biofuel, land and environmental issues: The case of SEKAB"s biofuel plans in Tanzania." In Matondi, P., K. Havnevik and A. Beyene (eds) *Biofuels, Land Grabbing and Food Security in Africa.* London: Zed Books.

Havnevik, K. and M. Hårsmar (1999) *The Diversified Future: An Institutional Approach to Rural Development in Tanzania.* Expert Group on Development Issues (EGDI). Stockholm: Swedish Ministry for Foreign Affairs.

Havnevik, K. and A. Isinika (eds) (2010) *Tanzania in Transition: From Nyerere to Mkapa.* Dar es Salaam: Mkuki na Nyota Publishers.

Hayes, K. (2008) *Artisanal and Small-scale Mining and Livelihoods in Africa.* Amsterdam: Common Fund for Commodities.

Hobsbawm, E. (1995) *Age of Extremes: The Short Twentieth Century 1914–1991.* London: Abacus.

Hogendoorn, J.S. and K.M. Scott (1981) "The East African groundnut scheme: Lessons of a large-scale agricultural failure." *African Economic History* 10: 81–115.

Igoe, J. (2003) "Scaling up civil society: Donor money, NGOs and the pastoralist land rights movement in Tanzania." *Development and Change* 34(5): 863–85.

Iliffe, J. (1979) *A Modern History of Tanganyika.* Cambridge: Cambridge University Press.

Jønsson, J.B. and D.F. Bryceson (2009), "Rushing for gold: Mobility and small-scale mining in Tanzania." Development and Change 38(3): 379–92.

Lange, S. (2006) *Benefit streams from mining in Tanzania: Case studies of from Geita and Mererani.* Report No. R2006.1. Bergen: Chr. Michelsen Institute.

Lange, S. (2008) *Land tenure and mining in Tanzania.* Report No. 2. Bergen: Chr. Michelsen Institute.

Lugalla, J.L.P. (1995) "The impact of structural adjustment policies on women's and children's health in Tanzania." *Review of African Political Economy* 22(63): 43–53.

Marx, K. (1992 [1867]) *Capital.* Vol. 1. London: Penguin Classics.

Matondi, P., K. Havnevik and A. Beyene (eds) (2011) *Biofuels, Land Grabbing and Food Security in Africa.* London: Zed Books.

Msambichaka, L.A., A.A.L. Kilindo and G.D. Mjema (1995) *Beyond Structural Adjustment Programmes in Tanzania: Successes, Failures, and New Perspectives.* Dar es Salaam: Economic Research Bureau.

Mwaikusa, J.T. (1993) "Community rights and land use policies in Tanzania: The case of pastoral communities." *Journal of African Law* 37(2): 144–63.

Nordlund, S. (2013) "The latest and greatest Loliondo land grab." Available at http://notesandrecords.blogspot.co.uk/2013/04/the-latest-and-greatest-loliondo-land.html (accessed 18 May 2015).

Nyerere, J.K. ([1958]) "*Mali ya Taifa.*" (English translation: National Property). In Nyerere, J.K. (1966) *Freedom and Unity: A Selection from Writings and Speeches, 1952–65.* Dar es Salaam: Oxford University Press, 176–87.

Nyerere, J.K. ([1967]) "*Socialism and Rural Development.*" In Nyerere, J.K. (1968): *Ujamaa: Essays on Socialism.* London: Oxford University Press, 106–144.

Ojalammi, S. (2006) "Contested lands: Land disputes in semi-arid parts of Northern Tanzania – Case studies of the Loliondo and Sale divisions." PhD dissertation, University of Helsinki.

Pratt, C. (1978) *The Critical Phase in Tanzania 1945–1968.* Nairobi: Oxford University Press.

Shanin, T. (ed.) (1976) *Peasants and Peasant Societies.* London: Penguin.

Shivji, I.G. (1975) *Class Struggles in Tanzania.* Dar es Salaam: Tanzania Publishing House.

Stein, H. (2013) "Land struggles in Tanzania: dispossession through formalization?," Paper presented at ECAS conference. Available at http://www.nomadit.co.uk/ecas/ecas2013/panels.php5?PanelID=2224 (accessed 18 May 2015).

Stein, H. (2014) "Formalization, Dispossession and the G8 Land Agenda in Africa." Presentation at Trinity College Dublin, Africa Event, "Imagining Land: Significance of Land in African Economics, Politics and Culture." Available at http://www.tcd.ie/tidi/assets/doc/Africa%20Day/Africa%20Day%202014%20Presentations/Howard%20Stein%20Presentation_Formalisation%20Dispossession%20G8.pdf (accessed 7 May 2015).

Stein, H. and K. Askew (2009) "Institutional transformation, accumulation and livelihoods in rural Tanzania: Land titling in Iringa district." AEGIS Conference Paper, Leipzig.

Stein, H. and K. Askew (2013) "Security, conflict and the formalization of property rights in rural Tanzania." African Studies Association paper, USA. Available at http://papers.ssrn.com/sol3/papers.cfm?abstract_id=2236947 (accessed 17 May 2015).

Sundet, G. (2005) "The 1999 Land Act and Village Land Act: A technical analysis of the practical implications of the Acts." RTF Draft. 1999_land_act_and villageland_act.rtf (accessed 9 May 2015).

Sundet, G. (2006) "The formalisation process in Tanzania: Is it empowering the poor?" Prepared for the Norwegian Embassy in Tanzania. Available at landportal.info/sites/default/files/theformalisationprocessinTanzania.pdf (accessed 9 May 2015).

Sulle, E. and F. Nelson (2009) *Biofuels, Land Access and Rural Livelihoods in Tanzania.* London: IIED.

Tanzania, United Republic (1994a) *Report of the Presidential Commission of Inquiry into Land Matters*, Volume I, *Land Policy and Land Tenure Structures.* Dar-es-Salaam: Ministry of Lands, Housing and Urban Development.

Tanzania, United Republic (1994b) *Report of the Presidential Commission of Inquiry into Land Matters,* Volume II, *Selected Land Disputes and Recommendations.* Dar-es-Salaam: Ministry of Lands, Housing and Urban Development.

Toye, J. (1994) "Structural adjustment: Context, assumptions, origin and diversity." In van der Hoeven, R. and F. van der Kraaij (eds) *Structural Adjustment and Beyond in Sub-Saharan Africa.* London: James Currey, 18–35.

Wangwe, S. (1987) "Impact of the IMF/World Bank philosophy: The case of Tanzania." In Havnevik, K. (ed.) (1987) *The IMF and the World Bank in Africa: Conditionality, Impact and Alternatives.* Uppsala: Scandinavian Institute of African Studies, 149–61.

World Bank (2006) *Tanzania mining sector review.* Report No. AB2029. Washington DC: World Bank.

World Bank (2015), *World Development Indicators.* Available at http://data.worldbank.org/data-catalog/world-development-indicators (accessed 9 May 2015).

Wuyts, M. and B. Kilama (2014) "Economic transformation in Tanzania: Vicious or virtuous Circle?" Special *Tanzania Human Development Report Issue*, Economic and Social Research Foundation, Discussion Paper No. 56.

Appendix I: Land Requested/Acquired for Producing Biofuel Crops as of 2009

	Investor	Crop	Location	Land requested (hectares)	Land acquired (hectares)	Operational project status	Planted land area* (hectares)
1	FELISA	Oil Palm	Kigoma	5,000	4,258	Land dispute in court for extra 350 ha obtained from 2 villages. No EIA done	
2	BioShape	Jatropha	Kilwa, Lindi	82,000	34,000	400 ha pilot farm planted. Integrity of EIA questioned	400
3	Sun Biofuel	Jatropha	Kisarawe, Coast	50,000	8,211	8,211 ha of land formerly belonging to 12 villages transferred to general land; derivative title being finalised	
4	SEKAB BT	Sugarcane	Bagamoyo, Coast	24,500	22,500	Seed cane planted and irrigation reservoir constructed	22500
5	SEKAB BT	Sugarcane	Rufiji, Coast	400,000	0	In land acquisition process	
6	Diligent Tanzania Ltd	Jatropha	Arusha; Babati, Manyara; Handeni, Tanga; Singida; Monduli, Arusha	n/a	n/a	Contracted over 4,000 farmers	
		Croton megalocarpus		n/a	n/a	Collecting seeds from natural and planted forests	
7	Donesta Ltd and Savannah Biofuels Ltd	Jatropha	Dodoma	n/a	2,000	200 ha planted	200
8	Trinity Consultants/ Bioenergy TZ Ltd	Jatropha	Bagamoyo, Coast	30,000	16,000	Surveying land to be granted	
9	Shanta Estates Ltd	Jatropha	Bagamoyo, Coast	n/a	14,500	Agreement with villagers signed	
10	Tanzania Biodiesel Plant Ltd	Oil Palm	Bagamoyo, Coast	25,000	16,000	Land not surveyed; land granted by district but not by TIC	
11	Clean Power TZ Ltd	Oil Palm	Bagamoyo, Coast	n/a	3,500	Project abandoned after realised high cost of doing land use plans	
12	CMC Agriculture Bio-energy Tanzania	White Sorghum	Bagamoyo, Coast	n/a	25,000	Land request approved but asked to do land use plans	

13	ZAGA	Jatropha	Kisarawe, Coast	n/a	n/a	Applied for land	
14	African Green Oils	Oil Palm	Rufiji, Coast	n/a	860	Planted 360 ha and financing land use plans in 7 villages	360
15	InfEnergy Co. Ltd	Oil Palm	Kilombero	n/a	5,818	Land lease pending. Cultivating rice while growing oil palm	
16	Bio Massive	Jatropha and Pangamia	Lindi	n/a	50,000		
17	JCJ Co. Ltd.	Jatropha	Mwanza, Mara, Shinyanga, Tabora	n/a	n/a	Aimed to sensitize local communities but project abandoned due to alleged lack of government support	
18	ABERC	Croton megalocarpus	Biharamulo, Kagera	n/a	20,000	No operational progress due to lack of funds	
19	Prokon BV	Jatropha	Mpanda, Rukwa	n/a	10,000	Contract farming with 2,000 smallholders; does not own any plantation land	
20	Mitsubishi Corporation	Jatropha	Arusha, Dar es Salaam, Coast	n/a	n/a	Looking for land in these regions	
21	Kapunga Rice Project	Jatropha	Mbarali, Mbeya	n/a	50,000	Planned to replant rice with jatropha; President recently ordered that rice cultivation patterns not be changed	
22	DI Oils Tanzania Ltd	Jatropha		n/a	n/a	Abandoned plans for Tanzania	
23	Kikuletwa Farm	Jatropha and Aloe Vera	Kilimanjaro	n/a	400	Growing Jatropha	400
	TOTAL			616,500	283,047		23,860

Source: Chachage and Baha (2010) compiled from Gordon-Maclean, Laizer, Harrison and Shemdoe (2008), Sulle and Nelson (2009)

Appendix II: Status of large-scale biofuel investments in Tanzania (2014)

No	Investor (year started production)	Crop	Area requested (hectares)	Area acquired (hectares)	Location	Operational project status	Planted land area (hectares)*
1	Sun Biofuels, UK (2007)	Jatropha		9 000	Kisarawe	Liquidated 2011, sold to Thirty Degrees East (Mauritius) in 2012	
2	Agro EcoEnergy, Sweden	Sugarcane	20,000	20,000	Bagamoyo	Seed cane production 200 ha, expecting financial closure 2013	
3	Eco Energy, Sweden	Sugarcane	400,000		Rufiji	Left the area due to e.g., lack of finances	
4	Diligent, NL (2004)	Jatropha	10,000	none	Arusha etc	Using only seeds from existing hedges, voluntary liquidation 2012, sold to Eco Carbon, France	
5	Prokon Renewable Energy Ltd, Germany (2007)	Jatropha	10,000	none	Mpanda, Rukwa	Only outgrower schemes liquidated in March 2011	
6	Felisa Ltd, Belgium/ Tanzania	Oil palm	10,000	100 + 4,258	Kigoma	Rumours about bankruptcy 2013	5,358
7	Africa Agrofuel and Emission Reduction Co. Ltd. USA/TZ (2007)	Croton Megalocar-pus		20,000	Biharamulo, Kagera	Land acquired, abandoned due to lack of funds	
8	Donesta Ltd and Savannah Agrofuels Ltd, Tanzania	Sunflower and Jatropha		2,000	Dodoma	Land lease pending 2010	
9	InfEnergyUK (2005)	Oil palm	10,000	5,818	Movmero, Kilombero	Switched to rice with new name: Agrica	5,818
10	BioMassive, Sweden (2006)	Jatropha and Pongamia	50,000	none	Lindi		

No.	Company	Crop			Location	Status
11	Bioenergy Tanzania Ltd	Jatropha	16,000		Bagamoyo	In the process of getting derivative rights 2010
12	Africa Green Oil, Norway/UK	Oil palm	10,000	860	Rufiji	Left land with palms or uprooted palms and departed
13	Kapunga Rice Project Ltd	Jatropha, rice		50,000	Mbarali, Mbeya	Renting land to smallholders 100,000 Tsh/ha/yr
14	CAMS-Agri-Energy, UK	Sweet Sorghum	45,000		Tanga and Handeni	
15	Trinity Consultants Bioenergy Tanzania Ltd	Jatropha	18,000		Bagamoyo	Surveying land (2010)
16	Shanta Estates	Jatropha	11,250		Bagamoyo	District authorities "not sure of existence" (2012)
17	D1 Oils, UK (2003)	Jatropha and Moringa oleifera			Kilimanjaro	Abandoned plans for Tanzania
18	Tanzania Biodiesel Plant Ltd	Oil palm	20,500		Bagamoyo	District authorities "not sure of existence" (2012)
19	CMC Agric-Bioenergy	White sorghum	25,000		Bagamoyo	District authorities "not sure of existence" (2012)
20	Synergy	Sugarcane	20,000		Rufiji	Has not appeared in district since 2010 (alleged lack of water)
21	Wilma, USA	Croton spp.			Biharamulo Kagera	Abandoned plans due to long land acquisition process
22	Mitsubishi Corporation, Japan	Jatropha			Arusha, Dar es Salaam	Abandoned plans
23	SAVANA Agrofuels Ltd	Sunflower and Jatropha	5,000		Handeni, Dodoma, Kongwa	
24	BioShape, NL	Jatropha	80,000	58,000	Kilwa	Ceased activities, still hold land lease
25	JandJ Group (Pty) Ltd, South Africa	Jatropha	20,000		Tabora	Abandoned due to alleged lack of government support

		Biodiesel crop				Abandoned
26	Kitomondo, Italy/ Tanzania		2,000		Bagamoyo	
27	Eurotech, South Korea	Jatropha and Castor oil	1,000			Planning to grow 100,000 ha and to invest more than US$ 20 million.
28	TM Plantations, Malaysia	Oil palm			Kigoma	
29	Sithe Global Power, LLC, USA	Oil palm	50,000			
30	Agri Sol Energy, USA	Corn sorghum soybeans sugarcane ethanol	320,000	14,000	Kigoma, Rukwa	Land acquisition in process 2010, abandoned plans for biofuels
31	Info Energy, UK	Jatropha			Mvomera, Morogoro	Switched to rice because of regional plan
32	Clean Power Tanzania Ltd	Oil palm	3,500		Bagamoyo	Abandoned due to high cost of land use planning
33	Biodiesel EA Ltd, Kenya	Jatropha	10,000		Bahi district	
	TOTAL		666,250	130,678		11,176

Source: Abdallah, Engström, Havnevik and Salomonsson (2014), 21-4.

Land cannot give birth to new land

Stig Holmqvist

Standing alongside Giamu Marish watching the smouldering remnants of his burnt-out house, I have the nasty sensation that history repeats itself. Nearly 40 years earlier, my wife Aud and I were gazing at Basotu Plains, a highland area in central Tanzania, where land was being cleared to prepare for a Canadian development project. The intention was to cultivate wheat on a large scale. This was supposed to be the flagship for other agricultural projects in Africa. It had the blessing of the Tanzanian authorities, including the president, Julius Nyerere, who took a personal interest in its development.

Giamu Marish now tells me that at that time, many years ago, his home was located up there on the plains. This land was called *muhajega* by the Barabaig people and it was considered to be the best grazing land.

"I was young then," says Giamu. "But I had two wives and three children and we had enough cattle to support our livelihood. We had a good life. There was water in the lake and honey in the trees … But one day the authorities came and told us that we had to move. We asked them why. 'Because you do not have any right to live here,' said the officials, who were accompanied by police officers. We explained that this is our land and that we Barabaigs have lived here long before the ancestors of these officials were born … But nobody listened. When we refused to move, they came back with big machines and drove them over my homestead. Then they set fire to everything."

Giamu Marish sighs, and silently watches the smouldering remnants of what was until very recently his home. There are an additional eight homesteads that have been set alight here in the open savannah landscape south of Lake Manyara National Park. But no one has been killed and the cattle have been rescued. Nevertheless, nine families now live like refugees among Fever Trees and sparsely growing palms. It is a woeful sight. Scattered household utensils (pots and pans, skins, calabashes and cloth) are hanging on branches in the shade of the trees.

Several naked children are staring at me, but nobody is afraid. On the contrary, they approach me politely and bow their heads, as one is supposed to do when greeting an elder. Somebody even dares to pass his hand over the hairs of my arm. All the dogs seem to have escaped the fire unscathed, at least a dozen lie stretched out on the ground, panting in the heat.

One of the older women, Dagabonga, who has a furrowed face, approaches me. "You can see how we are doing now! We live like wild animals. We live like the hyenas that come here at night … But even the hyenas have a home to return to when they want to sleep!"

She points to her grey hair. "Do you think my hair got this colour because I have slept in the sun? No! I'll tell you. All our problems started the year the French investor arrived. Before then we lived in peace. I have given birth to my children here. I have worked hard all my life. And now all is gone. Look around, this is all we have got left …What are we supposed to do? No one pays any attention to us, no one respects us."

Dagabonga is interrupted by a younger woman, who turns to me almost furiously: "Why is it that only you have come? Why did you not bring the president along? We want to see him here! Only he can do something about our situation. We won our case in court! Duncan helped us with that."

The young woman is right. A few months ago the Barabaigs here in Vilima Vitatu won a victory in the Court of Appeal of Tanzania with the help of a daring lawyer in a case that had been dragging on for five years. They had lost in the lower courts but now had triumphed in the highest instance.

But despite the final verdict, local authorities and the French investor seem not to care. They still try to chase away the families. If nothing else works, they are prepared to use brute force.

To me, it is incredible that the French investor would want to expel the locals who have lived here for so long. In 2008, he acquired, under strange circumstances, a concession to build a few exclusive tourist resorts. I think it is obvious that tourists would welcome the possibility of visiting the authentic homes of the original people after viewing the game.

To the investor, a former big game hunter, wild animals are, however, more interesting than local people. Over the years, he has worked to displace them, supported by corrupt local officials.

In this part of Tanzania, conflicts between agriculturalists and pastoralists go a long way back in history. Yet as long as there was no immediate land shortage, as long as the land frontier remained open, the different peoples could co-exist. Today, when the farming family survives on a small agricultural plot that they prepare, plant and weed, it is a disaster if roaming cattle and goats intrude on the farm and eat the growing crops.

In Tanzania, as in many other African countries, access to customary land and secure rights over it is a burning political question. The rapidly growing population sees access to a *shamba*, a plot of cultivable land, as a security in an insecure world. However, many international investors are also eyeing Africa's 'virgin soil,' either for large-scale agricultural investments or as tourist resorts, and free of local inhabitants.

In this clash for land, the losers are the Barabaigs, the Maasai and other groups who insist on maintaining their pastoralist way of life, grazing their herds over vast areas and occasionally farming small plots. As minority groups they are marginalised and lack political influence. Both small farmers and large investors cast their eyes at this land. It is commonly felt that the pastoralists are unproductive and that their land could be better used for farming, not least for large mechanised estates.

As we stand near the still smoking ashes of Giamu Marish's homestead, he pokes the dying embers, the tears rolling down his cheeks. "We won our case in the court. But still the authorities want to get us out of here. They tell us that the best we can do is to move away. They say that if we move then all the problems will be solved …"

He is interrupted by the keen young woman, the one who thought that I should have brought the president up here to listen to their grievances. Now she hisses: "The authorities … what do they understand? A human being can give birth to a new human being. But land cannot give birth to new land. There is no more land than there is now. Maybe the authorities can give birth to new land? Where is that new land that they tell us to move to?" Her beautiful brass bracelets glisten in the sunlight as she gestures with her arms towards the open savannah landscape.

Sometime later, in the coastal region of Bagamoyo north of Dar es Salaam, I remember her words as we sit with four Barabaig women in the shadow of bushes close to a signpost proclaiming *EcoEnergy.*

"Now we have moved all the way to the shore of the big sea. We cannot move on further …" says the woman called Gharibo, as she points east towards the Indian Ocean.

We met these women on the road and I asked Margaret Maina, my interpreter, if they would have time to stop for a chat. "Oh yes we have time," said Gharibo. Actually they were in a hurry to visit a woman who had given birth to a baby and to congratulate her with a calabash of milk, but they still wanted to tell us about their situation.

Gharibo is the oldest of the women, two others are her co-wives, one is a neighbour and the youngest is her daughter-in-law. All of them are dressed in pearl-embroidered skin skirts. Three of them wear brass rings around their arms and necks, and all have traditional wave-shaped Barabaig tattoos on their chins and cheeks. It strikes me how keen these women are to maintain their cultural identity, just like the women I met in Vilima Vitatu and in other isolated areas where Barabaigs have moved. Now they tell me about their lives in that open and fearless way I have so often admired among Barabaig women. Gharibo leads the conversation. Margaret laughs every now and then at some comment before translating for me.

Gharibo recalls that she came here to Bagamoyo in the 1990s. She and her family had been on the move across Tanzania for almost 20 years. She is originally from Hanang, and as a newlywed she lived on the Basotu plains, close to

TCWP – the Tanzania Canada Wheat Programme.[1] It is estimated that the wheat scheme over the years confiscated some 100,000 hectares of land, burning down homesteads in the process, while the authorities at the same time started moving people by force into collective *Ujamaa* villages. Gharibo and many other families took their cattle and moved away in search of new pastures. "When we at last arrived in this area, close to the sea, there were not many other people around. The grazing was good and we settled here. For a number of years our life was good. The cattle grew fat and the children were healthy. We had a lot of milk."

Gharibo's two co-wives agree. Yes, they are still having a good life here. Their husband is a considerate man who takes good care of his family. Even though there are things to complain about, the women think that their life is okay. "Other people who live here leave us alone ..." "But now we are worried," interrupts Gharibo, as if she thinks that the other women's account is too idyllic. "There are many things happening here," she continues. "There are rumours. The authorities and people from *EcoEnergy* have come to talk to us a couple of times. There is a lot of talk, but nobody has told us what will happen. Somebody said that we have to move away because all this land will be planted with sugarcane."

Gharibo nods towards the dense high grass where we are sitting. "They say that we will get assistance to move to another piece of land. There has been so much talk for such a long time ... but we know nothing."

Margaret Maina, my assistant, who is herself a Barabaig and has struggled hard to get an education, has at certain times worked for *EcoEnergy*. Her task was to support and prepare the 10 families living here for what in all likelihood will happen – departure.

"But nobody really knows how that will take place," Margaret had told me once when we were discussing *EcoEnergy's* plans. "The project management would like everything to take place correctly, otherwise they will not get any money from Sweden. I have heard that you Swedes are very particular when it comes to following procedures," Margaret says, giving me a wry smile.

Maybe I sensed a slight irony in her smile. For good reason –Swedish involvement in the *Eco Energy* project is controversial.

In 2005, the Swedish energy company SEKAB, based in Örnsköldsvik, began to eye Tanzania. Already active in Mozambique, SEKAB intended to develop an ethanol project, as they had already done in Sweden. The conditions in Tan-

---

1.   It was established in the late 1960's. It changed name to NAFCO – National Agriculture and Food Corporation – when the Canadian aid agency withdrew from the project after heavy internal criticism in Canada. The Tanzanian government then tried to run the scheme as a parastatal, albeit with little success.

zania seemed ideal. The government had given the assurance that free land was available, Swedish development cooperation had prioritised the environment and SEKAB had proposed an enterprise focusing on environmentally friendly energy development. This should have a fair chance of attracting Swedish funds from the development cooperation budget.

Two areas were selected – Rufiji in the southeastern part of the country and Bagamoyo in the east-central part. Both areas are criss-crossed by perennial rivers, which would be the water sources for the plantations that would produce the sugarcane to be converted into ethanol and sugar. These products were to supply the domestic market.

Feasibility studies were undertaken and the company launched an information drive emphasising that the Bagamoyo sugarcane project would be a win-win for the Tanzanian economy, the environment and the local people. But the Barabaigs I met did not share this optimism – they were just worried. And soon international environmental organisations started to question the rosy picture painted by SEKAB.

It is not my intention to analyse the feasibility reports and the debate in development forums, for that has been done elsewhere.[2] Let me just summarise what happened.

By 2009, criticism of the planned project had become profound and Sida (the Swedish International Development Cooperation Agency) decided against guaranteeing additional loans to SEKAB's subsidiary in Tanzania. At the same time, the parent company decided not to invest additional money in the Bagamoyo project. However, a week before this decision was made public, SEKAB's board had entered into an agreement with another company *Eco Development in Europe AB*. The three owners of the latter (who happened to be SEKAB board members) were to acquire all the shares in SEKAB's subsidiaries in Tanzania as well as in Mozambique. The price paid by the new owners amounted to the modest sum of 400 Swedish kronor (some USD 50) for a 170 million investment. It was pointed out in the SEKAB records that these board members did not take part in the decision.

Of course Gharibo and her family did not know anything of these international dealings. However, during my visit they told me of the rumours about the big farming project that was about to start. In March 2014, a group of dignitaries arrived in the area to inaugurate *EcoEnergy*. Feasibility studies had been modified, doubts and questions about the approach to and organisation of the proposed project had been reconsidered and rectified. The Tanzanian authorities

---

2.   See Havnevik, K. and H. Haaland (2011) "Biofuel, land and environmental issues: the case of SEKAB's fuel plans in Tanzania" in Matondi, P., K. Havnevik and A. Beyene (eds) *Biofuels, Land Grabbing and Food Security in Africa*. London/New York: Zed Books and Nordiska Afrikainstitutet. See also the article by Bryceson in this volume.

had issued a licence and everything seemed to be in good order for project start-up. Moreover, Sida had reassessed its earlier position and had decided to provide a credit guarantee for a first commercial loan to *EcoEnergy*. Thus it would now be possible to move on from the pilot project to a project on a large scale.

A few months after the formal inauguration, the Tanzanian newspaper *The Guardian* issued a special edition about the green revolution in the country. *EcoEnergy* was featured as an example. According to the newspaper, *EcoEnergy* would become the largest agricultural project in East Africa. It would generate 4,000 new jobs, produce 130,000 tons of sugar annually as well as 10 million litres of ethanol, and would in addition provide electricity to 100,000 house-holds. One hundred per cent of the potential of sugarcane would be utilised. The importance to the national economy would be significant. Currently, Tanzania imports half of the sugar it consumes and most of its fuel. The investments in infrastructure would, moreover, contribute to the general development of Bagamoyo region. President Jaya Kikwete, who was born in the region, was gladdened by the fact that the investment would benefit his supporters there.

Thus wrote *The Guardian*. I am convinced that the agricultural sector in Tanzania will remain the most important source of livelihood for the population years ahead. The majority still live off the land by cultivating small *shambas*. Former President Julius Nyerere's words are probably still relevant: "The hoe in the soil is the best friend of the poor". But the hoe has to be modernised. Tanzanian subsistence farmers do survive, even during years of bad weather, but their farms lack the potential to produce tangible surpluses for investment.

So, how do you ensure rural development? Through the reallocation of resources from the urban sectors to rural communities, or through large-scale, mechanised and often foreign-funded agricultural investments? Nyerere had the first alternative in mind, conceived as the *Ujamaa* policy. But his ideas were implemented through the forcible resettlement of people and the confiscation of land. The results were catastrophic for many small farmers, pastoralists and for the national economy as a whole.

Most probably a combination of small scale and large scale is necessary, but with meaningful consultation and real alternatives for local communities, not by force. In the best of worlds, the *Eco Energy* sugar plantation and ethanol factory would be a success, for the Barabaigs and other communities living in the area as well.

However, as I sit together with Gharibo and her friends I am still gripped by uneasiness. That time long ago comes to my mind, when my wife Aud and I talked to Barabaigs in Hanang about what was to happen in their area when the Canadian development project was established. That too, was supposed to be one of the greatest development projects in Africa, bringing increased production and welfare to the nation. International experts and Tanzanian politicians were convinced about its bright future. Today nobody wants to talk about the project.

But for Gharibo, the memories from Hanang are vivid. Now she is afraid that everything will be repeated and that she and her family will once again be evicted when *EcoEnergy* starts clearing the land. She admits that the concerned families have been promised compensation and access to new land. "But where is that land?" snorts Gharibo. "Maybe out there in the sea …" she says, pointing eastward to the Indian Ocean. "And how much land have we been promised? Only enough for a small *shamba*, not land for our cattle."

Gharibo explains that her family owns a hundred heads of cattle. Never before have they had to beg for anything from anybody. "We have always been self-sufficient," she emphasises, and asks Margaret to explain that precisely to me.

"So what will happen the day the clearing machines arrive?" Gharibo and the other women remain silent long after Margaret has asked the question. Then suddenly, with a dramatic gesture Gharibo covers her face with her hands. She starts shivering. Margaret embraces her. We remain seated like that in deep uneasiness, while I regret having put the question. The future?

Gharibo's story about a lifetime on the move, without security in land, is a story of a way of life in disintegration. Gharibo, her family, as well as the Barabaigs as a people see no future in a world where a French wildlife entrepreneur can buy the loyalty of local authorities or, for that matter, politicians are being charmed by Swedish aid money.

However, it is difficult to look into the future. Just as I finalise this article (in May 2015), I learn that the future of *EcoEnergy* is again in question. The Swedish project managers have not succeeded in mobilising the necessary investment capital, and Sida has discontinued its disbursements (the 50 million kronor already paid out may be accounted for as disbursements to a badly planned and executed development project).

What this means for Gharibo and the Barabaigs in Bagamoyo nobody knows. Maybe they will have a few more years of grace. But the story of *EcoEnergy* reminds me of the Canadian project in Hanang. The *muhajega* pastures taken from the Baragbaigs were never returned to them.

Small-scale and large-scale agriculture: Tanzanian experiences[1]

Andrew Coulson

According to Marx and Engels (in the 1848 *Communist Manifesto*) small farmers should not exist: they should long ago have been driven out of business by large highly mechanised "agribusiness" with close links to processing companies and produce markets. This view is shared, in broad terms, by writers such as Paul Baran on the left, or Paul Collier on the right of the political spectrum, or geographers such as Deborah Fahy Bryceson, who write about "deagrarianisation". Henry Bernstein is not explicit on this, but writes very warmly about large scale agriculture.

But small farmers do exist – in India, most countries in South Asia and Central America and, since the land reforms of the late 1970s, in China. In many parts of Africa, including Tanzania, their numbers are probably still increasing, despite rapid urbanisation, climate change and alternative means of raising income in rural areas, such as artisanal mining, and failures in the marketing of most of the crops grown for export.

The theory of how small farms compete with large ones owes much to the agricultural economist Alexander Chayanov, who studied small farms in Russia before the First World War. He influenced the "populist" or "*narodnik*" writers and politicians who argued against Lenin's and Stalin's determination to achieve economies of scale through collective farms.[2] In the 1960s and 1970s, agricultural economists in Tanzania undertook pathbreaking studies of the ways in which labour was used on small farms (e.g. Ruthenberg 1964, the six studies in Ruthenberg 1968, and the work of Michael Collinson). More recently, development specialists have shown how the innovations of the "green revolutions" in India can be implemented on small farms as well as large (e.g., Lipton 2010).

In Tanzania, small and large farms have coexisted for more than 100 years,

---

1.   Some of the material in this chapter was presented at the 19th Annual Research Workshop of REPOA, Dar es Salaam, in April 2014, under the title *Small and Large-scale Agriculture: Contrasting Contributions to Economic Development in Tanzania*. A paper on cotton was presented at the Colloquium in honour of Lionel Cliffe on Democracy, Land and Liberation in Africa Today, Cape Town, 20-21 October 2014. The author would like to acknowledge the contributions of participants at both these events, but also the work of countless Tanzanian farmers, and that of researchers who have sought to understand them, especially the pioneering agricultural economists of the 1960s and 1970s.
2.   For a detailed discussion of this, see Coulson (2014a).

making it possible to test whether this theory stands the test of time.[3] The total value of production by small farms far exceeds that of large. However, the last few years have seen determined efforts to encourage production on large farms – in some cases supplemented by small-scale "outgrowers" growing crops on contract.

This chapter looks first at the theory and extends it. It then summarises the history, looking also at some of the myths or misunderstandings that have been used by proponents of large-scale farming in Tanzania to suggest that small scale has little potential. It concludes by reviewing the present position. The evidence suggests strongly that many Tanzanians will continue to be small farmers for at least the next 20 years, and that they can produce surpluses of many crops.

The Theory: How Small Farms Compete with Large

Many studies have found a shocking "inverse relationship": small farms have greater yields per unit of land than large farms on similar land in the same country.[4] This is a tendency or a statistical relationship, not a law. It is found in local situations, not in cross-country comparisons – average yields of maize and wheat are higher in the US than in Africa (other than parts of South Africa), regardless of the size of farm. They may also be higher in a single country if the large farms are on better land or have better water supplies or access to inputs that are not available to small farmers.

Why should the inverse relationship, or anything close to it, exist, given the resources available to large-scale farmers? Chayanov (1925) pointed out that small farmers use more labour per unit of land than large, i.e., they "exploit themselves," and especially women and children. They use the labour of a whole family, which enables them to undertake tasks that are costly for a commercial farmer – such as building stone walls, terraces or irrigation canals, or making green manure, or scaring away monkeys. Pingali *et al.* (1987) pointed to the high costs of supervising labour on large farms. Bernstein (2009: 60–1) adds the initial costs of the waiting time before a farm is developed and its first crops harvested – as with tree crops such as tea or coffee. Small farmers have shown that they can undertake complex agricultural procedures, such as curing tobacco, as

---

3.   In this chapter, the term "small farm" does not refer to a particular size of farm. It does refer to existing patterns of land use, in which farm families grow much of their own food and sell surplus production. Some of these farms are substantially bigger than others. The paper does not discuss differentiation among farmers in rural Tanzania and the emergence of large African-owned farms.

4.   This "inverse relationship" was found in the German agricultural census of 1895 (David 1903) and in the Russian *zvemstvo* statistics studied by Chayanov and Lenin . Amartya Sen discovered it in India in 1962 (Bernstein and Byres 2001, fn.38 p. 22). Berry and Cline (1979) found it in six countries, Cornia (1985) in 15. A special issue of *World Development* explored it in 2010 (including an introduction by Wiggins, Kirsten and Llambí and an important article by Lipton).

efficiently as large farmers, and that if fertilisers, sprays or improved seeds are available they will use them when the risks are not great and the operations are profitable. Chayanov also recognised that many of the disadvantages of small scale could be mitigated if the small farmers worked together in cooperatives, especially for the marketing of their crops, as in Denmark (Mitrany 1951: 44ff.; Coulson 2014a: 411).

The inverse relationship may have other causes. Thus many of the Tsarist land-owners neglected much of their land. The same was true of many of the settlers in Zimbabwe – which was why production could increase when the land was allocated to war veterans and others from 1999 onwards (Stoneman and Cliffe 1989: 130–1; Hanlon, Manjengwa and Smart 2013). Much of the huge area given to agribusiness companies in Africa, including Tanzania, in recent years (Locher and Sulle 2013, 2014) is underused.

Small-scale farmers also get increased production by using technologies that are difficult to implement at large scale. In Tanzania, much of this technology was invented and implemented before the German conquest (Kjekshus 1977: 26–50). Thus on Kilimanjaro and in the Usambaras and many other places, small farms benefit from complex systems of irrigation channels. The carrying of green material to make manure up to higher levels made possible the banana agriculture of Karagwe (now sadly threatened by viruses and nematode worms). The "Matengo pit" cross-cutting ridges are extremely effective ways of green manuring, and also protect the soil from heavy storms (Stahl 1961: 49a, 95–6). Farmers used both green and animal manure, and systems of crop rotation.

Other good practices involve mixed- or inter-cropping, that is, growing more than one crop on the same plot. Large farmers often prefer a single crop in a field for convenience of mechanical planting and harvesting and the use of chemicals to control weeds. But there are at least eight scientific reasons why intercropping may produce higher total yields: if one of the crops grows quickly and covers the surface of the soil, then soil erosion is reduced; so is evaporation of water; with a lower density of any one crop, pests and diseases spread more slowly; if two crops use nutrients at different levels in the soil, both may get good yields; less weeding is needed – in effect one of the crops replaces weeds; a legume such as beans may "fix" nitrogen from the atmosphere and so fertilise another crop, such as maize; if one of the crops fails, for instance because of drought at a critical time, the other may not only survive, but have more space in which to grow; and one crop may provide much appreciated shade for the other.

To these can be added arguments specific to small-scale cultivation: small farms also have animals or birds – chicken, goats or cattle – which provide eggs, milk and meat, and also manure for the agricultural crops; a farmer can give special attention to, and so get more product from, small parts of the farm such as a damp patch or a patch with different soils, or close to a dwelling house and therefore easy to manure; hoe or ox-ploughing does less damage to the soil than tractors; there is less risk of damage to machinery from tree roots[5] – and trees may also provide shade as well as fruits or nuts; on fertile soil but steep slopes (for instance, the volcanic soils of Mounts Kilimanjaro or Rungwe in Tanzania) the hoe is often the most productive method of cultivation. On larger plots, with less steep gradients, ox cultivation may be efficient. Pingali *et al.* (1987) demonstrated that when tractors can only work for a short period in which crops have to be planted before the soil becomes too dry, they are often not cost-effective.

Supporters of large-scale farming, or agribusiness, are often influenced by the agriculture of the plains of the mid-West of the United States, where huge farms grow just a few crops (often just one) with high levels of mechanisation and often irrigation, and produce yields which on average are higher than anywhere else in the world. They forget that these are extremely capital intensive systems, that they are dependent on very high (and often increasingly high) use of fertiliser, insecticides, weed killers and other inputs (most of which have high energy and hence carbon contents) and the use of genetically modified (GM) seeds.[6] Much of the large-scale agriculture to produce biofuels in Brazil, Argentina, Paraguay and some other Latin American countries has similar characteristics. There are attempts to reproduce this in Africa, but as Kaag and Zoomers (2014) show, a number have already failed.

Small farmers are not peasants.[7] From colonial times onwards (arguably earlier) most small farmers have been integrated into the global economy (Bern-

---

5.   Pingali *et al.* (1987) give the costs of removing tree roots as a major disincentive to tractor cultivation, other than in soils which are permanently cultivated or in areas without trees. Tree roots that destroyed mechanical implements were one of the causes of the failure of the Groundnuts Scheme in Tanzania in the 1950s (Coulson 2013: 79-82). In some very wet conditions, tractors may get stuck, while hoe cultivation is possible.

6.   The case against GM crops that are bred to resist weed killers is not that they are a risk to health, but that in the long run they will not be sustainable because weeds will emerge that are resistant to the weed killers or require very high levels of weed killer to remove them. These weeds will have no competition, so they will spread fast.

7.   Anthropologists who try to understand what motivates those who live in rural villages use the word peasant as a term of approval. But Deborah Bryceson (2000: 1) notes that in day-to-day English usage it denotes someone uncultured or obstinate, and is associated with descriptions such as "primitive," "backward," "uneducated" and "obstructive," Thus the word "peasant" can be used to imply that small farmers are unskilled, ignorant or misguided. The majority of scholars – from Chayanov to the present day – have no illusion that small-scale farming is often backbreaking hard work, for very uncertain returns, and understand that most small farmers continue only because it gives them a possibility for keeping themselves and their families alive, and there is nothing better available. Conversely, the words "modern," "commercial," "efficient" and related terms can also be weapons and used as terms of praise or aspiration, often without meaningful support from evidence. In the discourse of linguistic analysis, these words are "empty signifiers" (or "floating signifiers": words without unambiguous meanings used with little or no accompanying evidence to promote or discredit a writer's point of view (see Jeffares 2007: 44–69; 2014). Henry Bernstein now concedes that the term "peasant" is problematic, or "anachronistic" (Choonara 2013), and avoids it where he can.

stein 2010). They sell crops or other products. They purchase what they cannot make individually. To fund those purchases they obtain money, much of it by selling agricultural products, but also from sales of animal products, hunting, poaching, fishing, charcoal, craft items or from other parts of the informal sector, including small-scale manufacturing, artisanal mining and migrating in search of labour, or working for other farmers. In years of poor harvests, or when prices for their crops are low, they may, up to a point, withdraw from markets, but there are limits on how much and for how long this may be sustained.[8]

When faced with the demands of the outside world, small farmers have two choices: they can increase production and sell surpluses, or they can resist, reducing production and consumption and surviving in other ways (Wolf 1966: 14–5).[9] The resistance can be very subtle, as with the social and political strategies adopted by the small rice farmers in Malaya studied by Scott (1985), who were threatened with loss of income when large farmers mechanised, or the case studies in Scott and Kerkvliet (1986), or the different tactics adopted after forced villagisation in the 1970s by three different *Ujamaa* villages in Tanga Region (von Freyhold 1979) or Rungwe District (Thoden van Velsen 1975). The common feature of all these studies, and others concerned with the adoption or non-adoption of new seeds, is that when anthropologists or other researchers talked to the farmers, they uncovered good reasons for these decisions.

---

8. The rural sector also provides a "reserve army of labour," or a "sponge" (Wuyts and Kilama 2014)), which absorbs labour not yet needed for manufacturing or other industries. However, in the years of structural adjustment in the 1980s, when marketing was disrupted and farm prices were often very low, agriculture was not attractive, those who could turned to other ways of making money, such as artisanal mining. Bryceson (e.g., 1997; 2000; 2014) is one of a number of writers who characterise what is happening in the rural areas of many parts of Africa as, "depeasantisation," or even "deagrarianisation." This is often associated with "desertification," and especially the march southwards of the Sahara Desert, affecting countries in West Africa, Southern Sudan and the northern parts of Uganda, Kenya and Ethiopia. However, the arithmetic of population growth is such that in countries such as Tanzania, which are less directly affected by desertification, the absolute number of small farmers is still increasing. It is misleading (as Bryceson would surely agree) to write small farmers off as marginal, or in all cases unable to be self-reliant or to contribute to their own survival.

9. Some writers assert that it is still possible for small farmers to survive outside the market economy. That was Göran Hydén's position in 1980, when he wrote of an "uncaptured peasantry" in Tanzania, and argued that there would be no progress until the state "captured" it, though by 1983 he was advocating the extension of the market. Waters, who worked with refugee families in the far west of Tanzania in the 1970s and 1980s, claimed that near self-sufficiency was still a viable way of life in remote places in Tanzania, where there was unclaimed land. He also suggested another tactic: farmers may plant relatively risky crops, such as maize, in drought-prone areas, knowing that, if they fail, they can appeal to the government for famine relief (Waters 2007). Iliffe (1979: 314) suggests that maize, replacing the more drought-resistant sorghum and millet, was more attractive to farmers once the colonial government provided famine relief. This may be a factor in the calculations of some farmers, but it is a strategy too unpredictable to be a major part of the story.

For example, any innovation that does not take account of labour bottle-necks at key times in the year increases risk, or produces a product which is not as tasty or easy to cook as traditional varieties, will often be rejected. The assumption that farmers plant recently developed seeds using fertilisers and other chemicals, ignores the fact that many farmers (and Tanzanian consumers also) have preferences for traditional varieties, for their cooking properties, aromas and storage characteristics. Thus a farmer may plant two varieties of rice – one a quick-growing high-yield variety for sale, but alongside it a traditional variety for cooking and perhaps also sale. There is also an economic argument for planting crops that use labour at different times in the growing season. In America and Europe, extra resources can usually be hired if necessary. But where most of the labour is provided by the farming family, economists should look at *farming systems* – how farmers benefit from the complementarities of different crops and their needs for labour at different times.[10]

Small farmers respond to changes in prices – higher prices usually lead to increased areas planted. Ellis (1982: 270–2) showed that production of food crops rose and traditional cash crops fell in response to the price signals given by government-fixed prices in the 1970s. Eriksson (1993: 7–74) drew similar conclusions. Dercon (1993) studied the responses of cotton output in Tanzania to price changes. He was able to show not only that farmers adjusted their behaviour (especially to changes in relative prices between cotton and rice or maize), but that they grew more of the food crops and less cotton when there were shortages of consumer goods.

These studies also demonstrate the importance of the marketing infrastructure. If farmers are not paid a good price, or are paid very late or not at all for their work, they will be very reluctant to grow that crop. But that requires agents from the public or private sectors with sufficient money at the times it is needed and outlets ready to take the crops when they are purchased. If these conditions are not in place, there is no point running extension campaigns and it is irresponsible to criticise farmers who withdraw from growing those crops (Coulson 2015).

Small farmers run businesses (Collier 2010: 213; Bernstein 2010: 93–4). They make commercial decisions about what to plant, how much, and where. They buy and sell. They save and invest. They need cash. They allocate the family labour. They decide whether to hire additional labour at peak periods, for example, to bring in the harvest. They work hard, usually for very low returns, but they do have some discretion in what they do. There is a great range in how

---

10. This was how African agricultural economics was studied and researched in the 1970s, but this "farm systems analysis" has now largely been replaced by calculations of the gross margin for each crop separately. It is time for the earlier tradition to be revived.

successful they are – from large and successful farmers at one extreme, to those barely surviving at the other. Their position is comparable to other parts of the informal economy.

Since over-specialisation in a single crop will lead to labour shortages at the peak periods of labour need for that crop, farmers are rational in planting small quantities of a crop at different times (even if this reduces the expected average yield) and in dividing their time between several crop or livestock activities or other opportunities to earn money. This also lessens the risks involved if a single crop fails.

This is not to suggest that being a small farmer was, or is, easy. On the contrary, it involves hard physical work for much of the year for very low returns in cash. But farmers who grow most of their own food can, in most situations, survive.

Women are particularly exploited. On farms with male "heads of household," they do much of the back-breaking work – digging, weeding, cutting and carrying grass to feed stall-fed cattle, selling small quantities of produce. This is in addition to childcare and cooking. Most small farms in Africa could not survive without this labour. Koopman and Faye (2012) and other feminist writers are correct to categorise it as a form of exploitation. When there is no male head of household, for example, through widowhood or domestic violence, life can quickly become almost impossible – with women losing control of their land (see, for example, da Corta and Magongo 2011; Bryceson (ed.) 1995, especially the article by Bridget O'Laughlin).

Tanzania: The Coexistence of Small-scale and Large-scale Agriculture

One of the main motivations for the German conquest was to promote settlement, but the colonisers quickly discovered that it was often more efficient to persuade or force African farmers to grow the crops they wanted. In the 100 years since then, Tanzania's population has grown and the area under cultivation has increased, but the coexistence of small and large farms has continued (Coulson 1978; 2013). Small farmers grow food – maize and bananas, sorghum, millets, rice, cassava, potatoes, beans and other legumes, fruits, vegetables and nuts. They sell part of what they grow, including "cash crops" that require processing before use. Robusta coffee was indigenous in the Bukoba area, Arabica coffee was grown by small farmers on Kilimanjaro from the 1890s, and cotton was cultivated south of Lake Victoria before the First World War (Iliffe 1979: 154–5). Settlers had political support: if the First World War had not intervened, German East Africa might have become a state controlled by settlers. Plantations with large labour forces and processing factories were created, owned by companies with access to capital (today's agribusiness). They failed with rubber (after an initial boom) and cotton, but succeeded with sisal on land with access to the railways, mainly near Tanga, Morogoro and Dar es Salaam (Iliffe 145–7).

After the First World War, "Tanganyika" became a Trust Territory under the League of Nations, administered by the British, nominally on behalf of its local population. Many settlers went to Kenya or Rhodesia, where the legal position was clearer. But some of the German farms were rehabilitated, especially after Germans were allowed to return, and in the 1930s "settlers regained some of the influence they had lost" (Iliffe 373).

At the end of the Second World War, the British government needed raw materials and its former troops needed employment. This was the background to the Groundnuts Scheme, which attempted to grow groundnuts for their cooking oil in three underpopulated parts of the country – Kongwa near Dodoma, Nachingwea in Mtwara District and Urambo near Tabora. It was an abject failure in all three locations, technically and economically (Coulson 2013: 79–80). However, some of those who came to work on the scheme stayed on and some became settlers and were joined by others seeking a new life after the war. Kathleen Stahl (1961: 37–50) paints a picture of the settlers just before independence: there were 1,124 farms around Arusha and Moshi, in the Southern Highlands and around Lushoto. This was a small number compared with Kenya, where they were far more entrenched. That did not prevent settlers from trying to influence the colonial government. This was stopped by independence in 1961. Meanwhile, the Colonial Development Corporation (later Commonwealth Development Corporation) and international companies such as Brooke Bond and Unilever invested in plantations growing tea, pyrethrum, wattle and other crops.

In the years before and after independence, agricultural production and exports rose, most of it from small farmers. But the World Bank and other experts (as well as Nyerere and other Tanzanians) were impatient at the speed of change. They promoted both the "Improvement Approach" (small farmers) and the "Transformation Approach" (large-scale mechanised production on large farms or settlement schemes).

By 1966–67, the settlement schemes were seen to be economic failures, paving the way for Nyerere's version of *Ujamaa*, in which economies of scale were to be achieved from communal work, which was to be voluntary (Nyerere 1967; James 2014). This failed for many reasons, the main one being the difficulties in creating systems of rewards and incentives that would reward the efforts put into communal work (von Freyhold 1979; Thoden van Velsen 1973; Wisner *et al.* 1975; Ibbott 2014).

Instead, the ruling TANU (Tanganyika African Nationalist Union) party implemented a policy of forcing people to live in "villages" (Coulson 2013: 280–309). This often meant moving away from the best land, and involved a significant loss of the capital that farmers had invested in their houses. Agricultural production fell. The position became much worse when the price of oil trebled in the early 1970s, much faster than the prices of Tanzania's agricultural export crops.[11] The IMF saw the situation as one of a structural failure in the Tanzanian economy, which could only be corrected by reducing government budgets and opening the economy to market forces. Only in 1986, after Nyerere had stood down as president, did Tanzania accept the IMF conditions and its financial support.

Do we believe the figures?

An important qualification to any analysis of agriculture in Tanzania is the fact that the figures for agricultural production and prices are extremely unreliable, especially for crops grown for food and consumed locally, or marketed through unofficial channels. A number of academic writers have pointed this out (most recently Edwards 2014: 242–7; also Ponte 2002: 65–71; Skarstein 2010; ASDP 2013 Annex 2: 13–14, 16–21). Agricultural censuses are conducted from time to time: in 2006 more than 40,000 farms were surveyed. Cross-checking is done where possible (for instance, with information about rainfall, or estimates of consumption corrected for imports and exports). Aerial photographs can provide information about cultivated areas and livestock numbers. Small sample censuses are conducted at regional level. Statistics are also compiled from estimates by district agricultural staff of likely harvests in their areas.

But problems remain. Farmers' recall of quantities or areas may not be accurate. When crops are interplanted, the census returns figures for the "major crop." It is not clear how the figures deal with by-products, such as cassava leaves used for cooking when the main crop is the tuber, which may be harvested later. When prices fluctuate, the enumerators return "an average." Where crops have been sold outside official channels, farmers may be reluctant to disclose them. If they are not paid for (because, for example, of failures in the voucher system, or because there is no market for what they have produced), they may still be included in the figures. Both Edwards and the Agricultural Sector Development Programme (ASDP) authors suggest that the estimates by agricultural officers may be biased by pressure, for example, to report good figures, or bad figures if they are looking for famine relief. The discussion that follows should therefore be treated with great care.

---

11. Lofchie (2014) and Edwards (2014) both follow their mentor Bates (1981) in asserting that farm prices were deliberately kept low to create surpluses for industrialisation. There is some evidence for this, but inefficiency and corruption could have achieved the same results without deliberate conspiracy (Coulson 2014b:42ff). Whatever lay behind it, world prices were not passed on to farmers (a kilo of coffee was worth much more in Kenya than in northern Tanzania), unofficial exports increased, farm inputs became very hard to purchase legally and farmers were very dissatisfied (Lofchie 2014: 32ff.).

Impact of Liberalisation

There are many detailed studies of the impact of liberalisation. Gibbon, Havnevik and Hermele (1993: 52–64) showed that following devaluation of the Tanzanian shilling, better prices were not passed on to farmers and that, partly as a consequence, agricultural production was higher in the years immediately before the major devaluations than it was afterwards. Ponte (2002) showed how the opening up to the private sector of cotton ginneries and coffee pulperies had deleterious impacts on the production and export of those crops. The systems for providing inputs on credit broke down, as farmers could take their credit from one trader and sell to another without repaying their loans. In the scramble for business, quality deteriorated – traders were even prepared to buy crops before they were harvested, regardless of the resulting quality (Ponte 2002: 25–6, 27–8; Coulson 2015).

The situation for food crops was only a little better. Skarstein (2010: Table 1) noted that marketed production of maize and rice grew at around 3.5 per cent per annum in the supposedly chaotic years of the late 1970s, but fell in the years of structural adjustment from 1986–92. He considered many possible explanations for this, concluding that the growth was primarily due to the availability of subsidised fertiliser that made possible a "Green Revolution in the Southern Highlands," which became the bread basket (a better description would be maize basket) of Tanzania, at a time when production in the Arusha area rose little. When the subsidies for fertiliser were withdrawn, there were falls in production.

But in the Southern Highlands, Isininka and Msuya (2011) reported that once subsidies for fertilisers were reintroduced, around 2004, production increased: 73 per cent of the AFRINT II[12] sample of farmers in Iringa were using pesticide sprays on maize and 71 per cent on paddy, and 37 per cent of the sample were using improved seeds, mostly hybrids, for maize.

From the early 1990s, agricultural production was reported to be growing at around 4 per cent. Tanzania's urban populations were growing rapidly, but not sufficiently to prevent the absolute numbers living in the rural areas from also rising. In contrast to the situation considered by Skarstein (2010) in the years immediately after structural adjustment, the agricultural sector was able to contribute to feeding the growing urban population.

Figure 1, from a presentation in support of the agricultural commitments in *Big Results Now*, summarises the official figures from 2007 to 2011. In value and tonnage, maize was by far Tanzania's most important crop, although in 2009 the value of rice (but not the tonnage produced) exceeded that of maize. Sorghum and cassava benefited from increased prices. Food and Agriculture

---

12. See www.keg.lu.se.

Figure 1. Production of Key Crops 2007–11.

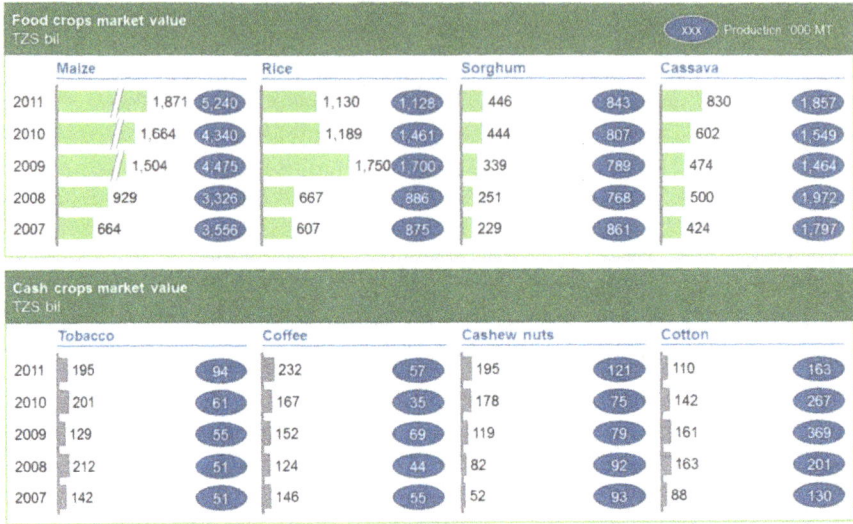

Food crops market value TZS bil								xxx Production '000 MT

	Maize		Rice		Sorghum		Cassava	
2011	1,871	5,240	1,130	1,128	446	843	830	1,857
2010	1,664	4,340	1,189	1,461	444	807	602	1,549
2009	1,504	4,475	1,750	1,700	339	789	474	1,464
2008	929	3,326	667	886	251	768	500	1,972
2007	664	3,556	607	875	229	861	424	1,797

Cash crops market value TZS bil								

	Tobacco		Coffee		Cashew nuts		Cotton	
2011	195	94	232	57	195	121	110	163
2010	201	61	167	35	178	75	142	267
2009	129	55	152	69	119	79	161	369
2008	212	51	124	44	82	92	163	201
2007	142	51	146	55	52	93	88	130

SOURCE: Ministry of Agriculture, Food Security and Co-operatives, Bank of Tanzania, Tanzania Revenue Authority, FAO Stats   4 TdV25!

Organisation figures also show rapid increases in the production of both round and sweet potatoes, onions and tomatoes, all of which had expanding markets in urban centres.

Growth in agricultural production at 4 per cent sustained over time is rare in comparative world terms. It was achieved when world prices for most of Tanzania's traditional agricultural export crops were falling, climate was poor in the north of the country, the impact of global warming was becoming apparent and there was evidence of increasing exhaustion of the soil and the drying up of water sources. The traditional cash crops contributed little to this, because prices fell so that even when there were years of high production, they contributed less value to the producers. The growth came in food products such as tomatoes, onions and potatoes, and above all in maize and rice production. It is clear, to say the least, that this was not a failing sector.

However, these results occurred in a context where national GDP, driven by rapid growth in mining and tourism, grew at close to 7 per cent. Thus agriculture contributed a smaller proportion of GDP: 28 per cent in 2005 but only 23 per cent in 2012, with the contribution of services rising from 46 per cent to 49 per cent, and industry (including mining) from 20 per cent to 22 per cent (ASDP 2013:5). Thus the high increases in GDP did little to reduce poverty or inequality (Atkinson and Lugo 2010, using data from the Household Budget Surveys).

In this period, Tanzania became open to proposals for large-scale agriculture from agribusiness interests in countries around the globe, some responding to opportunities to supply new markets for biofuels, others proposing to grow food grains for export, including propositions from the Middle East, which realised that it would be cheaper to supply food for their internal markets from Africa than from irrigating their deserts (Sulle and Nelson 2009; Chachage and Baha 2010; Chachage 2010; Pearce 2012). Tanzanians in the private sector and at Sokoine University of Agriculture started making the case for large-scale production – and influenced the policy statements discussed below, *Kilimo Kwanza* (2009), the "Southern Agricultural Growth Corridor of Tanzania" (SAGCOT) (SAGCOT 2010) and *Big Results Now* (2012). These can all be seen as reactions to the much more comprehensive *Agricultural Sector Development Programme,* which has relatively little to say about large-scale agriculture. These are considered in the sections which follow, along with some of the myths and misunderstandings on which they depend.

Agricultural Sector Development Programme

The *Tanzanian Development Vision 2025*, launched in 1999, aims to transform the country in 25 years "from a low productivity agricultural economy to a semi-industrialized one, led by modernized and highly productive agricultural activities which are effectively integrated and buttressed by supportive industrial and service activities in the rural and urban areas." It is linked with MKUKU-TA, the National Strategy for Growth and Reduction of Poverty, prepared in 2005 and revised in 2010. Its aim is to reduce poverty and inequality, primarily in the rural areas, and to meet the targets of the UN's Millennium Development Goals. The *Agriculture Sector Development Strategy* was prepared in 2001, and aimed to achieve a growth rate of 5 per cent per annum in the agricultural sector, rising to 10 per cent per annum by 2010, and to substantially reduce levels of rural poverty. The *Agricultural Sector Development Programme* (ASDP), developed in 2006, set out in detail how this was to be done. Three-quarters of the financial resources needed would be provided through "basket funding": donors would pool money to implement the programme on the basis of annual agreements with the Tanzanian government over how it would be spent. Three-quarters of the budget, including expenditure on extension services, was delegated to the district councils. The remaining quarter, including expenditure on government research stations and on irrigation, was allocated by central government departments. Proposals for a second phase of the ASDP were drawn up in 2013 (ASDP 2013: 6–9).

Near the start of the draft is the following quotation:

Tanzania has a total of about 7.1 million ha of high- (2.3 million ha) and medium-potential land (4.8 million ha), supported by rivers, lakes, wetlands and aquifers. Of the 2.3 million ha classified as high-potential, only 363,514 ha had improved irrigation infrastructure in 2012, accounting for only 1.3 percent of

the total land with irrigation potential. An estimated 55 percent of the land
could be used for agriculture, and more than 51 percent for pasture. However,
only about 6 percent of the agricultural land is cultivated, and the practice of
shifting cultivation causes deforestation and land degradation on pastoral land.
Tanzania is one of the few countries in Africa that still has extensive wildlife
resources and protected areas that account for about 25 percent of its total land
area. (ASDP 2013: 5–6)

This quotation includes a series of myths, misunderstandings, fudges or un-
truths, which appear in slightly different versions in documents produced by
Tanzanian government sources, donors and in newspapers. These have made it
very difficult to have a serious discussion about agriculture in Tanzania.[13]

The most misleading is the claim that 55 per cent of Tanzania's land could
be used for agriculture – and hence that there is a vast area of land just waiting
to be used. In areas of known high potential – the mountains of the north and
northwest, around Lake Victoria, the coastal areas, and much of the Southern
Highlands – most of the suitable land is already cultivated. Indeed, on Kilimanjaro and some other areas there is the opposite problem – many plots have
been divided so much that they are barely viable and there is encroachment
into forested areas needed to preserve water sources. There are areas that could
be cultivated in the far west and in the south. But much is game reserve (the
Selous), national park (Serengeti, Lake Manyara, Ruaha, Mikumi, etc.) or forest
reserve. Most of the land in the middle of the country has average rainfall of
less than 750mm, below which rainfed agriculture is hazardous. Much of the
so-called arable land (for example, in the Southern Highlands) is steep hillside,
often heavily eroded. Much land that is not planted is deliberately fallow – not
in use for agriculture that year, but it will be used in future – and the quotation appears to confuse shifting cultivation, where land is left fallow to recover,
with pastoralism. Furthermore, the soils in most of the unused areas are of poor
quality: they lack important nutrients, are poor at retaining organic matter and
include a silica content that makes them set extremely hard until the rains come.
Others are (or in some cases were) at great risk of soil erosion – for example, the
Ismani area north of Iringa, which in the 1960s and early 1970s was a frontier

---

13. The following quotation from a presentation by the chairman of the Agricultural Council
of Tanzania claims five times as much arable land and an unbelievable area with potential
for irrigation: "44 million hectares of good arable land but only 23% is currently under effective utilisation. 62,000 sq. kms of the fresh water resources available for crops, livestock
and fish farming which is grossly under utilised. 29 million hectares of irrigable land BUT
only 1% is currently under irrigation. 19 million cattle, 17 million sheep and goats, 50 million chicken which are not commercially exploited. 1,424 Kms of coastline and 223,000
Sq. Kms of Tanzania's Exclusive Economic Zone of the Indian Ocean which is not being
effectively exploited." (Shamte 2011, slide 6). The points about fisheries are fair comment.
The rest is oversimplified and misleading.

for African-owned tractor hire operatives, but is today a wasteland. Donors and government spokespeople should be extremely careful before they claim without qualification that Tanzania has large areas of surplus land that can be used for agriculture, because, at very least, this underestimates the problems.[14]

The targets for irrigation are also unrealistic. Tanzania does not have huge rivers flowing across flat alluvial plains, as in much of Pakistan, the Punjab and the great plains of China or Burma, whose water comes from the Himalayas. There is one substantial river, the Rufiji, fed by a number of tributaries. One of these, the Great Ruaha, has already effectively become a seasonal flowing river, not least because of the large out-take of water for irrigation at Mbarali near Mbeya, with adverse consequences for the hydroelectric schemes down the river at Mtera and Kidatu that supply Dar es Salaam. On the Pangani River, use of water for irrigation has reduced the quantities available for electricity generation at Nyumba ya Mungu. When the irrigation strategy was revised in 2005–06, the president proposed a target of 1 million hectares to be irrigated in five years. This was 20 times as much as had been created in the previous five years. Not surprisingly, it proved unattainable, even though almost 80 per cent of the money in the ASDP was allocated for irrigation. Almost all of this was spent on reconditioning existing schemes (Therkildsen 2011: 14–21; *Kilimo Kwanza* 2009: slides 20–21).

Very large areas of irrigation could be achieved by widespread use of boreholes, but boreholes are expensive in many parts of Tanzania, where the water is deep down and hard to locate. Can Tanzania justify sinking boreholes to supply water for irrigated agriculture when 60 per cent of the rural population does not have access to a source of piped water?[16]

The third problem with the quotation is its interpretation of pastoralism. Most of the land used by pastoralists would otherwise lie unused. It is true that they burn the scrub at the end of the dry season, but this kills insects such as ticks that affect cattle, and it fertilises the land so that grass grows quickly when it rains. The problems faced by pastoralists are how to survive the long dry periods, and recent extensions of crop agriculture on land formerly used for dry season grazing (and reserves for hunting where they are no longer permitted to

14. There is a further contradiction: if there is surplus land, intensification of the agriculture might not provide the optimum returns to labour – it might be better to find low-cost means to increase the area under cultivation.
15. That raises the question of how they were allowed to become derelict – suggesting that they were not highly profitable. In the past, some of these schemes have not produced more than one crop per year, that is, little more than they could have produced without the investment. This was true at Mbarali in the early 1970s, where farmers growing rice on swampland outside the irrigation project achieved similar yields to those on the irrigation project.
16. Small-scale irrigation from streams is often extremely viable. See Mdee (2014) for case studies in Morogoro region.

roam) mean that these important contributors to the Tanzanian economy and diet are in danger of dying out.

The ASDP focuses on a small number of crops: maize, rice, sugarcane, sunflower, sesame and horticultural crops. However, small farms minimise risk by planting a wide range of crops. Then, if one is attacked by pests, disease, or there is insufficient rain at the right times, there may still be output from the other crops. This also makes possible a balanced diet for the farm families. Risk is further minimised, and total production on average increased, by mixed cropping. Thus it should be normal to plant beans at the same time as maize, to plant bananas with coffee, to plant under fruit trees, and to plant a wide variety of quick-growing vegetables wherever the soil would otherwise be left exposed. The ASDP (and Big Results Now – see below) should consider systems of crops, and how farmers can minimise their risks: they are wrong to focus on a few crops.

There is some critical assessment of the strengths and weaknesses of extension. Extension workers should be able to help farmers with the problems that face them. Those problems may or may not be those highlighted in extension training. The ASDP points out that most farmers are already aware of the traditional messages about how crops should be grown: "What is lacking and gaining importance is focus on how farmers increase their incomes by engaging in more profitable activities including value addition and improved market efficiency" (ASDP 2013, para 29b).

The section of the proposed revision of the ASDP that supports the government agricultural research service does not recognise the crises it faces (Coulson and Diyamett 2012). Many problems are a consequence of inadequate recurrent funding over the years, which has left researchers not only with difficulties in maintaining equipment, but unable to carry out field trials with farmers, to listen to their problems, and to travel to conferences and meetings with other researchers.[17] The lack of core funding also makes it hard for Tanzania to appraise and make best use of agricultural research undertaken internationally, for example by IRRI,[18] ICRISAT,[19] ASARECA[20] and AGRA.[21] The research service is run through seven research zones, whereas responsibility for the extension ser-

---

17. The ASDP documentation reports that the total spending on agricultural research has increased, but most of it goes to academic institutions. These are also in a better position to get funding from external sources, including international organisations in the Consultative Group of International Agricultural Research (CGIAR).
18. The International Rice Research Organisation.
19. The International Crops Research Institute for the Semi-Arid Tropics, with an office in Nairobi.
20. The Assocation for Strengthening Agricultural Research in East and Central Africa, which potentially gives Tanzania access to work in Zimbabwe, Malawi and Zambia, among other countries.
21. The Alliance for a Green Revolution in Africa, a private NGO largely funded by the Bill and Melinda Gates Foundation, whose aim is to improve the productivity of small farmers.

vice has been delegated to the district councils, of which there were 169 on the mainland in 2012. This makes the extension service dependent on the political priorities of district commissioners, who may or may not liaise with the research services.

The ASDP includes some discussion of value chains: of storage, transport and other means of increasing the proportion of value added reaching farmers through, for example, better storage or local processing. It gives less attention to reducing unofficial deductions (such as cesses paid at road blocks), or government policies such as export bans or sudden unexpected imports,[22] or, above all, in ensuring that farmers actually receive what they are owed. The biggest conceivable disincentive to increased production by small farmers is a voucher system where (for whatever reason) the vouchers cannot be converted into cash, or, as appears to have been the case with much of the 2012 cashew nut harvest, there is insufficient money to purchase the crops. Improvements in marketing would almost certainly give much greater returns to farmers than investment in extension.

Policies more or less similar to the ASDP can be found in almost all African countries south of the Sahara and reflect the "Washington Consensus" of open borders, a maximum role for the private sector and identification of a small number of crops whose productivity can be raised through use of high-yielding new varieties together with fertilisers and other chemical inputs. The policies of AGRA are similar. The fundamental criticism of all these is that, in the last resort, they are top down. They do not start with the achievements of small farmers and the best means of addressing the problems they face. As a result, they look at crops one at a time, instead of relationships between the different crops that farmers plant in an area. They give too much weight to production (through new seeds and chemicals) and too little weight to marketing. If the support systems are in place, there is almost no limit to what small farmers can produce.

Kilimo Kwanza (Agriculture First)

This ambitious plan was launched by President Kikwete in 2009.[23] It was "formulated under the patronage of the Tanzania National Business Council" (Ngaiza 2012) and the Agricultural Council of Tanzania (both of which represent large-scale farmers), with technical support from academics at Sokoine University of Agriculture and elsewhere – but not in the Ministry of Agriculture. It is "a Private Public Initiative where the private sector is the engine of economic growth-mandated to be the lead implementing agent" (Ngaiza 2012, slide 15).

---

22. The market for rice was disrupted when the government suddenly authorised the import of large quantities of cheap rice in February 2013.
23. A year ahead of the 2010 elections.

Its policies are described in ten "pillars" (Government of Tanzania 2009). Much is uncontroversial, including measures to support small-scale farming. However, the place given to large-scale agriculture is much more overt than in any previous Tanzanian document. In particular Pillar 5 strengthens the power of the state to allocate land for large-scale agriculture. Pillar 2 commits the country to substantially increased spending on agriculture, and especially on irrigation, so meeting the Maputo Declaration target that 10 per cent of the government budget be spent on agriculture, and to creating a Tanzania Agricultural Development Bank, among other measures. But its target of 7 million hectares for irrigation is unachievable and irresponsible. In practice, the proposed budget allocations for agriculture have not been achieved – and budgets have become indicative only, with only fractions of the money released. The Agricultural Bank was created but concerns about its long-term future remain.[24]

The Southern Agricultural Growth Corridor of Tanzania (SAGCOT)

The concept of agricultural "corridors" in Africa appears to have been invented by the Norwegian fertiliser producer Yara International in 2008 and developed by the British consultants AgDevCo, with support from Syngenta, Monsanto, Unilever and a range of powerful international organisations and donors. The "Beira corridor" in Mozambique, running inland as far as Harare in Zimbabwe, was launched in 2009. SAGCOT was promoted, in a wave of publicity, by President Kikwete at the World Economic Forum in Davos, Switzerland in 2010. Its website describes it as "an inclusive, multi-stakeholder partnership to rapidly develop the region's agricultural potential."

The related map shows the area covered by this – close to a third of the whole land area of the country. It is not a corridor in any usual use of the term, though it includes areas that could be considered corridors, notably the Kilombero Valley, which is close to both a river and the TAZARA railway, and the area of the Usangu Plains around Mbarali.

Publicity materials suggest that land is available in large quantities, and that the beneficiaries will include large numbers of small farmer "outgrowers", growing crops on contract to supplement those produced on a central farm. It encourages international companies to come forward with offers to develop particular projects. The president takes a major interest. The board includes many of Tanzania's leading agriculturalists from the public and private sectors. Where possible, the project proposes involving small farmers as outgrowers, growing crops on contract to supplement those produced on a central farm. A detailed environmental report includes discussion of land acquisition and compensation

---

24. There are many problems with agricultural banks across Africa, and little to suggest that the situation in Tanzania will be different.

Map 1: The Southern Agricultural Growth Corridor of Tanzania

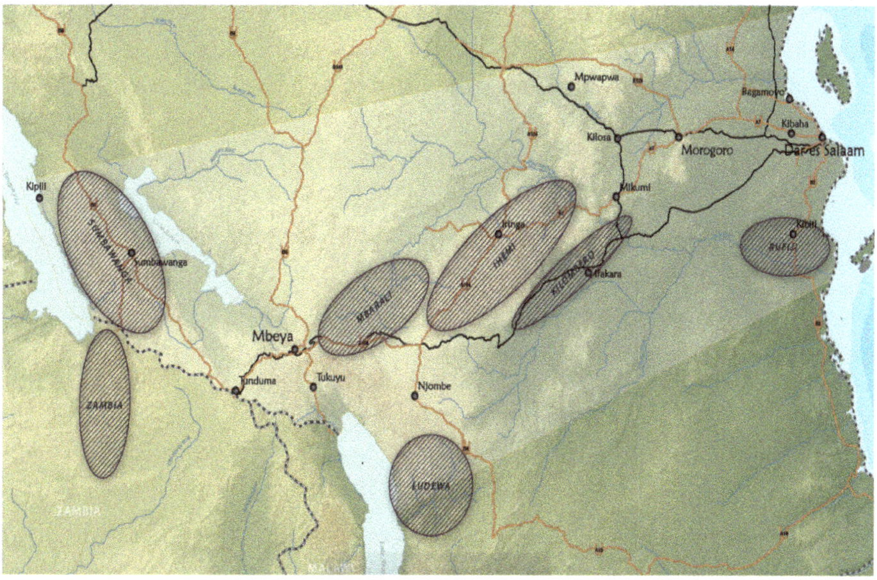

Source: SAGCOT

to smallholders, making it clear that many small farmers will lose land (ERM 2012), and a list of potential projects was identified.

However, on the ground development was slow. Potential investors hoped that the basic infrastructure would be in place or provided – access roads, electricity and water sufficient for at least supplementary irrigation – and that they would have a smooth path to getting rights to the land. It turned out that the Tanzanian government expected either the investors or the donors supporting them to provide this infrastructure. And investors applying for rights to land sometimes found that someone else was there first, or there were small-scale farmers who were very reluctant to lose their land. AgDevCo, which had a head start, did not have the resources to either buy land or develop infrastructure, and, as of 2013, its most advanced projects were on farms where it could get access to land that was already alienated for agricultural use.

Big Results Now

By the end of the 2000s, many Tanzanians began to realise that while an open economy and the ready availability of consumer goods was very desirable, completely unfettered markets were not necessarily in their best interests.[25] They looked to countries in Asia, especially Vietnam, which had survived a most

---

25. The point was made at the Annual Research Workshops of REPOA in 2012 by speakers from Vietnam and China, in 2013 by a keynote speaker from Malaysia, and in 2014 by speakers from Japan.

unpleasant war, followed by a period of socialism and then enforced structural adjustment, but where the state had kept control of key aspects of the economy. Growth in Vietnam was faster than in Tanzania. Tanzania also maintained good links with China, whose firms increasingly won building contracts in international competitions. But the most influential exchanges turned out to be with Malaysia, where leading politicians and civil servants were explicit about the need for an active and interventionist state (Tan 2013).

President Kikwete visited Malaysia in 2011, and was impressed with their "delivery lab" approach to planning, in which stakeholders in relevant sectors were closeted in a hotel for two or three weeks until they agreed on an action plan for their sector. The Malaysians agreed to send key experts from their Performance Management and Delivery Unit, PERMANDU, to explore how such an approach might work in Tanzania. In October 2012, six "focus areas" were agreed by the cabinet: agriculture, education, energy, transportation, water, and resource mobilisation.[26] Between February and April 2013, the six "labs" met and worked long hours at the White Sands Hotel outside Dar es Salaam. Their targets were then agreed by the cabinet, and key performance indicators were set for the managers of the chosen sectors. The commitments are summarised in Figure 1. The total cost was calculated at over USD 10 billion over three years. However, for the first year less than half of this was available from the government budget or other sources, and it was hoped that much of the balance would come from the private sector (BRN 2013a).

In contrast to *Kilimo Kwanza*, the targets for agriculture concentrate on just three crops: maize, rice and sugar (it was left open for oilseeds and horticultural crops to be added in a second phase). The maize sector would be addressed through 275 warehouse schemes in six districts in the southwest of Tanzania. The "collective rice irrigation and marketing schemes" develop and expand on the programmes of the ASDP, but with very specific and ambitious targets for both areas and yields. The proposal is to develop block farms, where land is prepared and irrigated collectively, but cultivated individually. This would include the irrigation projects recently refurbished or created.[27] But there is little evidence of a commitment to working closely with farmers – the projects are presented as expensive, and then as a more or less automatic process (BRN 2013b). Sugar and rice production would be expanded through 25 "commercial" farming deals, mainly on newly irrigated land.[28] These involve huge areas: 11 of them include "nuclear farms" of 20,000 hectares or more with substantial

---

26. Remarkably, given its importance in most discussions of development strategy, and that Tanzania's exports of manufactured goods exceed its exports of agricultural products, manufacturing was not one of the six "labs".
27. This is uncannily similar to the settlement schemes of the 1960s.
28. Continuing the emphasis on irrigation in both the ASDP and Kilimo Kwanza.

Figure 2. Big Results Now Targets

		Big Results by 2015
	Agriculture	• 25 commercial farming deals for paddy and sugarcane • 78 collective rice irrigation and marketing schemes • 275 collective warehouse-based marketing schemes
	Education	• Pass rate of 80% for primary and secondary school students • Improve students' mastering of 3R in Standard I and II by implementing skills assessment and training teachers
	Energy	• Increase generation capacity from 1,010 to 2,260 MW • Access to electricity to 5 mil more Tanzanians • Eliminate EPP reliance
	Transportation	• Passage of 5 mil tons per year through the Central Corridor • Increase port throughput by 6 mil tons, rail by 2.8 mil tons • Reduce road travel time from 3.5 to 2.5 days
	Water	• Sustaining water supply to 15.2 mil people • Restoring water supply to 5.3 mil people • Extending water supply to 7 mil new users
	Resource mobilisation	• Increase tax revenue by Tsh 3 trillion • Implementation of PPP projects valued at Tsh 6 trillion

Source: BRN 2013a: slide 11

extra land for outgrowers. The plan specifies that "to prepare the community for incoming investors" four visits will be made to each site and there will then be an additional visit "to discuss other matters (compensation and resettlement) … as necessary." Soil surveys, environmental analysis and social analysis were to be conducted over 16 days in the field for each project.

The development economist Brian van Arkadie, who has written extensively about Vietnam, commented at the 2013 REPOA Annual Research Workshop that this type of planning linked with administration, which has been successful in creating industrialisation in many Asian countries, derives from the military – and often uses the same kind of command centres, charts and maps. However, when applied to agriculture, there is too much detail and uncertainty for models of this sort to guarantee success. That is particularly true of large-scale agriculture, where the track record is, to say the least, mixed. The proposals for basing agriculture on large irrigated farms share many of the characteristics of the Groundnuts Scheme – on an even bigger scale. Agriculture can seldom be rushed. It requires time to work out the problems and develop the land. If the people who live in those areas are to be involved and to benefit, then it will take much longer than 16 days to win their hearts and minds.

Perhaps for the best, most of the very large agricultural projects have not been implemented as planned: the capital resources were not available, there were problems with land rights and water rights, and there were adverse reactions from some local populations. Even so, there will be long-term costs in terms of non-use of much of the land and uncertain ownership. It is a paradox that this programme is doing exactly what Malaysia did not do – come up with unfeasible targets and then throw resources at them. It is a route that can lead only to disillusion and despair.

Land Grabs

Proposals to subsidise the growing of crops to produce fuel, the high prices of food grains on world markets from around 2008 onwards, and the apparent availability of land suitable for agriculture made African countries a target for investors from Europe and America, but also from Asia and the Middle East. In Tanzania, even before *Big Results Now*, huge areas were at stake (Sulle and Nelson 2009: 16–17). An official in the Tanzania Investment Centre (reported by Sulle and Nelson 2009: 18) said that private investors had requested a total of more than 4 million hectares for the growing of biofuels. A ministerial speech in December 2008 indicated that 640,000 hectares had been "allocated," but rights of occupancy had been granted for only 100,000 hectares. Sulle and Nelson produced a table showing 280,000 hectares "allocated" to 17 projects. In 2013 Locher and Sulle updated this, having checked as many as possible of the projects on the ground (Locher and Sulle 2013; 2014). This showed that promises had been made or land transferred for more than 700,000 hectares, though many of the proposed projects had not proceeded much beyond upbeat press releases which indicated that an investor was in negotiation to gain access to a large area of land.[29]

Meanwhile Havnevik and Haaland (2011), and Abdallah, Engström, Havnevik and Salomonsson (2014) and Locher and Sulle (2014) have shown how those who set out to grow biofuels made slow progress or failed. However, even if large-scale agriculture proves non-viable, several of these developers will have long-term title to much land, especially as land leased by foreign interests through the Tanzania Investment Centre is protected under international law and cannot easily be challenged in the Tanzanian courts. Meanwhile, the way in which these projects are handled in the media, and the enthusiasm shown by leading Tanzanians, shows that the door is still open. It is therefore misleading to describe what is happening as "hype" (Kaag and Zoomers 2014). The consequences of these land transfers will be felt for generations to come.

In an influential review of a number of African countries, the World Bank economists Deiniger and Byerlee concluded that:

> The ... evidence suggests that large-scale expansion of cultivated area poses significant risks, especially if not well managed. As the countries in question often

---

29. Of this, 325,000 ha. is land presently farmed by refugees from Burundi and elsewhere in the far west of Tanzania. The refugees have been offered the prospect of Tanzanian citizenship, but only if they agree to move and disperse. Otherwise they run the risk of being forcibly returned to their countries of origin.

have sizable agricultural sectors with many rural poor, better access to technology and markets, as well as improved institutions to improve productivity on existing land and help judiciously expand cultivated area, could have big poverty impacts. Case studies illustrate that in many instances outside investors have been unable to realize this potential, instead contributing to loss of livelihoods. Problems have included displacement of local people from their land without proper compensation, land being given away well below its potential value, approval of projects that were only feasible because of additional subsidies, generation of negative environmental or social externalities, or encroachment on areas not transferred to the investor to make a poorly performing project economically viable. Many countries with large amounts of currently uncultivated land suitable for cultivation also have large gaps between potential and actual yields. Thus … large increases in output and welfare for the poorest groups could be possible through efforts to enable existing farmers to use currently cultivated land more productively. (Deininger and Byerlee 2011: xlii)

All these features have been identified on projects in Tanzania.

Conclusions

This chapter set out to test the theory that small farms can, in appropriate circumstances, compete with or outperform large. It presented theoretical evidence about how this can be; a historical survey that showed how large farms in Tanzania have often found it hard to survive; and summaries of Tanzania's current policies, which show support for the private sector and agribusiness on a scale not seen since before independence, but that these enterprises too are finding it hard to compete.

Small-scale farmers in Tanzania have repeatedly over the years shown that they can increase their production of crops for sale. The strongest recent evidence for this is the "green revolution" in the Southern Highlands, Ruvuma and Rukwa Regions, based on hybrid maize, rice and the opening up of markets for potatoes, tomatoes, onions etc. in Dar es Salaam and other urban centres. This depended on subsidies for fertiliser being available, but was achieved without much support from the extension service. In Urambo and elsewhere there was rapid expansion in the production of flue-cured tobacco. There were near-record productions of cotton in 2012 (Coulson 2015) and cashew nuts in 2011–12. However, in the case of cotton the *value* of the crop did not rise due to declines in world prices, while the cashew nut crop overwhelmed the purchasers: there was neither the money to buy all of it, nor the capacity to process it.

There were also failures and declines – in the production of coffee, and the growing of bananas in the northwest of the country. There are reasons for these failures: years of poor rainfall around Arusha, very low prices for coffee, attacks by viruses on banana plants. It is also unsurprising that, in areas of population pressure, some of the land that was brought into permanent cultivation 40 or 50 years ago is suffering from mineral deficiencies and soil exhaustion, and that some has been lost to soil erosion. Moreover, traditional water sources are affected by global warming and failures to maintain forest reserves that protect water sources (for instance, on Kilimanjaro) or to plant new trees when old trees are cut down or die.

In these circumstances, an increase in value of total agricultural production by just under 4 per cent per annum is a success (but note the outstanding questions about the accuracy of the official agricultural statistics), and it was achieved without significant extra contributions from large farms.

Meanwhile, Tanzanian planners have exaggerated the potential of large farms and the easy availability of land, and underestimated the challenges they face. In particular, they have exaggerated the potential of irrigation, producing targets that are unfeasible (such as irrigating 7 million hectares of land in a few years), and given insufficient consideration to the need to keep rivers flowing to supply hydroelectricity and to preserve biodiversity.

There is potential for large farms in the export of flowers to Europe, currently increasing at 9 per cent per annum, in the growing of improved seeds for sale, in sugar (despite its long-term consequences for health and obesity, which are leading Western countries to try and limit the consumption of sugar, especially for children) and in forestry. Irrigation will look more attractive if the newly created or refurbished schemes can achieve the high yields, and two or more crops a year, which are necessary if they are to cover the very high initial capital costs.

But overall, as it was for the Germans more than 100 years ago and for the British 60 years ago, the cheapest and quickest means to increase agricultural production in Tanzania is to support and trust small farmers by ensuring that marketing arrangements are in place that will give them fair prices for the crops they sell.

References

Abdallah, J., L. Engström, K. Havnevik and L. Salomonsson (2014) "Large Scale Land Acquisitions in Tanzania: A Critical Analysis of Practices and Dynamics." In Kaag, M. and A. Zoomers (eds) *The Global Land Grab: Beyond the Hype*. Zed Press and Fernwood Publishing.

ASDP (2013) *Agriculture Sector Development Programme II – Basket Fund*. Draft Programme. Volume 1, main report; volume 2, annexes. Government of Tanzania, 25 June.

Atkinson, A. and M. Lugo (2010) *Growth, Poverty and Distribution in Tanzania*. IGC Working Paper 10/0831.

Baran, P. (1973) *The Political Economy of Growth*, Penguin Books (also Monthly Review Press 1957).

Bates, R.H. (1981) *Markets and States in Tropical Africa: The Political Basis of Agricultural Policies*. University of California Press.

Bernstein, H. and T. Byres (2001) "From Peasant Studies to Agrarian Change." *Journal of Agrarian Change* 1(1): 1–56.

Bernstein, H. (2009): "V.I. Lenin and A.V. Chayanov: Looking back, looking forward." *Journal of Peasant Studies* 36(1): 55–81.

Bernstein, H. (2010) *Class Dynamics of Agrarian Change*. Kumarian Press and Fernwood Publishing.

Berry, A. and W. Cline (1979) *Agrarian Structure and Productivity in Developing Countries*. Johns Hopkins University Press.

BRN (Big Results Now) (2013a) *Presentation to PER Annual Review Meeting*, 4 October. Accessed at http://www.tzdpg.or.tz/fileadmin/documents/external/Aid_Effectiveness/PER_2012_-_2013/BRN_Overview_-_PER_Working_Group-4.pdf on 20 May 2014.

BRN (2013b) *Agriculture Lab: National Key Result Area*. Accessed at http://api.ning.com/files/cvkfPcnbiYq9PR6DzTVz3saawb7m2rnU96h17TYM-RoW05h7IZJORgtTxjn8yCmEM7DihrdqETDEGZWk*7JEm8cMxRJrVAn*/20130407AgLabdetailedreport.pdf on 20 May 2014http://api.ning.com/files/cvkfPcnbiYq9PR6DzTVz3saawb7m2rnU96h17TYM-RoW05h7IZJORgtTxjn8yCmEM7DihrdqETDEGZWk*7JEm8cMxRJrVAn*/20130407AgLabdetailedreport.pdf on 20 May 2014.

BRN (2013c) *Agriculture Lab: National Key Result Area*. Accessed at http://www.tzdpg.or.tz/fileadmin/documents/dpg_internal/dpg_working_groups_clusters/cluster_1/psdtrade/Documents/Policy_docs/20130408_AgLab_workstream_storyline_AS_PRINTED.pdf on 10 February 2015.

Bryceson, D.F. (ed.) (1995) *Women Wielding the Hoe: Lesson from Rural Africa for Feminist Theory and Development Practice*. Berg.

Bryceson, D.F. (1997) "Deagrarianisation in Sub-Saharan Africa: Acknowledging the inevitable." In Bryceson D.F. and V. Jamal *Farewell to Farms: Deagrarianisation and Employment in Africa*. Ashgate, pp. 3–20.

Bryceson, D. F. (2000) "Peasant Theories and Smallholder Policies: Past and Present." In Bryceson, D.F., C. Kay and J. Mooij (eds) *Disappearing Peasantries? Rural Labour in Africa, Asia and Latin America*. London: ITGD Publishing, pp.1–36.

Bryceson, D. F. (2010) "Agrarian Fundamentalism or Foresight? Revisiting Nyerere's Vision for Rural Tanzania." In Havnevik, K. and A. Isinika (eds) *Tanzania in Transition: From Nyerere to Mkapa*. Dar es Salaam and Uppsala: Mkuku na Nyota and Nordic Africa Institute, pp. 71–98.

Bryceson, D. F., E. Fisher, J. B. Jønsson and R. Mwaipopo (eds) (2014) *Mining and Social Transformation in Africa: Mineralizing and Democratizing Trends in Artisanal Production*. London: Routledge.

Chachage, C. (2010) *Land Acquision and Accumulation in Tanzania: The case of Morogoro Iringa and Pwani*. Pelum Tanzania. Accessed at http://www.docstoc.com/docs/131370391/Land-acquisition-and-accumulation-in-Tanzania on 14 March 2013.

Chachage, C. and B. Baha (2010) *Accumulation by Land Dispossession and Labour Devaluation in Tanzania: The case of biofuel and forestry investments in Kilwa and Kilolo*. Land Rights Research and Resources Institute (LARRRI/HAKIARDHI). Accessed at http://www.landforafricanwomen.org/fr/node/14 on 14 March 2013.

Chambers, R. (2009) "Foreword". In Scoones, I. and J. Thompson (eds) *Farmer First Revisited: Innovation for Agricultural Research and Development*. Practical Action Publishers.

Chayanov, A.V. (1986 [1925]) *The theory of peasant economy*, 2nd English ed., Thorner, D., B.Kerblay and R.E.F. Smith (eds.) University of Wisconsin Press.

Chetkovich, A. (2012) *A contract for development? Palm oil and Kigoma*. MSc Dissertation, University of Edinburgh.

Choonara, J. (2013) *"Interview: Agriculture, Class and Capitalism." International Socialism 138, April*. Accessed at http://www.isj.org.uk/index.php4?id=888&issue=138 on 22 May 2015.

Cliffe, L. *et al.* (1975) *Rural Cooperation in Tanzania*. Dar es Salaam: Tanzania Publishing House.

Collier, P. (2010) *The Plundered Planet: Why We Must, and How We Can, Manage Nature for Global Prosperity*. Oxford: Oxford University Press.

Collinson, M. (1972) *The Economic Characteristics of the Sukuma Farming System*. Economic Research Bureau Paper 72.5, University of Dar es Salaam.

Collinson, M. (1975) "Tanzania's Cooperative Movement and Farmer Credit in the 1960s." In Cliffe, L. et al. (eds) *Rural Cooperation in Tanzania*. Dar es Salaam: Tanzania Publishing House, pp. 254–77.

Cornia, G. (1985) "Farm size, land yields and the agricultural production function: Analysis for fifteen developing countries." *World Development* 13(4): 513–34.

Coulson, A. (1978) "Agricultural Policies in Mainland Tanzania." *Review of African Political Economy* 10: 74–100. Also in Judith Heyer, Pepe Roberts and Gavin Williams (ed.) (1981) *Rural Development in Tropical Africa*. Heinemann, pp. 60–76.

Coulson, A. and B. Diyamett (2012) Improving the Contribution of Agriculture to Economic Growth in Tanzania: Policy Implications of a Scoping Study in Tanzania. Working Paper 12/0093, London: International Growth Centre. Also at http://www.theigc.org/wp-content/uploads/2014/09/Coulson-Et-Al-2012-Policy-Brief.pdf.

Coulson, A. (2013) *Tanzania: A Political Economy*. Oxford University Press, second ed. with a new introduction (first ed. 1982).

Coulson, A. (2014a) "The Agrarian Question: The Scholarship of David Mitrany Revisited." *Journal of Peasant Studies* 41(3): 405–19.

Coulson, A. (2014b) "Book review of Aminzade (2013), Lofchie (2014) and Edwards (2014)" *Tanzania Affairs* 109: 42–8. Accessed at http://www.tzaffairs.org/category/issue-number/issue-109/ on 7 February 2015.

Coulson, A. (2015) "The Political Economy of Cotton in Tanzania." Submitted to *the Review of African Political Economy*. An earlier version was presented at the colloquium in honour of Lionel Cliffe on Democracy, Land and Liberation in Africa Today, Cape Town, 20–21 October 2014.

Da Corta, L. and J. Magongo (2011) *Evolution of Gender and Policy Dynamics in Tanzania*. Working Paper 203, Chronic Poverty Research Centre. Available at http://www.chronicpoverty.org/uploads/publication_files/WP203%20Magongo-DaCorta.pdf

David, E. (1903) *Sozialismus und Landwirtschaft* [Socialism and agriculture]. Leipzig, Berlin: Verlag der Socialistischen Monatshefte.

Deininger, K. and D. Byerlee (2011) *Rising Global Interest in Farmland: Can it yield sustainable and equitable benefits?* Washington DC: World Bank.

Dercon, S. (1993) "Peasant Supply Response and Macroeconomic Policies: Cotton in Tanzania." *Journal of African Economies* 2(2): 158–93.

Edwards, S. (2014) *Toxic Aid: Economic Collapse and Recovery in Tanzania*. Oxford University Press

Ellis, F. (1982) "Agricultural Price Policy in Tanzania." *World Development* 10(4): 263–83.

Eriksson, G. (1993) *Peasant Response to Price Incentives in Tanzania: A Theoretical and Empirical Investigation*. Research Report No.91. Scandinavian Institute for African Studies, Uppsala. Accessed at http://www.diva-portal.org/smash/get/diva2:273507/FULLTEXT01.pdf on 2 February 2015.

ERM (2012) *Southern Agricultural Growth Corridor of Tanzania (SAGCOT) Strategic Regional Environmental and Social Assessment, Interim Report*. Prepared for the Government of Tanzania. Accessed at http://www.sagcot.com/uploads/media/Interim_Report_-_SAGCOT_SRESA_Final_12_02.pdf on 12 May 2014.

ETG (nd.) *Export Trading Group*. Accessed at http://www.etgworld.com/wp-content/files_mf/etgcpmarketingdigitalfa.pdf on 20 April 2015

Gates (2012) *Developing the rice industry in Africa: Tanzania assessment July 2012.* Bill and Melinda Gates Foundation. http://www.inter-reseaux.org/IMG/pdf/20120803_Tanzania_rice_value_chain_analysis_external_.pdf Accessed 23 April 2015

Gibbon, P., K. Havnevik and K. Hermele (1993) *A Blighted Harvest: The World Bank and African Agriculture in the 1980s.* James Currey.

Government of Tanzania (2007) *Eastern Arc Mountains Strategy – Thematic Strategy: Mechanism for Payments for Water Environmental Services, Rufiji River Basin, Tanzania.* Forestry and Beekeeping Division. Accessed at http://easternarc.or.tz/downloads/07/CMEAMF_Rufiji_PES_Study.pdf 29 April 2015

Government of Tanzania (2009) *Ten Pillars of Kilimo Kwanza (Implentation Framework).* Accessed at http://www.tzonline.org/pdf/tenpillarsofkilimokwanza.pdf on 8 May 2014.

Green, M. (2014) *The Development State: Aid, Culture and Civil Society in Tanzania.* James Currey.

Hanlon, J., J. Manjengwa and T. Smart (2013) *Zimbabwe takes back its land.* Sterling VA: Kumarian Press.

Havnevik, K. and H. Haaland (2011) "Biofuel, land and environmental issues: The case of SEKAB's biofuel plans in Tanzania." In Matondi, P., K. Havnevik and A. Beyene (eds) *Biofuels, Land Grabbing and Food Security in Africa.* London: Zed Press, pp. 106–33.

Hydén, G. (1980) *Beyond Ujamaa in Tanzania: Underdevelopment and an Uncaptured Peasantry.* London: Heinemann.

Ibbott, R. (2014) *Ujamaa – The Hidden Story of Tanzania's Socialist Villages.* London: Crossroads Books.

Iliffe, J. (1979) *A Modern History of Tanganyika.* Cambridge: Cambridge University Press.

Isinika, A.C. and E. Msuya (2011) "Addressing Food Self-Sufficiency in Tanzania: A Balancing Act of Policy Coordination." In Djurfeldt, G., E. Aryeetey and A. C. Isinika (eds) *African Smallholders: Food Crops, Markets and Policy.* CAB International.

James, S. (2014) "Introduction". In Ibbot, R. *Ujamaa: The Hidden Story of Tanzania's Socialist Villages.* London: Crossroads Books.

Jeffares, S. (2007) "Why public ideas catch on: Empty signifiers and flourishing neighbourhoods." PhD thesis, University of Birmingham.

Jeffares, S. (2014) *Interpreting Hashtag Politics : Policy Ideas in an Era of Social Media: politics.* Palgrave Macmillan.

Kaag, M. and A. Zoomers (eds) (2014) *The Global Land Grab: Beyond the Hype.* Zed Press and Fernwood.

Kjekshus, H. (1977) *Ecology Control and Economic Development in East African History.* Heinemann Educational Books.

Koopman, J. and I. M. Faye (2012) "Land Grabs, Women's Farming, and Women's Activism in Africa." Presented at the conference on Global Land Grabbing, Cornell, October. Available at http://www.cornell-landproject.org/download/landgrab2012papers/Koopman.pdf.

Lenin, V.I. (1967 [1899]) *The development of capitalism in Russia. The process of the formation of a home market for large-scale industry.* Collected works, Vol. 3. Moscow: Progress Publishers.

Lenin, V.I. (2010 [1917]) *Imperialism: The Highest Stage of Capitalism* (English transl.). London: Penguin.

Lipton, M. (1989) (with Richard Longhurst) *New Seeds and Poor People.* London: Unwin.

Lipton, M. (2010) **"From Policy Aims and Small-farm Characteristics to Farm Science Needs."** World Development 38(10): 1399–1412.

Littlejohn, G. (1984) "The agrarian Marxist research in its political context: State policy and the development of the Soviet rural class structure in the 1920s." *Journal of Peasant Studies* 11(2): 61–84.

Locher, M. and E. Sulle (2013) *Foreign land deals in Tanzania - An update and a critical view on the challenges of data (re)production.* LDPI Working Paper 31, Institute for Poverty, Land and Agrarian Studies, University of the Western Cape. Accessed 30 April 2015 at http://www.plaas.org.za/plaas-publication/ldpi-31

Locher, M. and E. Sulle (2014) "Challenges and Methodological Flaws in Reporting the Global Land Rush: Observations from Tanzania." *Journal of Peasant Studies* 41(3–4): 569–92.

Lofchie, M. (2014) *The Political Economy of Tanzania: Decline and Recovery.* University of Pennsylvania Press.

Mdee, A. (2014) *The Politics of Small-Scale Irrigation in Tanzania: Making Sense of Failed Expectations* (with E. Harrison, C. Mdee, E. Mdee and E. Bahati). Working Paper 107, Future Agricultures Consortium (University of Sussex and Mzumbe University). Accessed 10 February 2015 at http://r4d.dfid.gov.uk/Output/197577/

Mitrany, D. (1951) *Marx against the Peasant: A Study in Social Dogmatism.* London: Weidenfeld and Nicolson.

Mwami, A. and K. Ng'wanza (2011) *Land Grabbing in a Post Investment Period and Popular Reaction in the Rufiji River Basin: A Research Report.* Hakiardhi, Dar es Salaam. Accessed at http://farmlandgrab.org/uploads/attachment/LAND%20GRABBING%20IN%20A%20POST%20INVESTMENT%20PERIOD%20AND%20POPULAR%20REACTIONS%20IN%20THE%20RUFIJI%20RIVER%20BASIN..pdf on 29 April 2015

Ngaiza, R. (2012) Presentation by the Ministry of Agriculture, Food Security and Cooperatives at the FAO-University of Nairobi Regional Workshop on an Integrated Policy Approach to Commercializing Smallholder Maize Production, Norfolk Hotel Nairobi, 6–7 June. Accessed at http://www.fao.org/fileadmin/templates/esa/Workshop_reports/Smallholders_2012/Presentations_1/Ngaiza_Kilimo_Kwanza_Tanzania.pdf on 29 January 2015.

Nyerere, J. (1967) "Socialism and Rural Development." Reprinted in Nyerere, J. *Freedom and Socialism,* Oxford University Press 1968.

O'Laughlin, B. (1995) "The Myth of the African Family in the World of Development." In Bryceson, D.F. (ed.) *Women Wielding the Hoe: Lesson from Rural Africa for Feminist Theory and Development Practice.* Berg, pp. 63–91.

Pearce, F. (2012) *The Landgrabbers: The New Fight over who owns the earth.* Eden Project Books.

Pingali, P., Y. Bigot and H.P. Binswanger (1987) *Agricultural Mechanization and the Evolution of Farming Systems in Sub-Tropical Africa.* Baltimore MD: Johns Hopkins University Press.

Ponte, S. (2002) *Farmers and Markets in Tanzania.* London: James Currey.

Rasmussen, T. (1986) "The Green Revolution in the Southern Highlands." In Boesen, J., K. Havnevik, J. Koponen and R. Odegaard (eds) *Tanzania: Crisis and Struggle for Survival.* Uppsala: Scandinavian Institute of African Studies, pp. 191–205.

Ruthenberg, H. (1964) *Agricultural Development in Tanganyika.* Munich: Springer-Verlag.

Ruthenberg, H. (ed.) (1968) *Smallholder Farming and Smallholder Development in Tanzania.* Munich: Springer-Weltforum.

SAGCOT (2010) Southern Agricultural Growth Corridor of Tanzania.

Scott, J.C. (1985) *Weapons of the weak. Everyday forms of peasant resistance.* New Haven: Yale University Press.

Scott, J.C. and B.J. Tria Kerkvliet (eds) (1986) Everyday forms of peasant resistance in South-East Asia. Special issue of *The Journal of Peasant Studies* 13(2).

Shamte, S. (2011) *Investment in Agriculture in Tanzania.* Presentation, London, 7 May. Accessed at http://www.slideshare.net/ABST/kilimo-kwanza-investment-presentation-to-tanzania-diaspora-may-2011-shamte on 11 May 2014.

Skarstein, R. (2010) "Smallholder Agriculture in Tanzania: Can Economic Liberalisation Keep its Promises?" In Havnevik, K. and A. Isinika (eds) *Tanzania in Transition: From Nyerere to Mkapa,* Dar es Salaam and Uppsala: Mkuki na Nyota Publishers and Nordic Africa Institute, pp. 99-130.

Stahl, K. (1961) *Tanganyika: Sail in the Wilderness.* The Hague: Mouton.

Stoneman, C. and L. Cliffe (1989) *Zimbabwe: Politics, Economics and Society.* London: Pinter.

Sulle, E. and F. Nelson (2009) *Biofuels, Land Access and Rural Livelihoods in Tanzania.* London: International Institute for Environment and Development. Accessed at http://pubs.iied.org/pdfs/12560IIED.pdf on 15 May 2015.

Tan, C. (2013) "Problems vs. Polarities: The Importance of Understanding Stakeholder Nuances in Your Quest for Inclusive Growth". Keynote address, REPOA Research Workshop, 3 April 2013. Accessed at http://www.repoa.or.tz/documents_storage/KN.pdf 12 May 2014.

Therkildsen, O. (2011) *Policy making and implementation in agriculture: Tanzania's push for irrigated rice.* Danish Institute of International Studies Working Paper 26.

Thoden van Velsen, H.U.E. (1975) "Some obstacles to Ujamaa: A case study from Rungwe." In Cliffe, L. et al. (eds) *Rural Cooperation in Tanzania.* Dar es Salaam: Tanzania Publishing House, pp. 346-59.

USAID (2010) *MicroCLIR/CIBER assessment: The legal, policy, regulatory, and institutional constraints to the growth of maize and rice in Tanzania – Agenda for Action.*

Von Freyhold, M. (1979) *Ujamaa Villages in Tanzania: Analysis of a social experiment.* Heinemann.

Waters, T. (2007) *The Persistence of Subsistence Agriculture: Life beneath the level of the market place.* Lexington Books.

Wiggins, S., J. Kirsten and L. Llambí (2010) "The Future of Small Farms." *World Development* 38(10): 1341–48.

Wisner, B., A. Kassami and A. Nuwagaba (1975) "Mbambara: The Long Road to Ujamaa." In Cliffe, L. et al. (eds) *Rural Cooperation in Tanzania.* Dar es Salaam: Tanzania Publishing House, pp.370–39. Also "Postscript to Mbambara" by the Tanzania Year 16 Project, *ibid.,* pp.392–5.

Wisner, B. (2014) *Is Banana-Millet Beer the Answer to Climate Change? Small farmer and pastoralist climate adaptation in northeastern Tanzania.* Seminar presentation, Britain Tanzania Society, London, 30 January.

Wolf, E. (1966) *Peasants.* Prentice Hall.

Wolter, D. (2008) Tanzania: The Challenge of Moving from Subsistence to Profit. OECD Development Centre.

World Development (2010) Special issue on the Future of Small Farms. *World Development* 38(10): 1341–1526.

Xiaoyun, Li (2012) *Why Has not Growth in Africa Been Pro-poor? Tanzania's case from Chinese perspective.* Presentation at REPOA Research Workshop, 28 March. Accessed at http://www.jica.go.jp/uk/english/office/topics/pdf/topics120316_18.pdf on 12 May 2014.

Xiaoyun, Li (n.d.) *What can Africa learn from China's success in agriculture?* Accessed at http://www.iprcc.org/userfiles/file/Li%20Xiaoyun-EN(1).pdf on 12 May 2014.

The rise and fall of the Paris Agenda in Tanzania

A study in trust and mistrust

Bertil Odén

Introduction

Over the years, Kjell Havnevik has published a significant number of texts on macroeconomic policy and development cooperation, including the links between these two fields, and often with empirical material from Tanzania. In some cases he was also commissioned by aid agencies and international organisations to evaluate or assess the results of development cooperation in a specific country or through the use of a specific aid modality. It therefore seems appropriate that my chapter reflects upon the fate in Tanzania, during the period 2005–15, of the Paris Declaration principles to improve aid effectiveness. This topic is also an excellent example of the important and, at the same time, underestimated role of mutual trust in all sustainable development cooperation.

The chapter starts with a brief historical exposé of aid relations from independence until the launch of the Paris Declaration in 2005. The second and main part covers the period from 2005 until early 2015, during which development cooperation relations moved from euphoria to disappointment. Concluding comments end the chapter.

The discussion is focused on relations between the government of Tanzania and the aid donor community established in Dar es Salaam. This gives an exaggerated picture of the role of development cooperation compared to other factors. It also reduces the importance of domestic policy decisions and domestic relations. This is a deliberate and almost unavoidable effect in a brief text focusing on aid relations.

Historical relations between Tanzania and its aid donors
– travels down a bumpy road

Honeymoon – from independence to the oil and debt crisis

Overall relations between the government of Tanzania and the aid donor community have changed significantly over the years since independence. During the 1960s, the previous British colonial administration was transformed into a national government, with quite a number of British staff still working in the administration of the recently independent country. Gradually, a number of other countries as well as international organisations offered support and new forms of public development cooperation emerged. The volume of aid increased rather rapidly, but the state administration was thinly staffed, in spite of the inflow of external specialists and material resources.

After the Arusha Declaration in 1967, the policy of self-reliance, including a number of rapid and ambitious economic policy reforms, was introduced. These reforms included nationalisation of most of the major financial, commercial and manufacturing enterprises, rapid state-financed expansion, the *Ujamaa* village system, introduction of universal primary education, expansion of primary health facilities and rural water supplies, and a new basic industries policy. As a result, the public sector expanded rapidly.

This also meant that Tanzania launched a development policy, in which some parts were at odds with the mainstream market-based development thinking of most donors at the time. In spite of this, Tanzania under President Nyerere became popular among donors, including the World Bank, which was prepared to support the country with substantial credits. Very early Tanzania had thus become a favourite laboratory for the main donors, in which full-scale experiments in the fields of development strategy and aid policy, methods, etc. were undertaken.

For some donors, Tanzania was also regarded as an arena of Cold War competition between East and West. The Soviet Union supported the country tepidly and China financed and constructed its largest development cooperation project of the time, the Tazara railway from Dar es Salaam to the copper belt in Zambia, after the World Bank had declined to do so.

Many of the initiatives and reforms implemented in Tanzania during "the *Ujamaa* era" turned out to have effects that were the opposite of those intended. Production stagnated, the needed economic surplus did not materialise and private external capital was not interested in investing. The government became more and more dependent on development aid, official loans and inflationary deficit domestic financing. For a couple of years, aid donors went along with Tanzanian policies and supported their implementation, contributing to projects and programmes that were later deemed to have contributed to the crisis of the 1980s.

Some researchers argue that lack of development in the agricultural sector, and hence the absence of an increasing investible surplus to sustain growth in other sectors, was a major cause underlying the onset of the crisis in the late 1970s. To this should be added an overambitious and too hurried industrialisation programme, running parallel with a rapid expansion of social services. An important factor aggravating the situation was the high inefficiency of surplus utilisation (Boesen, Havnevik, Koponen and Odgaard (eds) 1986). To that should be added a number of strong external factors. The most commonly mentioned was external economic shocks, such as the tripling of world oil prices twice during the 1970s, which quickly eroded the forex reserves. The armed intervention in Uganda to remove President Idi Amin from power also took a heavy toll in both human and economic terms.

The 1980s – economic crisis, structural adjustment, eroded mutual trust

In the late 1970s and early 1980s, the Tanzanian crisis manifested itself in an acute shortage of foreign exchange and drastic reductions in manufacturing, which resulted in increasing scarcity of basic consumer commodities and inputs. For example, at the beginning of the 1970s Tanzanian exports corresponded to 75 per cent of its imports, but by the beginning of the 1980s this share had fallen to 45 per cent. It became more and more difficult to cover the rest with development aid and commercial credits (Boesen et al. 1986).

The underlying negative trend in agricultural development, resulting in a stagnating agricultural surplus that was heavily taxed by the state, in particular the crop authorities, caused concern among the political leadership.

It was also recognised that the system of long-term five year plans could not address the situation of acute crisis. A National Economic Survival Programme (NESP) was launched in 1981, which envisaged a rapid increase in agriculture exports, a restructuring of the economy and increased industrial capacity utilisation supported by sizeable external loans and grant aid. As the conflict with the IMF over the economic policy continued, little external support was forthcoming, and soon it became clear that NESP would not meet its targets.

The first years of the 1980s saw an international shift towards neoliberal economic policy and the emergence of President Reagan in the US and Prime Minister Thatcher in the UK as leading political figures internationally. In this context, the more or less general donor support for Tanzania gradually gave way to an almost unanimous attitude among donors that Tanzania had to agree with the IMF and the World Bank on a stabilisation and structural adjustment programme. Only thus, it was felt, would Tanzania be able to get out of an unsustainable debt situation and improve the conditions for economic structural reform.

The most hesitant followers of this international trend were the Nordic countries. They supported the government of Tanzania when it tried to launch the "home-brewed" National Economic Survival Programme in order to avoid the stringent conditions set by the IMF and World Bank. Soon after its launch, it became clear the programme would be impossible to implement. Based on these conclusions, the Nordic countries informed (in November 1984) the Tanzanian government that they could not continue their aid unless Tanzania accepted the IMF conditions.

Tanzania's unwillingness to accept the IMF's loan terms was remarkably strong, considering the country's acute need for additional foreign assistance. In the early 1980s, the national leaders stated that giving in to these conditions would compromise the Tanzanian development model (Wangwe 1987). It required a shift in the political leadership to change that view. The 1984/85 budget signalled that the Tanzanian government was prepared to change its policy, in particular in the fields of agricultural producer prices and devaluation. In 1986, Nyerere resigned as president and was replaced by Ali Hassan Mwinyi. After that, an economic stabilisation agreement between Tanzania and the IMF was signed in August that year. In agreement with the World Bank, a Tanzanian government Programme for Economic Recovery for 1986/87 – 1988/89 was also launched (Boesen et al. 1986).

From then until the mid-1990s, stringent stabilisation economic policy and significant structural economic reforms were agreed and at least partly implemented and lending and grant aid from both the Bretton Woods institutions and bilateral donors was resumed.

Early 1990s – continued liberalisation and deteriorating aid relations

The first Tanzanian Economic Recovery Programme was based on the principle of "getting prices right." In the second programme, covering 1989 to 1992, the reforms revolved around social adjustment and institutions. These later stages required more political commitment than the earlier ones.

Donors began to express concern in the early 1990s regarding what they considered insufficient political commitment by the Tanzanian government. They felt that Tanzania was failing to implement the reform programme and had not mobilised sufficient domestic resources. The Tanzanian government, on the other hand, claimed that donors were interfering too much and were undermining national ownership of the development agenda (Wangwe 2010). This stand-off led again to a deterioration in the aid relationship between the government and foreign donors. The situation was cause for concern among many actors in Tanzania and within the donor community, particularly among Nordic donors.

Relations with the donor community were not very harmonious, as the level of corruption increased and what was minted as "aid fatigue" grew among donor governments. The latter pushed for still stronger reforms, which the Tanzanian government felt would erode its ownership of national economic policy. Mutual trust between the development partners eroded and very few constructive attempts to improve the situation were made.

From the mid-1990s: Tanzania as a Paris Declaration frontrunner

In 1994, the Nordic countries, with Denmark the driving force, decided to take action to improve the relationship. They launched a process that led to the appointment of a group of independent advisors under the leadership of Professor Gerry Helleiner of the University of Toronto. The advisors undertook a study, which was published in 1995. Subsequent discussions between the government and donors were based on this report. Opening up such a dialogue became a new policy priority. The result was the compilation of a set of "agreed notes" (in the form of 18 points) stating, among other things, that there was a need to improve government leadership of development programming and to achieve greater transparency, accountability and efficiency in aid delivery (Wangwe 2010). Reports assessing the progress made by both parties were presented to consultative group meetings (formal meetings between a partner country and the donor community) in December 1997, March 1999 and May 2000.

The government of Tanzania launched the Tanzania Assistance Strategy (TAS) in 1998-99 as a coherent national development framework for managing external resources to achieve stated development objectives and strategies. TAS represented the national initiative to restore local leadership in promoting partnership in the design and execution of development programmes. It contained a three-year national strategy covering various aspects of the national development agenda set out in the government's Poverty Reduction Strategy, which had also been endorsed by donors. Moreover, it contained best practices in development cooperation and a framework for monitoring its implementation.

TAS was followed by an action plan from 2002/03, which set out more practical implementation steps in four areas: promoting government of Tanzania leadership, improving predictability of external resources, increasing capture of aid flows in the government budget and improving domestic capacity for aid coordination and management of external resources (Wangwe 2010:211). The government and donors agreed to set up monitoring and evaluation mechanisms that would review the progress in improving the aid relationship and discuss reports submitted to the Tanzanian government and donors so that agreement could be reached on next steps.

The job of undertaking independent reviews was entrusted to an Independent Monitoring Group (IMG) appointed jointly by the government and donors. The IMG was thus a successor to the previous Helleiner group. Its first report (IMG 2002) was presented to the Consultative Group meeting in December 2002. Thanks to the impartiality of its authors, the report was able to raise a number of sensitive issues for discussion by donors and between donors and the government (Odén and Tinnes 2003).

It should be noted that this development took place three years before the launching of the Paris Declaration. Tanzania, as a frontrunner in the international trend towards more effective development cooperation, once again became a testing ground for donors.

The Paris Agenda saga – from euphoria to disappointment

As of 2005 the Paris Agenda set the stage for international development coop-eration negotiations.[1]

The second IMG report was presented in April 2005 and the third in Sep-tember 2010 (IMG 2010). They reviewed the status of the government-donor relationship in Tanzania and assessed the progress made towards the principles and objectives set out in the TAS and the Joint Assistance Strategy for Tanzania (JAST) (see below). What follows is to a significant extent a summary of the findings of the latter report.

JAST: Succeeding the TAS was JAST, signed in 2005 and covering the years 2006-10. Based on experience thus far in implementing a new aid relationship with Tanzania, it was designed to take the TAS to a higher stage of national ownership and leadership, and to reduce transaction costs by enhancing harmo-nisation and alignment with national priorities and national systems.

JAST tried to align each donor country's assistance strategy with the govern-ment's long-term outlook for the period up to 2025. It stated that donor funds should be used collectively for implementing the second Poverty Reduction Strategy, called MKUKUTA. JAST was formulated in a consultative process in-volving the government, donors, non-state actors and parliamentarians. The key issues in JAST included the division of labour based on comparative advantage, the use of technical assistance for capacity development, and recommendations for the increased use of general budget support. It was signed by 19 donors,[2] of which some had never participated in similar ventures before.

Focus on harmonisation and alignment

The strong lead taken by the government of Tanzania at the time of the imple-mentation of JAST, together with the donors' interest in "piloting" and honour-ing the commitments made in the Paris Declaration, led to a situation in which

---

1. The Paris Declaration (2005) adopted by the Organization for Economic Co-operation and Development (OECD) is a practical, action-oriented roadmap to improve the quality of aid and its impact on development. It gives a series of specific implementation measures and establishes a monitoring system to assess progress and ensure that donors and recipi-ents hold each other accountable for their commitments. The Paris Declaration outlines the following five fundamental principles for making aid more effective: *Ownership:* De-veloping countries set their own strategies for poverty reduction, improve their institutions and tackle corruption. *Alignment:* Donor countries align behind these objectives and use local systems. *Harmonisation:* Donor countries coordinate, simplify procedures and share information to avoid duplication. *Results*: Developing countries and donors shift focus to development results and results get measured. *Mutual accountability:* Donors and partners are accountable for development results.
2. African Development Bank, Belgium, Canada, Denmark, European Commission, Fin-land, France, Germany, Ireland, Japan, Netherlands, Norway, Sweden, Spain, Switzerland, United Kingdom, United Nations, United States and the World Bank.

development cooperation with Tanzania became more aligned and harmonised than it had been at any previous time.

The MKUKUTA strategy formed the point of departure for most development cooperation. It required donors to get together with the Tanzanian government to discuss priority areas and sectors for each intervention, an exercise that drastically cut the number of donor-funded projects. The result was not only fewer donor interventions, but also larger commitments, and this in turn led to more general budget support, sector support and basket funding.

The donors were also working together more closely when operating in a specific sector. For each joint activity, a special group was created under government leadership and agreed on all the necessary details from content to reporting procedures. Disbursements were generally triggered by a set of quantifiable indicators that were based as far as possible on the MKUKUTA strategy. All this led to a high degree of alignment. Moreover, the interventions were to a larger extent channelled through the government budget system and were reported jointly, in accordance with the reporting and accounting system adopted by the Tanzanian government.

Harmonisation was reflected in a proliferation of donor working groups. Every individual donor was involved in fewer sectors. The number of donors providing general budget support also increased. The prominence of aid modalities such as budget support and basket funds, including sector-wide approaches (SWAPs), made it more important for donors to participate in the Tanzanian Public Expenditure Review (PER), since this gave them an insight into and a degree of informal influence on the budget process and on Poverty Reduction Strategy implementation. It also meant that they had substantial information on the effectiveness of public funds in the Tanzanian priority sectors.

The aim of the PER was to provide input for the preparation of the government budget and enable assessment of its implementation. The PER assessed overall fiscal discipline, analysed government resources and spending on key priority areas, and acted as a check on whether the government's strategic priorities were in line with the country's overall macroeconomic and fiscal situation (Odén and Tinnes 2003). After a couple of years the PER process slowed down, but in 2012 the government and the main donors decided to revitalise it.

General budget support

The Tanzanian government made it clear that it found project support the most challenging modality in terms of management, as it tended to create parallel systems, raise transaction costs and drain government capacity.

General budget support (GBS), on the other hand, was the Tanzanian government's preferred aid modality. It enhanced the predictability of resources, national planning, the use of government systems, national ownership, accountability and transparency. GBS first started to be used in its present form in 2001 and was facilitated by a common performance assessment framework, whose reviews were undertaken annually prior to each financial year. During its peak period, 14–15 donors were providing GBS.

GBS changed government/donor relations and working habits considerably, and detailed project discussions gave way to macro dialogue on economic and political matters. However, after a few years of implementation, major questions were raised both about procedural matters and the dialogue as such. On procedure, the way in which the annual review was implemented was questioned by both sides. On the dialogue, concern was raised about the structure, level of participation by government and the content of the dialogue, which was more process- than results oriented.

Both donors and government were blamed for this development. A major problem on the donor side was the different criteria used for finally releasing funds, in particular the variable tranches after the joint decision had been made in the annual review process. The reasons for this were manifold but most of them stemmed from the considerable scepticism with which GBS was viewed in donor countries. On the government side, the handling of difficult political questions related to political and economic development complicated the dialogue. GBS as a government policy is also more susceptible to media criticism in donor countries. In particular, this is true of serious cases of mismanagement, including corruption. More recently, the government side's enthusiasm for GBS has also declined (see below).

Basket funding, which also increased, is based on the principle of donors and the Tanzanian government pooling resources for a specific sector or thematic area, and is normally specified in a memorandum of understanding. At their peak, there were 10–15 such funds operating in various areas and sectors, such as the Primary School Programme and Legal Sector Reform Programme (Government of Tanzania 2006).

As donor concerns regarding the potential of GBS funding gradually increased, more attention was given to the effectiveness of basket funding, including SWAPS, and donor interventions using this modality increased. Concerns about "projectisation" of this modality were raised, in particular because of the many new factors involved, such as vertical funds (funds in a specialised field, often operating outside the government administration).

A second issue which emerged was that the joint working groups formed to overview the implementation of the baskets worked slowly and in much detail (micromanagement). As a result, the basket funding often had not been agreed upon in time to be included in the government's budget. This led to difficulties in the implementation of important reform measures after agreement on them had finally been reached.

Project assistance. During the period of strong support for GBS very little thought was given to making project aid more effective and in line with the Paris Agenda. The subsequent reduction of GBS gave rise to a situation in which project aid again became the dominating aid modality.

Capacity development

For Tanzania, improvement of domestic capacity has always been a key issue. The aim was that staff responsible for implementing and coordinating the budget should be sufficiently competent to comply with all the new obligations and live up to all expectations.

Increased ownership, harmonisation and alignment, plus the emergence of new aid modalities, underscored the importance of effective institutions and regulations. The government enacted a number of important new laws and regulations. A Presidential Commission Against Corruption presented in December 1996 an agenda for eradicating corruption. One of the most encouraging developments was the introduction of a new integrated financial management system for recording and managing spending. By 2010, this system was considered successful. Other new laws were passed on public procurement and the budget process.

Donors also supported the improvement of capacity in Tanzania. A number of basket fund programmes to develop capacity in the government sector have been launched. These include reform programmes for each of the civil service, legal sector and private sector. A major problem is how technical assistance can be more effectively provided in the new aid architecture.

For donors, one important problem was – and still is – the lack of continuity among staff responsible for maintaining the dialogue and the different perspectives of field and home offices.

Dialogue structure and transaction costs. The dialogue structure developed during the implementation of TAS was further refined during the first years of JAST and was again revised in 2009. It comprised a large number of working groups at different levels and became so complicated that it became difficult to oversee. There were too many meetings and there was too much concentration on process rather than on substance. In many cases, the joint meetings did not seem to function.

The reasons for the problems on both sides were manifold. Among them, the most commonly cited was the fact that limited government capacity reduced the possibility of taking ownership. Donors also found that the level of government representation was not always appropriate to the questions to be discussed. Concern was also raised over the lack of meetings on overarching subjects. The dialogue on GBS was considered good and a similar calibre of dialogue was considered necessary for other modalities.

Transaction costs seemed to be higher than had been expected after all the years of harmonisation and alignment and the increased share of programme aid. This was particularly so on the government side, especially the Ministry of Finance. However, no study has compared transaction costs over time. Most probably, they were lowered. They were also concentrated on fewer actors, who therefore felt an increased burden. Simultaneously, the absolute amount of aid has increased substantially, new actors have entered the scene and latterly the share of projects has again increased, which in turn has counteracted any savings.

Most recent developments. The movement away from the Paris Agenda principles has continued during the most recent years. The government's enthusiasm for GBS has cooled and the dialogue platforms associated with it are not very active.

The government has also introduced parallel structures in its own budget, the main one being the *Big Results Now* initiative of 2013, originally covering six sectors (energy, education, transport/harbours, water, agriculture[3] and resource mobilisation). Recently, two more sectors have been added (private sector environment and health). The number of GBS providers declined to 11 in early 2015, and a few more are considering abandoning this modality. An increasing number of programmes are using special accounts to channel external funds.

Concluding comments

According to the Tanzanian analyst Samuel Wangwe, by 2005 the government had become more assertive, better organised and made better preparations for dialogue with development partners. Progress had been made in terms of leadership and ownership, as seen in the second national Poverty Reduction Strategy. Wangwe's overall assessment was that "Government of Tanzania leadership and ownership of the development agenda, its content and implementation, has indeed been strengthened during the first half of the 2000 decade" (Wangwe 2010:209).

Nonetheless, ownership was still rather narrowly based in the government, with many sector ministries showing little interest in it. Wangwe raised four specific concerns that needed to be addressed: 1) The number of active change agents within the government was still quite small, making the process rather fragile. 2) The spread of the government leadership was still narrow. Some ministries had a low level of awareness and capacity to play their role as leaders in policy dialogue. 3) The incentive structure should be improved to underpin efforts at enhancing harmonisation and ownership. That should include pay reform and how to deal with the power and resources that are often associated

---

3.   See also Coulson, in this volume.

with projects and parallel programmes. 4) The policy coordination system between the two parts of the Union (between the Mainland and Zanzibar) had not been functioning.

Dialogue institutions and rules to improve harmonisation and coordination were included in JAST, which expired in 2012. Since then, there have been attempts to replace JAST with a Development Cooperation Framework, DCF. This was supposed to be based on the principles adopted at the International High-level Meeting in Busan in late 2011. By early 2015, an agreement on DCF had still not been reached.

Problems related to the dialogue structure have deteriorated further. The dialogue and the ownership shown by the Tanzanian government have often been considered weak by donors. The harmonisation processes among OECD Development Assistance Committee (DAC) donors have declined and some major donors seem to have lost interest in this activity and in the principle of ownership. There is also a trend among major donors within the EU group and more widely to move ahead with individual agendas. Nor has coordination between traditional and emerging DAC donors really been achieved to date. The practice of using Tanzania's own budget, reporting, monitoring and procurement systems has slowly eroded, and a larger share of aid therefore flows beyond the control of the Tanzanian government.

The basic factor behind this is a further decline in the trust between many traditional donor agencies and the government. This trend has been accentuated by the government's weak attempts to implement accountability principles, resulting in a number of corruption cases or what donors regard as bad governance. On the other side, the government has encountered increased micromanagement by donor agencies as well as increased unwillingness by donors to abide by their disbursement pledges.

Thus, overall donor-government relations are beginning to resemble the situation of 20 years ago, while the economic, social and political contexts within Tanzania and globally have altered significantly.

Tanzania is today much less dependent on aid flows from DAC donors. However, the government is still to a degree dependent on such aid to further improve social services, infrastructure and government institutions. For as long as the level of trust is not restored, such initiatives will face an uphill struggle. A revival of the process that emerged during the first years of the millennium would be very helpful in this regard.

Most recently, some general trends within the donor group have been:
- A clear shift of interest towards growth sectors such as energy, agriculture, private sector development, which may increase competition between donors.
- A return to more short-term projects and programmes and increased fragmentation of donor portfolios.

- Stronger emphasis on visible results directly linked to specific donor interventions.

Discussions occur within the EU group about how to improve cooperation in a functional and pragmatic way, even though most member states are moving towards country strategies for which the sectors and focus are decided a number of years ahead. China and other emerging countries are investing substantially in Tanzania, but normally do not participate in DAC coordination forums. The Tanzanian government's responsibility for development issues –overseas development aid (ODA) financed or not – has become more fragmented, which in turn reduces the potential for accountability.

Present trends are likely to increase aid fragmentation and transaction costs. They may also contribute to a less focused policy agenda and policy dialogue. Alleged corruption cases have also contributed to a weakening of trust between cooperating partners and to the climate of cooperation. A spectacular example from 2014 is the alleged corruption case involving Independent Power Tanzania, Ltd (IPTL), which is believed to have high-level links with the political sphere. A report by the Public Accounts Committee was published in the autumn of 2014 and by the end of November parliament had made recommendations to government on how to handle the matter. However, by April 2015 government had still published no decision on the issue.

Pending a government move on the IPTL affair, including legal action against the culprits, donors have frozen the disbursements committed for fiscal year 2014/15, a total of US$ 558 million. Only US$ 84 million were disbursed at the end of 2014. The remainder was put on hold. However, in an update meeting between donors and government in March 2015, during which the government provided more information on the actions to be taken, some donors agreed to disburse another US$ 44 million. Even so, most of the committed GBS for 2014/15 remains undisbursed (*Development Today* 2015).

It could be assumed that reduced aid dependence would improve the conditions for increased ownership, clearer accountability and the potential to require aid agencies to use Tanzania's budget structure and other institutions for channelling aid. As already noted, the main obstacles to such outcome are the current lack of trust between the development partners.

As important are the changing priorities on both sides. Donor agencies, for instance, are fully preoccupied in preparing for three high-level international meetings in 2015: the UN global sustainable development goals, to replace the millennium development goals in New York in September; the conference on sustainable development in Addis Ababa in July; and the high level climate meeting in Paris in December. These international meetings reduce the incentives to implement in Tanzania and more generally the aid effectiveness principles decided at Busan in late 2011, aimed at updating the Paris Agenda.

It may also be assumed that global challenges such as increased armed conflicts, failed states, climate change, environmental problems, access to water, arable land for food production and international tax evasion may also divert international aid resources into global or international responses, programmes and processes. This would further reduce the scope for long-term bilateral cooperation.

Still, such cooperation with countries like Tanzania will continue to be an important complement, even in the new global political economy. However, the principles and modalities will have to be adapted to a new situation, and this can only be done through open-minded discussion between concerned partners. The result will not be a literal revival of the Paris Agenda. Instead, development cooperation will become much broader than the present ODA, and old structures will need to be replaced by more suitable ones, with fewer distorting side-effects. Still, to be sustainable, cooperation will have to be based on ownership, alignment, harmonisation, mutual accountability and trust.

References

Boesen, J., K. Havnevik, J. Koponen and R. Odgaard (eds) (1986) *Tanzania – crisis and struggle for survival.* Uppsala: Scandinavian Institute of African Studies.

Development Today (2015) "Donors continue to withhold Tanzania budget support," No. 3.

Government of Tanzania (2006) "Practical Experience on how Aid works in Tanzania," Dar es Salaam: Ministry of Finance.

IMG (Independent Monitoring Group), Tanzania (2002) *Enhancing Aid Relationships in Tanzania: Report of the Independent Monitoring Group.* Dar es Salaam: Economic and Social Research Foundation.

IMG, Tanzania (2010) *Assessment of Effectiveness of Development Cooperation. External Resources and Partnership Principles in Context of the Mkukuta/Mkuza Review.* Dar es Salaam: Economic and Social Research Foundation.

Odén, B. and T. Tinnes (2003) *Tanzania: New Aid modalities and donor harmonization.* Norad Report 8/2003.

Wangwe, S. (1987) "Impact of the IMF/World Bank Philosophy, the Case of Tanzania." In Havnevik, K. (ed.) *The IMF and the World Bank in Africa.* Seminar Proceeding No. 18, Uppsala: Scandinavian Institute of African Studies.

Wangwe, S. (2010) "Changing aid modalities and Tanzanian development assistance partnerships." In Havnevik, K. and A. Isinika (eds) *Tanzania in Transition. From Nyerere to Mkapa.* Uppsala: Nordic Africa Institute in cooperation with Mkuki na Nyota Publishers, Dar es Salaam and Sokoine University of Agriculture, Morogoro.

Promoting gender equality on land issues in Tanzania: How far have we come?

Aida C. Isinika and Anna Kikwa

Background

Since independence, there have been various efforts to promote equality between women and men in different spheres of life, including political representation, education and healthcare, and with different levels of success. There is general consensus, however, that efforts to promote gender equality in land matters have achieved only limited gains. This conclusion stems from the manner in which the gender debate has been contextualised and strategised within the wider debate on land tenure reform in Tanzania and also in Africa at large.

Land tenure has commonly been defined according to evolutionary theories of land ownership as a bundle of rights a person possesses over a piece of land.[1] These rights prescribe what the person can or cannot do on the land, and include rights of access, disposal and exclusion. Restrictions on these rights impinge on one's security of tenure, while unrestricted, continuous use and disposal rights enhance tenure security. As pointed out by Place, Roth and Hazell (1994), security of land tenure is not discretely observable. However, one may use indicators to monitor variables as tenure evolves in response to changing economic, political, institutional and technological conditions. Insecurity of tenure arises from inadequate or poorly defined property rights, inadequate duration of any of the rights, lack of assurance in asserting those rights, and the high cost of enforcing the rights (Isinika and Mutabazi 2010; Van Donge 1993).

In the African context, the evolutionary theory of land tenure is viewed as progressively evolving over time from a predominantly communal/customary system towards individualised tenure as land markets become more dominant. This is consistent with modernisation discourse. Such evolution is driven by population pressure and agricultural commercialisation, both of which lead to rising demand for individualised land access. It is on the basis of such arguments that many African states (including Tanzania) have embarked on land reform programmes that involve the demarcation and registration of land.

It is important to note that under the evolutionary theory of land tenure, there is little discussion of the gender dimension: indeed, gender as an analytical tool is lacking (Yngstrom 2002). Mbilinyi and Shechambo (2009), therefore recommend the need for conceptual clarity in analysing land and gender issues.

---

1. See the article by Opira and Ståhl, in this volume, for a general discussion on land tenure in East Africa.

In Africa, women's rights to land are subsumed under their customary position within the household as wives, daughters, sisters or under their position within the community or clan. While the literature on women's land rights claims that individualised tenure would provide more security to landowners, including women, this argument, it has been asserted, is based on a shallow understanding of African customary land tenure and the relative position of women (Manji 1998; Whitehead and Tsikata 2003).

It is true that under customary tenure, women get derivative rights to access land as wives, daughters and sisters (Yngstrom 2002). Studies have shown that such rights are quite robust, even in the face of evolving unregistered land markets, because African systems of land access are socially embedded and created by negotiation. For instance, Isinika and Mutabazi (2010) cited examples from Koda (2000) and BACAS (1999) wherein parents and grandparents increasingly opt to bequeath land to their daughters, sometimes disguised as gifts, to prevent such inheritance being challenged by other clan or family members. Women's claims to land are therefore stronger and more diverse than is usually presented in the literature (Whitehead and Tsikata 2003). Several studies across Africa (Daley and Englert 2010) and even in Tanzania (Koda 2000; Isinika and Mutabazi 2010) have actually established that a majority of women do not perceive their land rights to be insecure as long as their households remain stable. However, such security erodes with widowhood or divorce, especially if the woman has not given birth to children.

Meanwhile, there is ample evidence that economic changes, which are cited as strong arguments to justify land reform in the direction of individualised ownership, have reduced women's access to land because of the skewed distribution of resources within many communities and families. Women often lack capital and therefore cultivate less land, use fewer inputs and have less access to extension services and credit. Moreover, simple titling and registration does not transform land held under customary tenure into economically viable pieces of leasehold or freehold land. To improve agricultural productivity, there must be other changes that occur concurrently with or subsequent to land reform. It is on the basis of this background relating to land ownership that the land tenure reform process in Tanzania is discussed from a gender perspective.

Gender perspective of land tenure reform in Tanzania

The history of land tenure reform in Tanzania is rather short. Most of it was gender-blind until gender was brought into land reform discourse in the last two decades. The Land Tenure Ordinance of 1923 is cited as the basis of all land laws in mainland Tanzania. This ordinance established the prevailing dual land tenure system, which recognises granted or statutory rights of occupancy and deemed rights of occupancy. Before independence statutory rights were supported by documentary evidence while customary or deemed rights were claimed on the basis of occupation and use (URT 1994). The radical title to land both occupied and unoccupied was vested in the governor who held all land in trust for the people (URT 1994). In the event, customary land was subjected to continuous alienation to the foreigners who applied for statutory land rights, mostly for agricultural development.

After 1923, reform efforts to recognise customary land tenure were limited to providing statutory recognition in 1928 and to adding provisions to the law in 1950 regarding consultation with native authorities. Efforts in 1958 to promote individual land ownership according to the recommendations of the East African Royal Commission failed due to the strong opposition of the natives through political forums (URT 1994; Sungusia 2003). When communities lost land through alienation, both men and women were affected, but there is no evidence that there were any efforts to address the impacts on women separately or specifically.

In 1962, after independence, only minimal changes were made to the land ordinance: the radical title was transferred to the president; all freehold titles were converted to leasehold titles of up to 99 years, and in 1967 leasehold was converted to granted rights of occupancy (Sungusia 2003; Gondwe 1986). The reforms of 1962 also abolished the semi-feudal *nyalubanja* system in northwestern Tanzania (Kagera Region). Through the radical title, alienation of land in the public interest continued to provide land for national parks and game reserves, which occupy over 40 per cent of the land, as well as for other public purposes. Despite all these land reforms, there is no evidence that there was any analysis of their likely impacts on affected communities, women and men included. As long as the land frontier was still open, communities sought alternative land, to which women and men had uninhibited access for subsistence use under customary law. In areas such as Kilimanjaro, Kagera and Rungwe, however, population pressure was already high, agricultural intensification was on the rise and the vulnerability of divorced and widowed women in terms of land access was becoming more evident (Whitehead and Tsikata 2003).

There were other government policies and programmes implemented after independence that had a bearing on land tenure – though unintended. The villagisation programme relocated rural Tanzanians from their customary lands to new locations, in the process alienating customary land in many communities. Villagisation also gave power to elected leaders of village governments to serve as land administrators and in that capacity to allocate village land. The village land committee was also the first level of land adjudication. It was expected that the village government would provide equal access to land to women and men, but as land became scarcer the rights of women were marginalised under the influence of customary norms and practices. Village leaders have by no means been invariable saints. They have also been associated with corruption and nepotism in land allocation. Two examples illustrate this point.

> During the villagization programme in Uhekule village, Njombe district, single (unmarried) women had been granted equal rights to apply for land that was allocated by the village government. This right was however withdrawn later on the pretext of protecting the village women from opportunistic men who courted and married women who had acquired land from the village as a strategy to secure land rights in the village through marriage, only to divorce the women later. The village had enacted a bylaw prohibiting non-villagers from acquiring land in the village by allocation. After a couple of divorce incidents involving such women, the village enacted another bylaw, prohibiting single women from being allocated village land (Isinika and Mdoe 2001, p. 22).

While the decision to ban allocations of land to single women was made on the pretext of "protecting" those women, the action violated their basic human right as enshrined in the constitution, in terms of which all human beings are equal. Specifically, articles 12 and 13 prohibit gender discrimination.

Another example is cited by Mwanda (2001). Young women in a village in Ruvuma Region were allocated less land than their male counterparts on the grounds that they would marry and could use land held by their husbands' families. What, however, about women who never marry? By having less land, such women were condemned to a lower standard of living, which is likely to affect them for the rest of their lives and their offspring thereafter.

Land reform and a market economy

Since 1986, Tanzania has been shifting towards a market economy. This has entailed changes to various aspects of the economy, including land tenure institutions and organisations.

In response to the land conflicts that had escalated across the country, a Land Commission was appointed in 1991 to look at various aspects of land policy in Tanzania. It submitted a report to government in 1994[2]. A land policy followed in 1995.

The stated objective of land reform in Tanzania included providing tenure security to smallholders, promoting private sector investment and freeing up the land market (URT 1994; Havnevik 1995). Subsequently, the Land Acts of 1999 were enacted – Act Number 4 for public land and Act Number 5 for village land.

---

2.   "The Presidential Commission of Inquiry into Land Matters" was led by Professor Issa Shivji (University of Dar es Salaam). Its work led to the publication of several reports including the widely known "Shivji Report", published later in 2 volumes. See also Bryceson, in this volume, for a discussion of the work of the commission.

The land policy did not incorporate many of the Land Commission's substantive recommendations, such as vesting radical title in the village assembly.

Nonetheless, the publicity surrounding land issues raised awareness and prompted debate on various aspects of land, including those related to gender. The period leading up to the approval of the land policy and the land laws witnessed rekindled activity among various organisations and interest groups in assessing and discussing the proposed land policy and instruments through the prism of gender. A coalition of NGOs, the Tanzania Land Alliance (TALA), was established to form a common front and collectively lobby for favourable reforms in terms of gender equality and improved democratic processes and governance. TALA was part of a larger coalition, Feminist Action Coalition (FemAct). In terms of gender, the agenda was to foster equal access to land for women in their own right as individuals within families and communities.

While TALA failed to secure a bottom-up land administration and adjudication framework – particularly the proposal to vest the radical title in the village assembly – some milestones were achieved in relation to gender. First, customary tenure, which governs more than 70 per cent of the land in Tanzania, was given legal recognition. Second, Part IV section 161 (1) of the Land Act (Cap 113) stipulates that "the title for land jointly owned by husbands and wives shall bear the names of both." Part IV section 36 (1)(i) of the Village Land Act (Cap 114) gives priority to wives as beneficiaries when a man (husband) surrenders his customary rights of occupancy. It has, however, been argued by some analysts that this clause is diluted by Part II clause 10 (b) and 25 (d) recognising marriage under customary law and hence land inheritance under customary tenure, which is perceived to undermine women's land rights (Rwebangira 1996, 1999). The inheritance law similarly undermines women's rights to land inheritance. Under the Local Customary Law Declaration Order, No. 4 (1963) males inherit movable and immovable properties absolutely, but females inherit immovable property only for their use during their lifetime. They cannot sell such immovable property unless there are no male members in the family. Daughters are placed in the third degree of inheritance after the oldest son (first degree) followed by other younger sons who fall in the second degree. According to this law, daughters of a deceased can only inherit land if they are the only surviving member of the family. To manoeuvre around this law, parents increasingly bequeath land to their daughters before their death, sometimes disguised as gifts (Isinika and Mutabazi, 2010; Koda 2000).

Some researchers have argued that the gender dimension of land reform was marginalised by the Land Commission in the first place (Manji 1998; Daley and Englert 2010), because it did not consider the land problems faced by women as being capable of explicit analysis. To the extent that the Commission undertook an analysis, it focused only on succession, which is more informed by the

Marriage Act and the Law of Inheritance. The Commission's report, in turn, influenced subsequent analysis and discussion, which was likewise shallow and focused only on succession rather than on the wider context of land use and agricultural production systems. According to Daley and Englert (2010), NGOs and women's advocacy groups in Tanzania did not effectively challenge the marginalisation of gender issues in the land reform process because they failed to engage in the debate, and their arguments were not based on in-depth analysis of how women relate to land both as owners and as users of land for productive and social purposes. According to Manji (1998), the Commission failed to capture the multitude of ways in which women interact with land in their role as food producers and producers for the market, and the complex nature of the discrimination they face in relation to land.

Manji presents four arguments to show why the agenda of women was marginalised or why efforts by feminists and other activities groups failed to have an impact on the land reform debates and other processes. First, he argues that women's movements, including the Tanzania Gender Network Programme (TGNP), as well as feminist literature had focused on employment rather than on land ownership as a significant factor affecting women's position in society. Second, the Tanzania land debate lacks theorisation on how the proposed reforms affect women: there is no independent policy position regarding women's relationship with land. Feminists, activist groups and even researchers have reacted to government proposals, often proposing simplistic legalistic solutions. Third, the women's movement in Tanzania has an inherently urban bias, and is therefore slow to react to rural concerns. Fourth, the land-gender debate highlights class differences among women, with middle class women standing to benefit by legislation that enhances their statutory land ownership rights, since they can afford to acquire land on the market and also the cost of litigation related to land contestation. Most feminist and activist groups are middle class, and middle class women are likely to face conflicts of interest in land reform debates.

Manji (1998) continues his critique of subsequent literature by pointing to the narrow focus of the arguments regarding the purpose of land reform as between the state and the people, and to the failure to address the implications of the multifaceted relations between women and men, as if the society and households were undifferentiated. From the government perspective, the reforms created a conducive environment for investment in land by large-scale buyers and set up an efficient market in land. It is on this basis that the Land Act 4 of 1999 was amended in 2002 and 2004 to facilitate investment in large-scale farming, ranching and tourism and the use of land for mortgage (Katundu, Makungu and Mteti 2013).

In retrospect, as if to amend the shortcomings of the Commission's report in relation to gender, Shivji (2009) presented a reflection on the issue of women and land. He clarifies that gender issues cannot be simply subsumed under the larger context. Instead, he presents a contextual analysis distinguishing between different levels of analysis (family and the larger clan) and identifying the following land problems: (i) ownership and access (ii) control of the fruits of the land, (iii) participation in decision-making and (iv) inheritance and divorce. Land ownership is said to encompass several aspects, including transferability or negotiability, security and a clear definition of interests. For Shivji (2010) and Whitehead and Tsikata (2003), land ownership under customary tenure does not mean exclusive access and the ability to dispose. Rather clansmen and family elders play a key role in matters related to land disposal and inheritance, and they may from time to time be biased against women. Village government leaders have also been found to be corruptible. While the Village Land Act (1999) provides for equal opportunity for representation of women and men on Land Committees (Part IV 53 (2)), women are often not effectively and actively involved in land administration and management. Village assembly meetings are also dominated by men.

The above discussion has raised a number of issues, including the argument that while reform that takes land away from customary tenure towards individualised ownership will continue, titling is not a magic wand for all land tenure problems. In particular, studies from Kenya and elsewhere (Whitehead and Tsikata 2003; Manji 1998; Yngstrom 2002) offer a number of lessons suggesting that titling and land registration should be handled cautiously. Some of those lessons are that such practices:

- open new possibilities for conflict and enhance the possibility of land grabbing
- have often resulted in greater insecurity for landowners
- have not improved the efficiency of production systems or had discernible effects on investment on agricultural land
- have been said to serve as a means to transfer wealth in favour of educated economic and political elites
- do not extinguish customary claims on land; and
- did not transform land tenure from customary to freehold title.

In addition, sometimes the law in relation to land may be favourable to women, but they may not benefit either because those women lack awareness or the laws are not enforced. Moreover, women often lack the resources to pursue litigation, or may wish to avoid exposure and humiliation (Isinika and Mutabazi 2010). Finally, land registration in the name of the household head gives men exclusive rights to the land.

Meanwhile, the fact that various studies have shown that women do not perceive their land rights as insecure as long as relations within the household and community remain stable (Leonard and Toulmin 2000), has led some researchers and activists to reconsider the option of improving the customary tenure system. Arguments have been made by Whitehead and Tsikata (2003), for example, that there is a developing consensus among non-gender specialists in favour of the evolution of customary practices in order to deal with conflict and disputes over land access. They argue further that, since land markets do not require formalised property rights, returning to customary tenure would not impede their growth.

However, such arguments are countered by legalistic feminists and activists on the grounds that women's security of tenure continues to be jeopardised by customary inheritance practices, inadequate legislation and failure to observe legal measures intended to protect women. Other limitations include the male dominance of local land administration institutions. All of these factors imply that a return to customary tenure would pose challenges. For these reasons, this group sees the law as a better avenue for securing women's land rights (Whitehead and Tsikata 2003). In a study based on court cases involving land litigation and a survey, Isinika and Mutabazi (2010) established that over 60 per cent of respondents, especially women, were unaware of the ongoing land reforms, and that less than 25 per cent of male respondents and none of the female respondents perceived that titling and registration would enhance their tenure security.

Conclusions

The analysis presented in this study has shown that while titling is often chosen by governments as an important step in land reform, empirical evidence from other African countries indicates that most of the expected positive impacts of such land reform programmes have been negative, while some of the expected positive results have not materialised. The different acts governing access to land and subsequent rights to use and transfer land are contradictory, since the land laws are interpreted against the background of customary law and religious practices, which have provisions that undermine women's rights.

Many of the recommendations in the papers reviewed are based on limited empirical studies and often lack a gender-based analytical framework. Gender and land activists should therefore develop an analytical framework for land that takes specific account of gender. The framework would involve setting and monitoring the goals and milestones to be achieved. Expanding awareness and knowledge among villagers through training and other related activities would also help the target audience to make informed decisions before and after land titling and registration initiatives. Training and education in their legal rights would also enhance the ability of women and men to avoid deals that undermine their land rights. As more land is transferred from customary to statutory tenure, it is prudent to set up mechanisms to monitor unregistered land markets, which exist with regard to customary land. This will reduce the potential of land being concentrated in the hands of fewer people, a trend that is very likely to affect women more than men.

References

BACAS (1999) *Production systems in Kigoma region.* Vol. II, a report for UNDP coordination and micro-projects in Kigoma region.

Daley, E. and B. Englert (2010) "Securing land rights for women." *Journal of Eastern African Studies* 4(1): 91–113.

Gondwe, Z.S. (1986) "Agricultural policy in Tanzania at the crossroads." *Land Use Policy* 3(1): 31–6.

Havnevik, K., (1995) "Pressing land tenure issues in Tanzania in light of experiences from other Sub-Saharan African countries." *Forum for Development Studies* 2(2): 267–84.

Isinika, A. C. and M. Mutabazi (2010) "Gender dimension of land conflicts: Examples from Njombe and Maswa Districts in Tanzania." In Havnevik, K. and A. Isinika (eds) *Tanzania in Transition: From Nyerere to Mkapa.* Dar es Salaam: Mkuki na Nyota, pp. 131–57.

Isinika, A. C. and N. S. Y. Mdoe (2001) *Improving farm management skills for poverty alleviation: The case of Njombe district.* REPOA research report No. 01.1.

Katundu, M., I. M.A. Makungu and S. H. Mteti (2013) "Nature and magnitude of land acquisition: Analyzing role of different actors, key trends and drivers in land acquisitions." Paper presented at international conference organised by Future Agricultural Consortium on the Political Economy of Agricultural Policy in Africa, Pretoria, South Africa, 18–20 March.

Koda, B. O. (2000) *The gender dimension of land rights in Tanzania. A case study of Mshindo village, Same district.* PhD thesis (Development Studies), University of Dar es Salaam.

Leonard, R. and C. Toulmin, (2000) 'Women and Land Tenure'. Mimeo. IIED Drylands, Programme, UK.

Manji, A. (1998) "Gender and the politics of the land reform process in Tanzania." *Journal of Modern African Studies* 36(4): 645–67.

Mwanda, N. (2001) "The place of customary land rights in the Village Land Act the Land Act of 1999." Third year research paper in partial fulfilment of a LLB degree, University of Dar es Salaam.

Mbilinyi, M. and G. Shechambo (2009) "Struggles over land reforms of the Tanzania Gender Network Programme and Feminist Action Coalition." Available at http:// www.google.co.tz/...profile_mbilinyi_shechambo.pdf&ei. Accessed 3 May 2015.

Place, F., M. Roth and P. Hazell (1994) "Land tenure security and agricultural performance in Africa – Overview of research methodology." In Bruce, J. and S.E. Migot-Adholla (eds), *Searching for Land Tenure Security in Africa.* Dubuque, Kendall/Hunt Publishers, pp. 15–40.

Rwebangira, M. K. (1996) *The legal status of women and poverty in Tanzania*. Research report No. 100. Uppsala: Nordic African Institute.

Rwebangira, M.K. (1999) "Gender and the land registration in Tanzania with particular reference to the land bills of 1998." Paper presented at a workshop organised by the Forest Trees and People programme of the Department of Forestry Economics, Sokoine University of Agriculture, Morogoro, 19-20 February.

Shivji, I. (2009) *Where is Uhuru? Reflections on the Struggle for Democracy in Africa*. Edited by Godwin R. Murunga. Dar-es-Salaam, Cape Town, Dakar and Oxford: E&D Vision Publishing and Pambazuka Press.

Sungusia H.G. (2003) "The Nyerere Doctrine of land value and the enactment of the Land Act (1999)." Unpublished research paper, University of Dar es Salaam.

United Republic of Tanzania (URT) (1994) *Report of the Presidential Commission of Inquiry into Land Matters*, Vol. I. Dar es Salaam: Ministry of Lands, Housing and Urban Development (in cooperation with the Scandinavian Institute of African Affairs).

Whitehead, A. and D. Tsikata (2003) "Policy discourses on women's land rights in Sub-Saharan Africa: The implication of return to the customary." *Journal of Agrarian Change* 3(1 and 2): 67–112.

Van Donge, J. K. (1993) "Legal insecurity and land conflicts in Mgeta, Uluguru Mountains, Tanzania." *Africa* 63 (2): 197–218.

Yngstrom, I. (2002) "Women, wives and land rights in Africa: Situating gender beyond the household in the debate over land policy and changing tenure systems." *Oxford Development Studies* 30(1): 21–40.

Land grabbing in Africa
– a variety of primitive accumulation

Rune Skarstein

Introduction

In the last 10 to 15 years an apparently new phenomenon has arisen in Africa, variously called land grabbing, land acquisition or land deals. Foreign corporations, local investors or even governments themselves occupy large areas of land for commercial agriculture, biofuel production, mining, hydropower construction etc., or for merely speculative purposes in the expectation of future rises in land prices. Several studies have argued that in this process large numbers of agricultural smallholders will be evicted from their land and in most cases left without alternative means of livelihood (cf. Matondi, Havnevik and Beyene 2011).

The purpose of this chapter is to put the phenomenon of contemporary land grabbing in Africa into the broader historical perspective of capitalist development by applying Marx's notion of "primitive accumulation." In the first part, the process of land grabbing is discussed, with emphasis on its consequences for agricultural smallholders. A presentation and discussion of Marx's analysis of primitive accumulation follows. The third section discusses Marx's changing view of history, which started with a type of optimism about the capitalist mode of production and ended with a sceptical view that capitalist expansion into pre-capitalist societies would play only a destructive and non-progressive role, even for capitalism itself. In this latter view, land grabbing in Africa can be seen as mere vandalism without any progressive effects, even in the longer term.

Land grabbing in contemporary Africa

Africa has a bloody history of external colonisation, including land theft by European settlers for plantations and mines. Even today this continent of rich natural resources is being exploited by transnational corporations hunting for oil, copper, diamonds, uranium and gold. And still local people are losing land or are being displaced, for example for extraction of oil in the Niger Delta or for gold mining in North Mara (Tanzania).[1] Mostly these activities take place in close collaboration with local elites. Here I discuss the more recent phenomenon

---

1. On gold mining in North Mara, see Lugoe (2011). Sometimes the resistance to destructive projects succeeds. One example is the impeded Stiegler's Gorge hydropower project in Tanzania, which would have destroyed the livelihoods of numerous rice cultivating smallholders and fishermen in the Lower Rufiji Basin. Cf. Havnevik (1993: 76-81, 263-83).

already noted, the grabbing of the land of smallholders by transnational and local corporations, with the support of state and even local authorities, to establish
large farms for the production of food or biofuel feedstock.

Land acquisitions by capitalist corporations are taking place not only in Africa. According to the *Land Matrix*, formal contracts with private corporations
on acquisitions of 39.6 million hectares (396,000 sq. kilometres) in the world
had been completed by the end of 2014. That is an area considerably larger than
the whole of Germany (349,000 sq. kilometres). In addition, contracts for about
16 million hectares were under negotiation (Table 1).[2]

Table 1: Formally concluded land acquisition contracts by end of 2014.

Region	Transnational contracts ha. (thousand)	Per cent	Domestic contracts ha (thousand)	Percent	Total ha. (thousand)	Per cent
Africa	16,078	52.8	1,982	21.6	18,060	45.6
Europe	2,903	9.6	1,791	19.6	4,694	11.9
America	2,707	8.9	1,012	11.0	3,719	9.4
Oceania	2,257	7.4	1,63	1.8	2,420	6.1
Asia	6,490	21.3	4,214	46.0	10,704	27.0
World	30,435	100.0	9,162	100.0	39,597	100.0

Source: http://landmatrix.org/en/get-the-idea/agricultural-drivers/ Retrieved 25 Feb 2015.

Africa, in particular sub-Saharan Africa, appears to be in the forefront of the
new wave of land acquisitions. However, the exact scale of land grabbing in
Africa is difficult to estimate. The main reason for this is the lack of transparency surrounding these transfers and the reluctance of "host governments"
as well as foreign investors to publish the content of contracts on land deals
(Cotula 2011: 1–3, 18; Mousseau and Mittal 2011: 16). The World Bank notes
that, "instead of relying on publicity of relevant documents, and independent
third-party verification, agreements are surrounded by an air of secrecy that
makes public reporting and monitoring near impossible" (World Bank 2011:
71). Among researchers there seems to be broad agreement that land grabbing
is largely underreported. The *Land Matrix* points out that particularly domestic
land acquisition contracts are strongly underreported.

According to information collected by the World Bank for the period 1 October 2008 to 31 August 2009, 48 per cent of the registered projects and 70 per
cent (39.7 million hectares) of the acquired area worldwide was in sub-Saharan
Africa (World Bank 2011: 51). A report from 2010 that reviewed the literature estimated that between 51 and 63 million hectares of land in Africa had
been transferred to foreign investors (Friis and Reenberg 2010: 11–12). For some

2.   Cf. Land Matrix – February 2015: www.landmatrix.org. The Land Matrix is a cooperative
     venture involving several research institutions and NGOs.

countries, the World Bank reports substantially lower figures than do Friis and Reenberg, while other studies report higher figures.[3] A report from the GRAIN organisation (GRAIN 2012) indicates that land deals in Tanzania amounted to more than 1 million hectares by January 2012. Of these deals, contracts for 542,400 hectares were classified as "done," which is almost twice the area of concluded contracts reported by the *Land Matrix* (Table 2).

Table 2: Land resources and known concluded land acquisition contracts in East Africa by the end of 2014

Country	Estimated agricultural area (million ha.)	Number of contracts	Total contracted land area. '000 ha	Contracted land as per cent of total agricultural area
Ethiopia	36.5	58	990.9	2.7
Kenya	27.4	5	188.4	0.7
Madagascar	41.4	9	592.6	1.4
Malawi	5.7	3	57.5	10.1
Mozambique	49.9	68	2,208.5	4.4
Rwanda	1.9	3	21.1	1.1
Tanzania	40.6	27	276.4	0.7
Uganda	14.2	11	47.0	0.3
Zambia	23.8	21	360.6	1.5
Zimbabwe	16.2	3	391.7	2.4
Total	257.6	208	5,134.7	2.0

Source: http://www.landmatrix.org/en/get-the-detail/by-target-region/eastern-africa/ Data on agricultural area: FAOstat land resource database, http://faostat3.fao.org/download/R/RL/E
Note: Agricultural area is defined as potentially cultivable land, not land that is actually cultivated.

For seven contracts, corporations are not reported or the contract company is domestic. The remaining 201 contracts (97 per cent) are signed by foreign corporations. Nine contracts in which the land area is not reported, are not included in the table.

Data from the *Land Matrix* database indicate considerably lower figures than most other reports. That database provides information on formally concluded contracts for a total of 18 million hectares of land in the whole of Africa, and formally concluded contracts of 5 million hectares of land in East Africa (Tables 1 and 2). Even so, Africa is in the forefront of global land grabbing, accounting

---

3.   The World Bank estimates that between 2004 and 2009, total land acquisitions in Ethiopia amounted to 1,190 thousand hectares, and in Mozambique 2,670 thousand hectares (World Bank 2011: 62). On the other hand, Katundu et al. (2013: 21, 28) report that in Tanzania 117 companies have acquired more than 2 million hectares of land corresponding to 5.9 per cent of the country's agricultural area. By contrast, Mousseau et al. (2011: 16) report that, with regard to foreign investors, "data obtained from national government officials suggests that less than 70,000 hectares had actually been formally leased as of December 2010."

for nearly 46 per cent of all concluded contracts and up to 53 per cent of all transnational contracts measured by land area (Table 1).

In East Africa, almost all land acquisitions are based on contracts between the "host country" and foreign corporations. As a share of the potentially cultivable agricultural area, the contracted land varies from almost nil (Uganda) to more than 10 per cent (Malawi), with an average of 2 per cent (Table 2). However, the potentially cultivable area is generally many times larger than the actual cultivated area. For example, in Tanzania an estimated area of 14.7 million hectares of land is cultivated (URT 2013: 46–8). Thus the contracted land area reported in Table 2 represents 1.9 per cent of the cultivated area.

There are five important drivers of the new "scramble for land" in Africa. First, the global economic crisis since 2008 has made international capital investments outside the US and Europe more attractive. Second, the price hike of food (maize, wheat, rice) in 2008–09, to a large extent caused by speculation, prompted investment in land for food production (World Bank 2011: 51).[4] Third, rising oil prices and fear of the future scarcity of fossil fuels, combined with policies to avert climate change, stimulated international investments in land for biofuel feedstock production, especially sugarcane, maize, jatropha and oil palms (Matondi, Havnevik and Beyene 2011).

Fourth, many governments in Africa consider smallholder agriculture an impediment to economic development, implicitly claiming that a transition to large-scale commercial agriculture is necessary in order to achieve higher agricultural productivity and exports, especially of food crops. This view prevails among the political class even in Tanzania, where smallholders probably enjoy better legal protection than in any other African country. In its draft biofuel guidelines of 2008, the government states that "smallholder farmers responsible for 90% of all farm produce underutilize arable land, as production systems remain archaic in tillage, storage and processing."[5]

This is consistent with the Tanzanian government's Agricultural Sector Development Strategy of 2001, which emphasises that, *"Government will work towards creating an enabling environment for medium and large-scale investors to make use of the abundant land resource in the country"* (URT 2001, not paginated, italics in original). This was followed up in the Kilimo Kwanza (agriculture

4. The World Bank reports a strong increase in foreign land acquisitions concomitant with the sudden rise in food prices. From 1 October 2008 to 31 August 2009, 464 projects involving a total of 56.6 million hectares were registered. As much as 70 per cent of this area (39.7 million ha) was acquired in sub-Saharan Africa (World Bank 2011: 51). These figures are much higher than those reported by the *Land Matrix*. The reason may be that the *Land Matrix* coverage is low, or that many of the projects the World Bank reported in 2011 have failed.

5. URT, Guidelines for Sustainable Liquid Biofuels Investments and Development in Tanzania (draft), Ministry of Energy and Minerals, Dar es Salaam 2008. Here quoted from Sulle and Nelson (2009: 36).

first) strategy launched in 2009 to modernise agriculture. One "pillar" of the strategy is making more land available to investors in order to increase capital flows to the sector.

It should be noted that governments in other sub-Saharan countries are also sceptical about the possibilities of improving smallholder agriculture. On Mozambique, Timothy Wise (of Tufts University) reports the following conversation with the economic advisor to the minister of agriculture, Luis Sitoe, about the huge and largely unsuccessful ProSavana land acquisition project, "the largest land grab in Africa":

> I asked Mr. Sitoe ... if the lesson of ProSavana was that agricultural development needed to be based on Mozambique's three million small-scale food producers. He smirked again. No, he assured me, the government is committed to foreign investment, with its capital and technology, as the path to agricultural development (Wise 2015: 4).

A fifth driver is the wrongly perceived abundance of land, which has encouraged international investors to target sub-Saharan Africa.[6] For example, in Tanzania, which is considered one of the most land-abundant countries in Africa, the government has stated that: "Unlike its neighbours, Tanzania has comparatively abundant land resources. Even though there are substantial areas under various forms of protection, and other areas infested with tsetse fly, there is still land available for expansion of cultivation" (URT 2000: 3).[7]

It is not only many African governments that apparently believe there is land abundance in sub-Saharan Africa. The World Bank claims that the potentially cultivable land area is 201 million hectares, corresponding to more than 45 per cent of total potentially cultivable land in the world (World Bank 2011: xxxiv).[8] This optimism ignores the fact that Africa's numerous smallholder families survive on very small holdings. For example, for mainland Tanzania, the National Land Policy of 1995 estimated arable land at 48.7 million hectares (NLP 1997: 4). However, the great majority of the more than 30 million people (almost 80 per cent of the population) involved in crop agriculture are members of 5.7 million smallholder families cultivating about 14.7 million hectares of land. The average land per household is 2.5 hectares. Mainly owing to cultivation with fallowing, an average of only 1.6 hectares is planted with annual crops (URT

---

6. For an example of the belief in land abundance, see Purdon (2013). For criticisms of this belief, see Andrew Coulson's chapter (in this volume), as well as Lugoe (2010) and Matondi, Havnevik and Beyene (2011): 7–10.

7. According to official estimates, about 12.9 million hectares, that is, 26 per cent of pastoral areas, are affected by tsetse fly and cannot be used for grazing (URT 2000: 28).

8. It appears from Table 2 that the FAO is even more optimistic, estimating that potentially cultivable land in East Africa alone amounts to 257.6 million hectares.

2013: 46, 48). Most of these households also need additional land for collecting firewood.

Moreover, there is a considerable population of pastoralists needing large grazing lands for their animals. Official figures indicate that Tanzania is made up of about 61 million hectares of pasture or grazing land, of which only 37 million hectares is permanent pasture. However, the aggregate figure of actually used pasture is about 44 million hectares (NLP 1997: 4). This means that a "sizable portion of grazing" is undertaken on about 7 million hectares of non-permanent pasture, which, "as experience has shown, is vulnerable to harsh weather and climatic conditions" (Lugoe 2010: 6).

In other words, under present conditions in Tanzania there is a large *deficit* of land for permanent pasture in livestock agriculture, while cultivating smallholders are in great need of more acreage. Land abundance turns out to be an illusion.[9] It should be added that more than 30 per cent of the land surface in Tanzania is protected, meaning that cultivation there is prohibited and grazing strongly restricted (USAID 2012: 25–8). A considerable increase in the area for large-scale commercial agriculture may lead to serious conflicts with cultivators and pastoralists, as well as hostilities between these groups, and have grave ecological consequences (USAID 2012: 56).[10]

In most of sub-Saharan Africa, land tenure has for generations been based on customary law, in terms of which the chief or the elders of the community allocate land to members. However, most states have superimposed national land laws on customary law. Even in countries where customary land rights enjoy legal protection, such as in Mali or Tanzania, national law considers most rural people as having qualified use rights to land "vested" by the (head of) state (Shivji 1998). Cotula summarises the situation as follows:

> The problem is that the customary rights of local people may have no or little recognition under national law. This circumstance is historically rooted in the colonial experience, when colonisers treated conquered lands without visible developments as being empty (*terres vacantes et sans maître*, in French) and brought them under the state ownership, and in decades of post-independence law-making shaped by single-party regimes or military dictatorships … Virtually all countries have legislation that enables government compulsorily to take [land] rights if it is in the public interest to do so (Cotula 2011: 17, 33).

---

9. Thus, Lugoe's comment appears to be highly relevant: "Statements floating around with regard to land abundance in Tanzania should be based on reality and not wishes as is currently the case" (Lugoe 2010: 7).

10. In the National Land Policy of 1995, this problem seems to be acknowledged: "There are growing social conflicts, environmental concerns and land use conflicts due to haphazard alienation of rangeland for large scale agriculture" (NLP 1997: 35).

We have noted that smallholders in Tanzania probably enjoy more secure land rights than smallholders in most other African countries. However, even in Tanzania customary law represents no guarantee of secure land rights. Following the abolition of a colonial act in 1963, the executive power of chiefs, headmen and elders in land administration based on customary law was replaced by elected village councils and assemblies. Customary law survived in reality, if not formally. This fact was recognised by the Shivji Commission (1992)[11], which recommended two forms of land tenure with equal legal status, namely "granted right of occupancy" and "customary right of occupancy." These two forms of tenure were upheld in the National Land Policy (NLP 1997) of 1995, as well as in the Village Land Act (VLA) of 1999. According to official estimates, 69.5 per cent the land area in mainland Tanzania is under customary law, whereas 15.8 per cent is land "owned by buying" and 5.5 per cent is land "under official land titles" (URT 2013: 46). However, customary tenure does not only apply to village land, but also to to "general land" and some "reserved land," as well as urban land and peri-urban areas (cf. Lugoe 2010).

According to the NLP and VLA, all land in Tanzania is public land and "vested in the President as trustee on behalf of all citizens." The legislation defines three categories of land: (i) *village land* within the demarcated boundaries of villages, which comprises customary, communal and vacant land; (ii) *reserved land* (about 30 per cent of Tanzania's total land area), which is set aside as protected areas for wildlife, forests and marine and coastal protection; and (iii), *general land,* which is neither village land nor reserved land and may also include unused or unoccupied village land.

Investors can acquire land in Tanzania only by obtaining a "granted right of occupancy." The transfer of customary land rights by citizens to non-citizens is prohibited (NLP 1997: 11). However, the president has the authority to "transfer any area of village land to general or reserved land for public interest," which includes "investments of national interest" (VLA, Part III, p. 26; NLP 1997: 15). If a company or a person wishes to invest in village land, the president must first convert that land to general land. Village land converted to general land falls under the administration of the Tanzania Investment Centre (TIC), which, acting as a "land bank," will lease it out to domestic or foreign investors by granting them so-called "derivative rights of occupancy."[12] The NLP (1997: 9) states that "consultation and consent of a Village Council will be required whenever alienation of Village lands is necessary." However, several reports argue that this requirement is not always followed. One study states that "the whole process happens at government level, from introduction of business idea to the TIC,

---

11. Cf. the articles by Bryceson and by Isinika andKikwa in this volume.
12. The leases are long term, 50 years and even 99 years.

finding of appropriate general land, approving of land by the Ministry of Agriculture and finally application for derivative right of occupancy from the TIC"
(Theting and Brekke 2010: 5).

An additional aspect is that the great majority of villages cannot protect
their interests by referring to official documents demarcating the village borders.
The World Bank notes that, "more than a decade after passage of Tanzania's
Land Acts, only 753, or 7 percent, of the country's 10,397 registered villages
have received a certificate of village land. Even where such certificates were issued, pastoralist rights continue to be neglected" (World Bank 2011: 102). The
World Bank points out that in this regard Tanzania is not an exception. In
Mozambique, only some 12 per cent of the 70 million hectares estimated to be
controlled by communities have been mapped (World Bank 2011: 102).

Another general aspect is that after leasing the land, the investor quite often
does not implement the proposed project. The World Bank study found that
"investors acquired land in quantities much larger than they could use, at least
initially" (World Bank 2011: 63). The general picture is that "actual farming has
so far started on only 20 percent of the announced deals, indicating that there
is a large gap between plans and implementation" (World Bank 2011: xxxii).
For example, in Mozambique an enormous area of 2.7 million hectares was
transferred to investors in the period 2004–09.[13] However, a land audit in 2009
found that more than 50 per cent of the projects had either not started or lagged
significantly behind their development plans. In the Amhara region of Ethiopia,
only 16 of 46 large-scale agricultural projects were being used as intended. In
other projects, the land was either put to other purposes or simply rented out to
smallholders "in explicit contravention of contract" (World Bank 2011: 62, 118).
A similar pattern was found in other countries, including Tanzania (Katundu ,
Makungo and Mteti 2013: 21–7).

The reasons for acquiring more land than "needed" may be to take advantage
of (too) favourable lease terms, eliminate future competition from other investors and profit from expected land price rises or from higher prices for food and
biofuels in the future.[14] In any event, the World Bank concludes that "many investments, not always by foreigners, failed to live up to expectations and, instead
of generating sustainable benefits, contributed to [smallholder] asset loss and
left local people worse off than they would have been without the investment"
(World Bank 2011: 71).

Especially biofuel projects demand not only land, but enormous quantities of
water. Water is therefore one potential source of conflict between biofuel inves-

---

13. Note that this figure is considerably higher than the 2.2 million hectares of concluded
contracts reported by the *Land Matrix* (Table 2).
14. One study suggests that the cost of land acquisition in Africa is only about USD 50 per
hectare (Mitchell 2011: 64–5).

tors and smallholders in sub-Saharan Africa. Even more than in other sectors of agribusiness, corporate profit in the production of biofuel feedstock is best assured when plantations are on the most fertile lands and have ample water supplies, especially for sugarcane production, and are close to major transport routes. However, millions of smallholders in Africa already occupy these lands and they have become the main obstacles to the biofuel rush. It is becoming clear that when biofuel crops are on the agenda, the pressure on smallholders to leave their land intensifies (cf. Matondi, Havnevik and Beyene. 2011).

Although Africa's wetlands cover only 4 per cent of its total landmass, they store more than half of the world's liquid fresh water (Sielhorst, Molenaar and Offermans 2008: 3). The most popular biofuel crops require large volumes of water. One litre of ethanol produced from sugarcane requires 4,000 litres of water, while maize needs 2,500 litres. On the other hand, the normal ethanol yield per hectare of land is 8,900 litres for sugarcane and 3,200 litres for maize, which makes sugarcane the crop preferred by international investors (Sielhorst, Molenaar and Offermans 2008: 31–2). Consequently, biofuel feedstock production may have a negative impact on both the water and land available to local smallholders in wetlands. For biofuel production to expand, smallholders will be forced to move to poorer lands and local food production may also be affected by the decreased availability of water, which is already a limiting factor in agriculture in large parts of sub-Saharan Africa (Sielhorst et al. 2008: 35–6; Matondi et al. 2011).

From India we know that the establishment of corporate-led hydropower plants and mining, highway construction, Special Economic Zone (SEZ) industrial projects, as well as commercial agriculture and forestry projects result in the forced displacement of very large numbers of people. These internally displaced persons (IDPs) and project-affected persons (PAPs), dispossessed of livelihood and habitat, are the true victims of land acquisitions. According to one estimate, the acquisition of 25 million hectares of land for industrial sites, hydropower plants, mines and highways resulted in around 60 million IDPs/PAPs by 2004, that is, *before* the SEZ Acts (2005/2007) facilitating more effective displacements for "public purposes" came into effect. This land area included 7 million hectares of forest and 6 million hectares of other common property resources (Fernandes 2011: 303).

In addition to destroying the livelihood of large numbers of "tribal" and lower-caste people (*adivasis* and *dalits*), accounting for about 25 per cent of the total population of India, the acquisition of land causes distress to small farmers, who are very often displaced to less fertile land. The ratio of landless agricultural workers to total agricultural working population has risen markedly. In 1951, about 72 per cent were cultivators and 28 per cent landless agricultural workers. In 2011, 45 per cent were cultivators and 55 per cent landless workers (Bhaduri

2015: 18, note 8). As Fernandes (2011: 309) points out: "An obvious result of landlessness is joblessness, because the land the IDPs/PAPs lose to the project is their sustenance, both in the form of food and work. So its loss deprives them of both." Hence landlessness equates with impoverishment, and impoverishment forces many IDPs/PAPs into debt or labour bondage, or into child labour, prostitution and crime. Displacement also leads to increased pressure on the remaining non-privatised land (Fernandes 2011: 310–11).

In Africa, too, forced displacement of large numbers of smallholders is becoming a reality. For example, an environmental and social impact assessment of a sugar plantation project in Mali concluded that land acquisitions will have a negative impact on local food security and pastoralists' access to grazing. The Resettlement Action Plan for the project estimated that 1,718 people would be directly affected, and that, among these, 1,644 people from 128 households would be physically displaced (Cotula 2011: 32). A study of five regions in Tanzania shows the same pattern. In Mvomero District, Morogoro Region, 247 smallholder farmers were displaced and dispossessed of their land to make way for land acquisition by foreign investors. The same happened to 14 smallholder farmers in Kisarawe, Coast Region, and eight smallholders in Kilolo, Iringa Region (Katundu, Makungo and Mteti 2013: 21).[15] These forced displacements not only mean economic ruin for many smallholders, but also destruction of their culture.

Marx on primitive accumulation

Karl Marx emphasised that a basic characteristic of emerging capitalism was that land (as a collective term for all natural resources) and labour are *commodified*.[16] Referring to the rise of capitalism in England – in Chapters 26–28 of the first volume of *Capital* – he analyses the process of commodification of land and labour, which he, alluding to Adam Smith, calls "so-called primitive accumulation" (Marx [1867]1976: 873–904).[17] He notes that primitive accumulation is a process that "precedes capitalist accumulation; an accumulation which is not the result of the capitalist mode of production but its point of departure" (Marx [1867]1976: 873). The "point of departure" of capitalism is theft from the immediate producers of their means of production and livelihoods – of the land, forests, water and other resources – forcing them to become vagabonds and beggars or, at best, people dependent on selling their labour power: "In actual history, it

---

15. Mainland Tanzania has 21 regions. The five regions of the study are Arusha, Iringa, Dar es Salaam, Morogoro and Pwani.
16. Of course, several other theorists share the view of Marx on this particular issue, e.g., Karl Polanyi (1957) and Max Weber ([1923]1991).
17. In the original German edition Marx, uses the expression "ursprüngliche Akkumulation" – "original accumulation" – which I think is a more accurate term.

is a notorious fact that conquest, enslavement, robbery, murder, in short, force, play the greatest part ... As a matter of fact, the methods of primitive accumulation are anything but idyllic" (Marx [1867]1976: 874).

In short, the basic feature of primitive accumulation is twofold. One aspect is the expropriation from the immediate precapitalist producers of their means of production and livelihood, thereby transforming land and other natural resources, as well as labour, into commodities that will serve as objects for capital accumulation. The other aspect is that the expropriated populations will have "nothing to sell but their labour power," and they are thus made ready to be exploited by capital as wage labourers. Marx's message is that for the capitalist mode of production to expand, land, natural resources in general and labour power have to submit to capital, that is, be made into material and human resources for the accumulation of capital. This process will be repeated whenever capitalism conquers and destroys precapitalist modes of production. Precisely because primitive accumulation takes place outside the circuit of capital, conquering land and labour for the accumulation of capital, "conquest, enslavement, robbery, murder, in short, force, play the greatest part." Therefore, primitive accumulation is a deeply political process. As long as the "never-ending circle of capital" does not encompass all natural resources and all labour power, there is scope for further expansion of the capitalist mode of production, implying industrialisation and "modernisation."[18]

Marx restricted his analysis of the history of primitive accumulation to England, noting that, "only in England, which we therefore take as our example, has it [primitive accumulation] the classical form." The broad aspects of his analysis have later been confirmed by several historical studies of the enclosure movements in England. I summarise some of their main points.

The first wave of enclosures (ca. 1400–1520) was in the aftermath of the Black Death (ca. 1350) and the subsequent outbreaks of the plague. At times of conflict with the Crown, big landlords, including the church and monasteries, enclosed vast areas of abandoned as well as still cultivated holdings, and also some common land. The enclosed land was turned into less labour-intensive sheep pasture, and wage labourers were hired as herdsmen and fence-builders. In this way, the landlords mitigated the lack of peasant serfs and succeeded in maintaining control over their land and reinforcing their property rights. Through wool exports to the Flemish market, landlords, as capitalists-to-be, established close networks with the urban bourgeoisie, which represented an important step towards a capitalist agriculture (Tawney [1912] 1967: 187–8). Gradually, the process which started with the enclosure of abandoned holdings

---

18. When Marx uses the term "so-called original accumulation," my understanding is that it was not original in the sense of taking place back in history, which is David Harvey's interpretation (Harvey 2005: 144–5).

led to displacements of numerous small peasants from their plots of cultivated land, and even from their pastures and from firewood resources in the commons. This process was so comprehensive that, between ca. 1450 and 1525, about 10 per cent of the villages in the southern part of the Midlands were destroyed (Allen 1992: 66, 163–7).

The second wave of enclosures (from about 1660 to the late 1700s) is often called the "parliamentary enclosures," because it was backed by law enacted by the parliament, in which only the landed nobility was represented. The main aspect of that wave was enclosure of the remaining open fields and amalgamation of the small peasant holdings into large farms, to be rented out to tenants for cultivation using wage labour. Enclosure of commons reduced access to pasture and firewood was probably the main reason for the landlords' success in purchasing virtually all land from the free tenants in the period ca. 1690–1780 (Allen 1992: 95–6). Under the pressure of competition and landlords' rent hunger, tenant farmers sought to reduce costs through the typical capitalist ploy of technical change, namely labour-saving innovations. An important aspect of these innovations was the rapidly increasing use of horses for traction and transport both in the countryside and in towns (Wrigley 2004: 73–7). Oxen as draft animals, as well as human labour, were replaced by horses. A horse's traction speed is on average 50 per cent higher than that of an ox, and the work carried out by a horse per hour is roughly equivalent to six hours of work by a man (Bairoch 1973: 465; Wrigley 2006: 461). Thus, the increasing use of horses resulted in a large increase in labour productivity in agriculture. In this process, many more peasants were evicted from their holdings, and the number of employed per acre fell to about half of what it was in 1600 (Wrigley 2004: 43). As a consequence, numerous displaced peasants were turned "from decent husbandmen into a mob of beggars and thieves" (Polanyi 1957: 34–5).[19] A large "industrial reserve army" (Marx) was created.

Robert Allen provides several examples of how the amalgamation of holdings into large farms implied a "social revolution" that actually represented the rise of agrarian capitalism. He concludes that:

> Not only were most rural people becoming exclusively dependent on wage income, but the demand for that labour was falling. Enclosures and large farms were the cause of the rise in productivity, but they also caused low wages and unemployment for the majority of the population, and high rents for the rich minority. *Inequality and productivity growth were inextricably linked* ... The conclusion is unavoidable – most English men and women would have been better off had the landlords' revolution never occurred (Allen 1992: 8, 21, my italics).

19.　See also Hill (1991: 39–56).

So far, the modern accounts confirm Marx's analysis of primitive accumulation in England. However, although Marx used England for his historical analysis, he also stressed that primitive accumulation is an ongoing process of capitalist expansion:

> In Western Europe, the homeland of political economy, the process of primitive accumulation has more or less been accomplished … It is otherwise in the colonies. There the capitalist regime constantly comes up against the obstacle presented by the producer, who, as owner of his own conditions of labour, employs that labour to enrich himself instead of the capitalist … Where the capitalist has behind him the power of the mother country, he tries to use force to clear out of the way the modes of production and appropriation which rest on the personal labour of the independent producer. (Marx [1867]1976: 931)

Marx's changing view of history

Until about 1870, Marx held the view that there is no such thing as "capitalist underdevelopment." On the contrary, he considered all *precapitalist* social formations as "backward" or "barbarian," that is, underdeveloped. In his writings up to the end of the 1850s, he even insisted on the Hegelian perspective that capitalist society is universalistic in its urges, drawing all, "even the most barbarian, nations into civilisation." Obviously, he meant that the injustices and cruelties of primitive accumulation are the necessary cost of economic and social progress. In his writings on India, he elaborated this perspective in more detail. In 1853 he wrote: "England has to fulfill a double mission in India: one destructive, the other regenerating – the annihilation of old Asiatic society, and the laying of the material foundation of Western society in Asia" (cited in Avineri 1969: 132–3).

He went on to argue that, "English interference … dissolved these small semi-barbarian, semi-civilized communities [in India], by blowing up their economical basis, and thus produced the greatest, and, to speak the truth, the only social revolution ever heard of in Asia" (cited in Avineri 1969: 93). At that time, he considered the extension of the railway system throughout India as a major vehicle for this revolution (Avineri 1969: 136).

There is no indication that Marx had abandoned his 1853 view of Indian society in the first volume of his magnum opus, *Capital* (1867). On the contrary, he reiterated his view that Indian society and Asiatic societies in general were fundamentally static, and that the intrusion of capitalism represented historical progress (Marx [1867]1976: 479). In other words, the process of capitalist colonisation would bring about a rapid development of productive forces even in those "backward" areas.

On this latter point, however, he obviously changed his mind as time went by. It was quite evident to Marx that the initial form of capitalist expansion in colonial areas at his time would be the expansion of commercial capital. In a theoretical discussion in the third volume of *Capital,* he emphasised that the intrusion of merchant capital into colonial areas did not necessarily imply that the precapitalist modes of production in those areas would dissolve or capitalist relations of production emerge:

> Trade always has, to a greater or lesser degree, a solvent effect on the pre-existing organizations of production, which in all their various forms are principally oriented to use-value. But how far it leads to the dissolution of the old mode of production depends first and foremost on the solidity and inner articulation of this mode of production itself. And what comes out of this process of dissolution, i.e. what new mode of production arises in place of the old, does not depend on trade, but rather on the character of the old mode of production itself (Marx [1894] 1981: 449).

He referred to the British colonisation of India as one of the examples that proved his point:

> The obstacles that the internal solidity and articulation of pre-capitalist national modes of production oppose to the solvent effect of trade are strikingly apparent in the English commerce with India and China. There the broad basis of the mode of production is formed by the union between small-scale agriculture and domestic industry, on top of which we have in the Indian case the form of village communities based on common property in the soil, which was also the original form in China (Marx [1894] 1981: 451).

He went on to argue that in India:

> ... the English applied their direct political and economic power, as masters and landlords, to destroying these small economic communities. In so far as English trade has had a revolutionary effect on the mode of production in India, this is simply to the extent that it has destroyed spinning and weaving, which form an age-old and integral part of this unity of industrial and agricultural production ... In this way it has torn the communities to pieces (Marx [1894] 1981: 451–2).

In the third draft of his letter of March 1881 to Vera Zasulich, he repeated this view, pointing out that, "the violent abolition of common property in the soil [in India] was only an act of English vandalism which pushed the indigenous people not forward but backward ... they [the English] have only succeeded in ruining domestic agriculture and redoubling the number and intensity of famines" (Marx/Engels 1972: 402, 405, my translation).

In other words, Marx became increasingly sceptical about the role of primitive accumulation and the potential for capitalist development in non-European precapitalist social formations. Eventually, he considered English colonialism in India as mere vandalism without any regenerating function. In accordance with this view, he also rejected Hegel's general philosophy of history, which in his famous letter of 1877 (which was never sent) to the editors of the *Otetschestwen-nyje Sapiski,* he characterised as "a master-key of a general philosophy of history, the greatest advantage of which is to be ahistorical" (Marx und Engels 1972:112, my translation).

Concluding remarks

The conclusion that the process of land grabbing in contemporary Africa is a variety of primitive accumulation is obvious. That this process causes injustice and suffering for large numbers of people, as well as explosive social conflicts, is also obvious. By contrast, it is not obvious that land grabbing will lead to economic and social progress in the long term. In this regard, I think it wise to share the scepticism of the older Karl Marx. African smallholder agriculture is truly stricken with problems. However, that does not mean that capitalist agriculture is the solution. In Europe, only England experienced the long-term "success" of capitalist agriculture, albeit at great social cost. An important condition for that "success" was the concomitant and rapid growth of demand for industrial labour, which eventually absorbed a large part of the population squeezed out of agriculture. In much of the rest of Europe, agriculture did not turn capitalist. Instead, smallholdings were moderately consolidated and transformed and relieved of surplus labour through rising demand for industrial labour and emigration to America. Agriculture remained characterised by family holdings enjoying allodial rights. This experience contradicts the presently dominant neoliberal dogma that the only route to economic progress is through the overall destruction of precapitalist modes of production in order to give the upper hand to free-market capitalism.

References

Allen R.C. (1992) *Enclosure and the Yeoman.* Oxford: Clarendon Press.

Avineri, S. (ed.) (1969) *Karl Marx on Colonialism and Modernization.* New York: Anchor Books.

Bairoch, P. (1973) "Agriculture and the Industrial Revolution 1700–1914." In C.M. Cipolla (ed.) *The Fontana Economic History of Europe, Vol. 3: The Industrial Revolution.* London and Glasgow: Collins Fontana, pp. 452–501.

Bhaduri, A. (2015) "A Study in Development by Dispossession." Unpublished draft manuscript obtained from the author, February 2015.

Cotula L., S. Vermeulen, R. Leonard and J. Keely (2009) *Land grab or development opportunity? Agricultural investment and international land deals in Africa.* London/Rome: FAO/IIED/IFAD.

Cotula, L. (2011) *Land deals in Africa: What is in the contracts?* London: IIED.

Fernandes, W. (2011) "Development-induced displacement in the era of privatisation." In Mathur, H.M. (ed.) *Resettling Displaced People: Policy and practice in India.* New Delhi/London: Routledge.

Friis, C. and A. Reenberg (2010) *Land Grab in Africa: Emerging land system drivers in a teleconnected world.* GLP Report No. 1. Copenhagen: GLP-IPO.

GRAIN (2012) Landgrab Deals, January 2012.

Harvey, D. (2005) *The New Imperialism.* Oxford: Oxford University Press.

Havnevik, K. (1993) *Tanzania – The Limits to Development from Above.* Uppsala and Dar es Salaam: Nordic Africa Institute and Mkuki na Nyota Publishers.

Hill, C. (1991) *The World Turned Upside Down.* London: Penguin.

Katundu, M. A., I.M.A. Makungo and S.H. Mteti (2013) *Nature and magnitude of land acquisitions in Tanzania: Analyzing role of different actors, key trends and drivers in land acquisitions.* Paper presented at the international conference on The Political Economy of Agricultural Policy in Africa, organised by Future Agricultures Consortium (FAC), Pretoria, 18–20 March 2013.

Lugoe, F. (2010) *Land – Pillar No. 5 of Kilimo Kwanza.* Dar es Salaam Institute of Land Administration and Policy Studies (DILAPS), September.

Lugoe, F. (2011) *The Land Factor in Mining Gold Reserves in Tanzania,* Dar es Salaam; ESRF Policy Brief No. 1.

Marx, K. (1964) *Pre-Capitalist Economic Formations.* London: Lawrence and Wishart.

Marx K. ([1867]1976) *Capital – Volume 1.* Harmondsworth: Penguin.

Marx, K. ([1894]1981) *Capital – Volume 3.* Harmondsworth: Penguin.

Marx, K. und F. Engels (1972) *Werke,* Band 19. (East) Berlin: Dietz Verlag.

Matondi P.B., K. Havnevik and A. Beyene (eds) (2011) *Biofuels, land grabbing and food security in Africa.* London and New York: Zed.

Mitchell, D. (2011) *Biofuels in Africa – Opportunities, prospects and challenges.* Washington DC: World Bank.

Mousseau, F. and A. Mittal (eds) (2011) *Understanding land investment deals in Africa. Country Report: Tanzania.* Oakland CA: Oakland Institute.

NLP (1997) [Ministry of Lands and Human Settlements Development], *National Land Policy,* 2nd edition, Dar es Salaam. (1st edition, 1995).

Polanyi, K. (1957) *The Great Transformation.* Boston: Beacon Press.

Purdon, M. (2013) "Land Acquisitions in Tanzania: Strong Sustainability, Weak Sustainability and the Importance of Comparative methods." *Journal of Agriculture Environment Ethics,* published online 15 March.

Shivji, I. G. (1998) *Not yet democracy: Reforming land tenure in Tanzania.* IIED/HAKIARDHI/Faculty of Law, University of Dar es Salaam.

Sielhorst, S., J. W. Molenaar and D. Offermans (2008) *Biofuels in Africa – An assessment of risks and benefits for African wetlands.* Report commissioned by Wetlands International, Wageningen/Amsterdam.

Sulle, E. and F. Nelson (2009) *Biofuels, land access and rural livelihoods in Tanzania.* London: IIED.

Tawney, R.H. ([1912]1967) *The Agrarian Problem in the Sixteenth Century* New York and London: Harper Torchbooks.

Theting, H. and B. Brekke (2010) *Land Investments or Land Grab? A critical view from Tanzania and Mozambique.* Oslo: Spire.

URT (United Republic of Tanzania) [Ministry of Agriculture and Food Security] (2000) *Tanzania Agriculture: Performance and Strategies for Sustainable Growth.* Dodoma.

URT (2001) *Agricultural Sector Development Strategy.* Dar es Salaam, October 1.

URT (2013) *Tanzania in Figures 2012.* NBS/Ministry of Finance Dar es Salaam, June.

USAID (2012) *Tanzania Environmental Threats and Opportunities Assessment.* Washington DC.

VLA [The Village Land Act, 1999], Passed in the National Assembly on the 11 February 1999. Dar es Salaam: Government Printer.

Weber, M. ([1923]1991) *Wirtschaftsgeschichte.* Berlin: Duncker und Humblot.

Wise, T. A. (2015) "The Great land Giveaway in Mozambique." *Triple Crisis Blog*, 11 March: http://triplecrisis.com/the-great-land-giveaway-in-mozambique/

World Bank (2011) *Rising Global Interest in Farmland – Can it yield sustainable and equitable benefits?* Washington DC: World Bank.

Wrigley, E.A. (2004) *Poverty, Progress and Population.* Cambridge: Cambridge University Press.

Wrigley, E.A. (2006) "The Transition to an Advanced Organic Economy: Half a Millennium of English Agriculture." *Economic History Review* LIX(3): 435–40.

Adjust or change?
The debate on African economic structures

Mats Hårsmar

A few years before the turn of the millennium, Kjell Havnevik was travelling through the Jomo Kenyatta International Airport in Nairobi, Kenya. At the immigration counter he was asked to declare his occupation.

"I am a professor of development studies," he conscientiously answered.

"You study development, huh? Then, what are you doing in this part of the world?" the officer replied. "Can you see any development taking place here?"

During the preceding decades economic growth had been faltering across sub-Saharan Africa, not least in the East African countries. The rapid growth of the immediate post-independence years had slowed and turned into recession. Foreign debt burdens had been piling up and macroeconomic imbalances were legion. The 1980s and 1990s were even seen as lost decades (Eriksen 2012:127). In sub-Saharan Africa (SSA) as a whole, real per capita GDP growth rates had been above 3 per cent from the early 1960s up until 1973. Following the first oil crisis in that year, real per capita GDP stagnated, wobbled but remained relatively unchanged until 1980, when it started to decline for more than a decade until the mid-1990s (Havnevik 1987:85; World Development Indicators 2015). The external environment had been hostile, with high oil prices, rapidly increasing interest rates, minimal or absent foreign investments and worsening terms-of-trade. Domestic African economic policies were often as bad, with overvalued exchange rates, galloping inflation and major unproductive investments.

In response to this dismal situation, the international financial institutions – the International Monetary Fund (IMF) and the World Bank – shifted their style of intervention on the continent in the early 1980s. The World Bank turned from projects to policy-accompanied programme and sector lending, while the IMF shifted focus from advisory services to more hard-nosed stabilisation lending. Thus, economic policy conditionality became a new element – and a hotly debated issue during the era known as the "structural adjustment period." Proponents argued that orderly adjustment was always a lesser evil than the spontaneous adjustment that was the only realistic alternative. Critics argued that the Fund and the Bank supported class-biased adjustment that hit the poor especially hard, that reforms were ideologically driven and that the harsh conditionalities that accompanied lending were an intrusion into young nations' sovereignty.

Havnevik was both instrumental to, and took part in, such critical discussions, not least by organising a seminar in January 1987 at the Scandinavian Institute of African Studies on the roles of "The World Bank and the IMF in Africa." The proceedings were later turned into a book, edited by Havnevik (1987).

At the heart of the discussion were two major issues. One concerned the distinction and tensions between economic growth and broader social development. The structural reforms promoted by the international financial institutions aimed at limiting the economic role of the state, privatising state-owned companies and deregulating markets. Critics claimed that this hampered the state's abilities to provide social services and drive social development more broadly (see e.g. Olukoshi 1998). Even critics from within the UN system argued that adjustment processes needed a more "human face" (Cornia et al. 1987).

The other major issue concerned the role of external factors and external agency in relation to national political sovereignty and human dignity. Reforms implemented as conditions set by international financial institutions and other outside agencies increased dramatically. Critics claimed that African governments instead needed greater "political space" (Olukoshi 2002).

These and related issues have been part and parcel of Havnevik's work ever since. This chapter will dwell on the current debate on structural change in African economies, but also make reference to how the debate – and African realities – have evolved since the 1980s.

Current economic situation

The debate about economic growth versus social development is still very much alive. Over the last two decades, rapid economic growth in several African countries has set "Afro-optimists" against "Afro-realists," positions that to a significant extent reflect the dispute over the primacy of economic growth or social development. One narrative claims that the rapid growth we currently see leads to reduced poverty and eventually will cause low-income African countries to catch up with richer countries (Devarajan and Fengler 2012). A competing story claims that poverty is sustained and even increased by rapidly rising inequalities brought about by the current character of economic growth. African countries may as a result be pushed even further into commodity-export dependency, sustaining poverty traps (Sindzingre 2013; Akyüs 2012).

It is generally acknowledged that current economic growth in SSA is mainly driven by the export of energy, minerals and other commodities together with growth in the service sector, in particular information and communications technology (ICT) and retailing. The factors underlying such growth include high commodity prices on the world market, the emergence of a new African generation of reform-oriented leaders, improved macroeconomic policies and a growing "middle" or "consumer class." A further factor is rapidly improving external balances as a result of international debt renegotiations and write-offs of African foreign debts (UNECA 2013). An increasing number of democratic elections add to the general optimism, although the links between democratic evolution and economic development are unclear.

Despite such seemingly good news, poverty is still widespread on the continent. The UN Millennium Development Goal to reduce poverty by half by 2015 – which would imply that 29 per cent of the population live below USD1.25 a day – will not be met. Even though reliable statistics are not yet available, reduction is off-track and in practice the objective is unreachable within the given timeframe. In 2008, 49.7 per cent of the SSA population survived on less than USD1.25 a day, a share that had shrunk to 46.8 per cent in 2011, according to the latest available statistics. Extrapolations indicate that around 43–44 per cent of the SSA population still lives below the USD1.25 per day threshold during 2015 (UNDP 2012; Povcal.net 2015). Of all the regions in the world, economic growth is least able to reduce poverty in SSA (Fosu 2011). Inequalities are rapidly increasing, due to Africa's strong dependence on commodity exports. Hence, there is no single representative image to describe the continent. Economies in SSA run on at least two separate speeds. This is why the two competing stories tend to persist.

However, the dividing lines are not the same as they used to be. The heated and often ideological debates of the 1980s over the character of economic reforms have been replaced by a fairly wide consensus that socioeconomic development in low-income African countries requires structural transformation and increased economic diversification. Since Africa's economic growth is mainly driven by energy and mineral exports, there is wide agreement on the challenge of creating jobs and promoting much more inclusive economic growth. Today's discussion rather concerns what the options are for reaching such much needed structural transformations. Can the current growth pattern become more labour intensive? Is industrialisation a realistic option, and if so, what are the key policy interventions needed to arrive at it? Put simply: in what economic sectors can jobs be created? What are the signs of structural change taking place?

We will, in the following sections, describe measures of structural change and how these play out in various countries. Following that we will move on to describe and discuss what the options are for job creation in various economic sectors from a continent-wide perspective. The issue of preconditions for structural change will then be dealt with by measuring economic vulnerability.

Structural change

It is often rightly claimed that structural factors work to the detriment of African economies. However, there are also structural factors that are beneficial. We will here mention two such factors. One of them reflects a positive future potential, the other is a current reality.

Table 1: Africa's international trade

	1995	2005	2011
Import			
Non-OECD (%)	36.1	45.1	51.2
OECD (%)	61	49.3	44.6
Total value (US$ billion)	125	257	570
Export			
Non-OECD (%)	34.2	30.6	43.8
OECD (%)	64.8	67.9	55.7
Total value (US$ billion)	113	319	582

Source: UNCTAD (2012)

The first beneficial factor is the "demographic dividend." The age structure of its population provides SSA with an enormous economic potential in international comparison. While the populations in Asia are growing older and population pyramids on that continent become increasingly similar to those of OECD countries, a majority in African countries is below 20 years of age. When SSA's youth and children reach productive ages, the potential for economic growth will be massive.[1]

The other beneficial structural factor concerns the rapid economic growth occurring in the populous Asian middle-income countries. Economic growth in these countries, as well as in Latin American middle-income counties, has among other things contributed to a "super cycle" of high commodity prices. A clear indicator that such increased demand has benefited African economies is the rapid expansion of international trade between the regions (see Table 1). Africa's international trade has increased fivefold during the last decade and most of this pertains to economies south of the Sahara. Outside partners whose trading shares have increased most rapidly include emerging economies like China, India, Brazil, Indonesia and Turkey. Traditional trading partners, such as the EU and the US, still represent the largest shares of trade with Africa, but in particular the shares of EU countries are decreasing (UNECA 2013).

Export from most SSA countries is dominated by very few products, and in many cases 80 per cent and more consists of oil, with minerals in second place. Among the few exceptions are South Africa, Kenya and Tanzania. Such dependency has been reinforced in recent years as the African index of export concentration has increased from 0.24 in 1995 to 0.43 in 2011 (UNECA 2013:78). These figures can be compared to the 2011 average for Asian countries (0.12) and for OECD countries (0.06) (Sindzingre 2013).

---

1. However, there are also potentially major risks with rapidly increasing populations, especially if those people are not put to productive work. Refer, for instance, to Oestigaard (2012).

Another indicator of how much Asian and Latin American growth benefits Africa is the evolution of Foreign Direct Investments (FDI). The FDI inflows into SSA peaked in 2008 and again in 2011, reaching a value of about USD 37 billion annually. Increasing shares of this inward FDI originate in emerging economies, mainly in Asia. Their share of new ("greenfield" as distinct from mergers and acquisitions) investments increased from 45 per cent in 2010 to 53 per cent in 2011 (Sindzingre 2013).

Most of the 2011 FDI inflows reached seven sub-Saharan African countries (South Africa, Mozambique, Nigeria, Ghana, Sudan, the Democratic Republic of the Congo, and the Congo), each receiving investment values above USD 2 billion. Fifteen countries received investments worth between USD 500 million and USD 2 billion, while the remaining SSA countries received investments lower than USD 400 million (UNCTAD 2014).[2] Greenfield investments are evenly distributed among economic sectors. In 2010, 23 per cent went to the primary sector (mining, agriculture), 33 per cent to services (banking, finance, ICT) and 44 per cent to industry, mainly energy plants and breweries (UNCTAD 2012:39f).

Increased trade, investments and other cooperation with middle-income countries such as China, India, Brazil and Turkey have strongly contributed to widening the "political space" that critics were so intensely arguing about in the 1980s and 1990s. African countries have, following the Cold War and especially during the last decade, had an increasing number of international partners to choose from for economic and other relations. Massive reductions in foreign debts have also contributed to the widening policy space. It is possible to argue that international trade, investment and finance regulation still place constraints on African governments. However, compared to the situation in the 1980s, their policy space is larger today. What impact this has had on African economies and societies is still an open question, though.

The larger trade flows and inflows of FDI obviously contribute to increased economic growth. However, there are risks when such developments come with a high, and possibly increasing, dependency on commodity exports (Sindzingre 2013; Akyüs 2012; Castaldi, Cimoli, Correa and Dosi. 2009). Historically, commodity prices have been falling over several decades, causing terms-of-trade to fall for commodity-exporting countries. Although experts talk of a fourth "super cycle" of high commodity prices, real values of most commodities are still lower than they were in the 1970s, and may have started to fall again. Another risk associated with high commodity export dependency is price volatility, making long-term planning difficult or even impossible. Furthermore, as

---

2. Countries that received FDI worth between USD500 million and USD 2 billion were Equatorial Guinea, Tanzania, Zambia, Mauritania, Uganda, Liberia, Ethiopia, Gabon, Madagascar, Namibia, Niger, Sierra Leone, Cameroon, Chad and Kenya.

revenues from a booming commodity sector are spent, demand and prices for non-tradable goods will rise, which causes the real exchange rate to appreciate. Such "Dutch disease" makes other export sectors less competitive. On top of this, windfall gains floating in from commodity exports tend to make governments and political leaders less willing to take on the political risks involved in promoting structural transformation and economic diversification. Hence, there are obvious risks that economies get stuck in commodity export and eventually – when commodity prices dip –find themselves back in poverty traps (Sindzingre 2013).

But risks are not natural laws. There are as well historical examples of countries that have succeeded in diversifying their economies despite high commodity export dependency (Gylfason 1999; Findlay and Lundahl 1999). To achieve this, well-functioning institutions, high quality governments and clear development visions are needed in order to transform mining industry expansion into broader social development. Recent growth has been extremely rapid in the sector. While 38 of 53 African countries are net oil importers, new oil- and natural gas fields have recently been found and exploited in countries like Uganda, Tanzania, Ghana and Mozambique, to be added to already established fields in Nigeria, Angola, Sudan, the Congo and Gabon. Over the last 20 years, oil reserves in Africa have grown by 25 per cent, while gas reserves grew by more than 100 per cent (AfDB/AU 2009). Supplies of minerals and metals in SSA are mainly focused on Central and Southern Africa. In many cases, SSA shares represent a quarter or more of global supplies. Hence, the challenge is to transform growth within these sectors into inclusive, employment-creating and sustained growth.

Sector-based analysis

How do SSA countries succeed in transforming their economies and in translating the increased trade and investment into job creation? This question is so essential that almost all of the flagship reports of international organisations published since 2011 and dealing with the continent's economy have focused on the challenge of job creation.[3] One of these reports is the McKinsey Global Institute's "Africa at Work" (2012). The findings of this report are especially interesting, since they concern prospects for job creation in various economic sectors, estimated at continental level. For the estimations the growth of the "consumption class" plays a key role. This class is defined as households earning more than USD5,000 purchasing power parity (PPP) a year, and it has grown from 60 to 90 million over the last decade. At times referred to as the "middle class," it is important to note that this category is defined by a lower threshold

----

3.   Examples are McKinsey (2012); Africa Progress Panel Report (2012); UNECA (2012) (2013); Filmer et al. (2014).

that amounts to USD2.5 /day/ person, which is just above poverty levels. In other parts of the world, most definitions of the "middle class" use USD10 a day as a lower limit. Furthermore, the "middle class" understood as a sociological term forms and expresses expectations, organises politically and becomes an important pressure group in society. The "middle class" in African countries is small in size, but increasing. Hence, it is motivated to critically discuss the McKinsey report estimations about job creation.

Projections of the increase in the African labour force are relatively straight-forward. During the period 2011-20 an additional 122 million persons will join the workforce, according to the report. For the same period, the estimations are that 72 million new jobs can be created in the formal sectors of agriculture, services, retailing and manufacturing. This will leave an additional 50 million people to be added to those who lack formal employment. However, as hinted, even these estimations turn out to be overly optimistic for SSA countries.[4]

Agriculture

In the agricultural sector, the McKinsey report claims that most of the additional 14 million agricultural jobs they project will come from large-scale land investments. At the time when the report was written, there was a surge in demand for agricultural land, which was intensely discussed, mainly under the label "land grabbing." However, the planned large-scale land investments have not been implemented at the speed suggested by the McKinsey report. A large number of previously announced deals are being delayed or cancelled, slowing down job creation. Cumbersome and prolonged processes for acquiring land, weak or missing infrastructure together with changing market outlooks for agrofuels contribute to lower profitability and increased risk. This pattern has emerged in countries such as Tanzania, Ethiopia and Liberia (Engström 2013; Matondi, Havnevik and Beyene 2011).

It has also been argued that large-scale agriculture may be less labour-intensive than small-scale agriculture, which implies that the single focus on large-scale investments may be a false start (Havnevik forthcoming; Coulson 2013). There are major opportunities in agricultural development, not least if increased access can be gained to global value chains in commodities such as cocoa, coffee, tea and vegetables. But smallholders have long struggled with low productivity, and they generally lack resources for investments. Changes to this situation are possible and due, but they will require concerted efforts by private

---

4. This over-optimism emerges primarily because the McKinsey study discusses the whole continent and uses a sample where North African and middle income countries are over-represented (McKinsey, 2012, p. 4, footnotes). We will in the following not discuss the exact numbers provided, but rather to what extent the order of magnitude in the estimations made in the McKinsey study are relevant for sub-Saharan Africa.

and public agents. This will take longer than envisaged by the McKinsey report. Hence, employment opportunities – other than continued production at near subsistence level – will not emerge as quickly as projected.

Agricultural potentials in SSA depend on continued access to land and water and on more productive use of the large peasant-farming labour force (Hazell 2006). Magnusson et al. (2012) describe four scenarios for African agriculture in 2050. These scenarios are based on analysis of economic, political, social, cultural, demographic and natural resource conditions. What emerges as critical to increased agricultural production is the increased and more productive use of marginal lands and drylands, along with the restoration of lands, increased use of livestock and aquaculture and more sustainable and productive farming systems. It will also be necessary to improve systems for risk management and investment, as well as for innovation and technology adoption. At the aggregated level, governance and market development are key.

To reduce poverty in poor countries, the focus will have to be on the development of small-scale agriculture. The largest gains in poverty reduction are achieved when labour starts to move out of agriculture into rural industries or non-farm service sectors. However, this is no easy task. Increasing productivity in small-scale farming involves many challenges, such as improved natural resource management, improving farming systems, infrastructure, credit provision, factor and product market functions, as well as innovation, among others (Hårsmar 2006, 2013).

Retail

Given its focus on the growing the "consumption class," the McKinsey report estimates that 13 million new jobs will come from retailing and "hospitality" (hotels, restaurants). Rapid urbanisation, quick economic growth and changing consumption patterns will lead to vast numbers of shopping malls emerging on the continent. However, a negative side of this is that as more formal jobs are created, informal street vendors are chased away from city streets and lose market share. Labour productivity will increase with such a process. The net short-term employment effect may even be negative (Teppo, personal comm.).

Public sector

The largest provider of formal employment in SSA is the public sector. McKinsey estimates that another 15 million new jobs can be created there. However, for this to happen there is a need to increase taxation and widen tax bases. Most African countries are trying hard to do this by replacing trade taxes with Value Added Tax (VAT) and increasing income tax. Still the latter account for a mere 4 per cent of GDP on average. Revenue from the mining sector also remains weak (Lundstol, Raballand and Nyirongo 2013).

Figure 1: Industry sectors' contribution to GDP (%) (Africa)

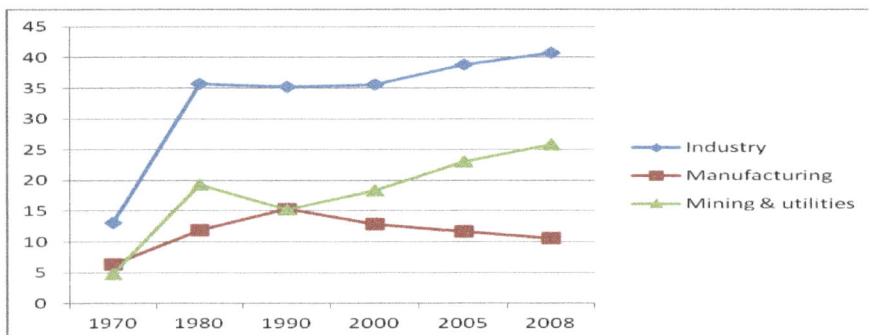

Source: UNCTAD/UNIDO (2011).

Taxation can improve the legitimacy of the state in ways that oil revenues or aid cannot. For this to happen, the state has to increase its capacity to deliver services, act in accountable and transparent ways and function efficiently. If the state does not succeed in this, efforts at raising taxes will most likely be in vain. Enormous tax evasion challenges remain for African countries. A World Bank study using Malawi and Namibia as examples estimates that tax evasion in those countries is the equivalent of 8 to 12 per cent of GDP. Corruption, in turn, is estimated at around 5 per cent of GDP (Yikona et al. 2011). Comparable countries are believed to have comparable problems. In the Transparency International Corruption Perception Index for 2012, 20 SSA countries are found among the 50 countries with the highest corruption levels. Only four SSA states are among the 50 least corrupt countries (Transparency International 2013).

Manufacturing

Hence, we note relatively bleak employment prospects in all three sectors discussed. What about the manufacturing sector, then? The McKinsey report estimates that 15 million new manufacturing jobs will be created. However, this would imply a radical turn-around. Since 1990, there has been a constant decrease in manufacturing in Africa in general and SSA in particular. This de-industrialisation has occurred against the backdrop of an already low level of industrialisation. The drop in labour-intensive manufacturing has been largest in textiles, for which changed WTO regulations may be one factor (UNCTAD/UNIDO 2011). It is true that increased investments have occurred in the mining and utilities sectors. However, these sectors create very few jobs. A perhaps extreme example is the Mozal aluminium smelter in Mozambique, which contributes 30 per cent of the country's GDP, but employs no more than 1,100 persons directly and some additional 1,600 as subcontractors (Mitsubishi Corporation 2006).

African countries differ significantly in their degree of industrialisation, although very few of them have reached any significant level. UNCTAD/UNIDO has divided countries into five separate categories.[5] A key challenge for future African industrialisation is the comparatively high labour costs. Industrial labour costs in 12 SSA countries are on average about 50 per cent higher than in a set of comparable low-income countries, such as Vietnam or the Philippines (Gelb, Meyer and Ramachandran 2013). Similar results had earlier been obtained by Söderbom and Teal (2004) for industries in Ghana. Badly functioning labour markets due, for instance, to regulation or missing institutions; high infrastructure costs limiting productivity increases; and highly valued exchange rates are some possible reasons, according to Gelb et al.

Some of these costs may be brought down by locating industries in clusters around "growth poles." Another important policy reform area concerns regional collaboration. African competitive positions versus other low-income countries would be improved if African countries achieved economies of certain size. Production may be organised more efficiently with subcontractors nearby, and possibilities for building stronger innovation systems would also increase.

In 2007, the African Union (AU) agreed on a joint Action Plan for the Advancement of Industrial Development in Africa (AIDA). The strategy outlined policy recommendations in seven separate fields – industrial policies; increased capacity in production and trade; infrastructure and energy; human resource development for industrialisation; research and technology development; finance and resource mobilisation; and sustainable development. But the strategy has so far not been very successful, partly because of political manoeuvring. The implementation and coordination unit, which is key to both financial and resource mobilisation and project implementation, has neither been funded nor started. There is, in addition, a severe lack of capacity within the AU. Most of the work has in practice been done by UNIDO (Matambalya 2014).

In 2012 another AU agreement was reached concerning a Continental Free Trade Area (CFTA) to be implemented by 2017 (UNECA 2013). This is important since intra-regional trade contains much larger shares of manufacturing and capital goods than Africa's intercontinental trade does. Currently, the share of intra-African trade is 10–12 per cent of total trade. Increased intra-regional trade would open possibilities for increased manufacturing. For this trade to increase, local productive capacity needs to improve, together with the expansion of infrastructure, among other factors.

---

5. The categories are *Forerunners:* Namibia (gemstones, uranium), the Seychelles, Tunisia, Egypt; *Acheivers*: South Africa, Libya, Mauritius, Swaziland; *Catching-up*: Sudan, Angola, Mozambique, Uganda; *Falling-behind*: Kenya, Senegal, Cameroon, Cote D'Ivoire, Zimbabwe; and *Infant stage*: Rwanda, DR Congo, Burundi, Mali, Sierra Leone, Liberia, Guinea among others.

However, even if this happens, the problem with high labour costs is likely to remain. Against this backdrop, UNECA as well as the Africa Mining Vision discusses possibilities of creating back-, forward- and horizontal linkages in order to industrialise based on existing extractive industries. As the productivity in this sector is high, labour costs could more easily be accommodated. Even if mining activities in themselves do not create many jobs, it is argued that such subsidiary industries can create considerable employment (UNECA 2013).

Strategies for commodity-based industrialisation have to be country-specific. There is no single policy proven to be effective, and conditions vary depending on what commodity is exported. "Soft commodities" (agriculture) usually demand wider networks of infrastructure. However, there are often gains to be made by moving just a few steps up the processing ladder when exporting cocoa, tea or coffee. As regards the coffee value chain, around 90 per cent of total income ends up in consumer countries. This share has even increased considerably over the last decades (UNECA 2013).

In sum, African economies should try to compete both with low prices in manufacturing and increase their degree of processing. This demands improved international competitiveness, which is possible to achieve from positions within global value chains. Such chains may be governed in various ways. The common denominator is enhanced efficiency through the organisation of inputs, services, production, design, marketing and distribution in chains (UNECA 2013:11). Manufacturing is a sector where gains can be made, making the McKinsey estimations less unrealistic, if only they are initiated and other reforms can gain speed and political energy.

ICT Services

The service sector is perhaps the sector with the largest job-creating potential. The world's fastest growing markets for mobile phones are currently in Africa. The number of mobile phone users increased from 16 to 500 million from the year 2000 to 2010, and network coverage is high – more than 60 per cent of the population is covered. In addition, new financial and market-supportive services can be offered through ICT (information and communications technology), not least in rural areas, where demand is high. Only one in five African households has access to formal financial services. The "M-pesa" payment system in Kenya and other parts of East Africa is spreading rapidly, and uses mobile phones for money transfers. Users with an ID document may deposit, withdraw and transfer money in local shops. However, in countries where identity systems are weak or absent, it is difficult to reach out with ICT services.

ICT is also important in sectors such as healthcare and agriculture. For instance, the Ethiopian Commodity Exchange (ECX) uses ICT to increase the efficiency of markets. The model is built on a few key foundations: national quality standards are defined for the most important crops, a national network of storage facilities is built, and prices are set through auctions at the exchange. As soon as the market price for each crop and each quality changes, peasants are instantly informed over mobile phones and the Internet about the value of their harvests. This is an effective way to bypass middlemen and increase the functioning of markets. There are plans to establish similar commodity exchanges in a number of other African countries (Nyamkye and Array 2012).

This example indicates that the ICT sector provides much needed linkages between the two different spheres that characterise current African economies – the fast-growing commodity export sectors and the often stagnant agricultural sector. These economic sectors need to be linked. Sustained and inclusive economic growth in SSA countries requires increased productivity in small-scale agriculture, while rural-based industry and services also need to emerge. The demand that could drive further industrialisation would come from increased incomes for the large proportion of the population that is currently active in small-scale agriculture. It is also well known that the greatest poverty reduction will come when smallholder labour is released to start working in activities linked to agricultural sectors with increased productivity (Christiaensen, Demery and Kuhl 2010).

Function-based analysis

The sector-based discussion above shows that great challenges remain for the creation of jobs, and thus for more inclusive growth. However, the options for structural change in SSA economies may also be analysed from a different angle, where key components of structural change are measured. The African Centre for Economic Transformation (ACET 2014) has recently analysed structural change in African economies with the help of a specially developed index called "DEPTH." This index measures: **D**iversification of production and exports; **E**xport competitiveness and gains; **P**roductivity increases; **T**echnology upgrading; and improvements in **H**uman economic well-being. Diversification is needed in order for countries to develop a wider set of economic activities to choose from for their subsequent specialisation, as well as for increased economic stability. Increased export competitiveness enables countries to better exploit their comparative advantages, earn foreign exchange and higher incomes. Productivity increases are needed to enlarge domestic markets, particularly in agriculture, where the challenge is also to enable labour to transfer to other economic sectors. Technology upgrading is necessary to sustain continued productivity increases and to bring the economy on to a higher level of knowledge content and enhanced learning (ACET 2014; Stiglitz and Greenwald 2015; Reinert 2008).

The DEPTH measures are summarised in an index measuring how far countries have come in terms of transforming their economies – the African Transformation Index (ATI). Of the 21 countries for which data are available, the vast majority remain in the 11–35 point range out of 100 possible. Only South Africa and Mauritius stand out as transformed economies with values above 50, reaching 66 and 73 points respectively. The weakest results were found in the areas of human economic well-being, productivity increases and technology upgrading (ACET 2014). Even though changes are occurring, many SSA countries are lagging in areas key to building more inclusive and hence sustainable economic growth. Not much economic transformation has occurred – despite rapid economic growth.

In a specific study, 15 selected African economies were traced on the DEPTH variables for the period from 1970 until today. The averages for these countries were compared with the average for SSA and with a group of transforming countries outside Africa. These comparisons showed that very little progress has been made in most areas, and that the transforming 15 differed very little from the SSA average. However, the comparative group outside Africa had made much better progress during their transformative periods (ACET 2014: 28ff).

Does this imply that critics are right in claiming that lack of structural change pushes SSA countries deeper into one-sided commodity-export dependency and hence poverty traps? Not necessarily. A key to that argument is that commodity-export dependency causes increased economic vulnerability, which in turn hinders inclusive growth and broader social development.

A closer look at how economic vulnerability has evolved over the last decade provides more positive signals. When studying what can be seen as *preconditions* for structural change, the picture is not as gloomy. Economic vulnerability may be studied with the help of the approach used in the UN's classification of "least developed countries" (LDC). Most LDC countries happen to be sub-Saharan. The classification of countries into the LDC category is based on several criteria, with economic vulnerability playing a key and critical role (see Appendix 1). Economic vulnerability is measured by the economic vulnerability index (EVI). Guillaumont (2009) defines "vulnerability" as the risk of being negatively affected by exogenous shocks. Hence, structural economic vulnerability depends on the size and probability of shocks that countries are exposed to, as well as their resilience to such shocks. Both natural/environmental and economic shocks are included, while an important distinction is made between shocks that are truly external and those that can be influenced through political action.

Figure 2 shows how economic vulnerability has evolved in SSA over the last 30 years. The critical value of 42 – which serves as a threshold for the classification of LDCs – has been surpassed ever since the mid-1980s, indicating high levels of vulnerability. There was a marked decline in economic vulnerability during the 2000s. This finding is also consistent with that of the African Development Bank (AfDB et al. 2013) that economic structural change in 19

Figure 2: Economic vulnerability index (EVI), sub-Saharan Africa

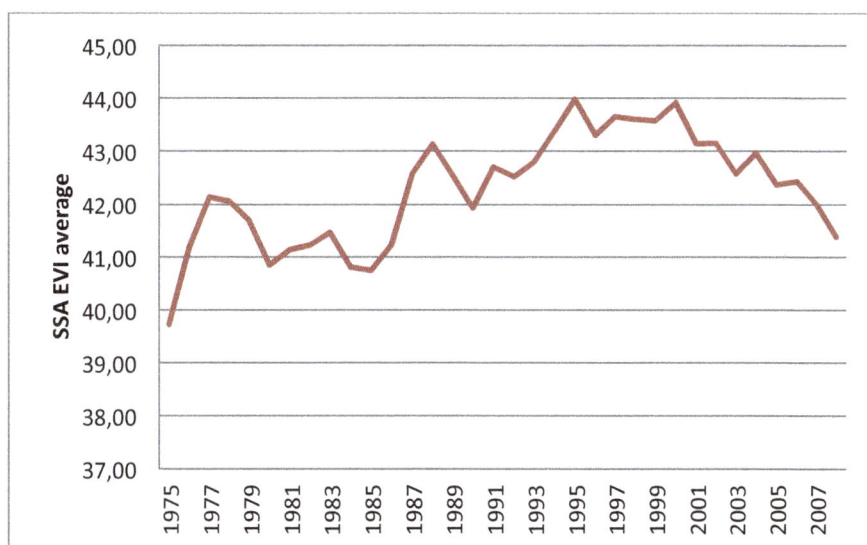

Source: Own calculations based on data available from FERDI, University of Clermont-Ferrand, France.

selected African countries was negative during the 1990s, but turned positive in the period 2000–05. "Structural change" is in the AfDB et al. study defined as labour moving from sectors with lower to higher productivity, most particularly from agriculture to the service sector. EVI data for the period 2006-12 also confirm that the decrease in economic vulnerability has continued in SSA. The two datasets are not fully comparable, since recent amendments to the EVI have been included in the later data set, making the averages higher (see Table 2).

Economic vulnerability has thus fallen in most SSA countries. Only 13 of 47 countries have experienced increasing economic vulnerability between 2006 and 2012, with the Gambia, Angola and Zambia worst hit. Two of them – Zambia and Angola – have, however, simultaneously experienced rapid export-led commodity growth.

The largest decreases in economic vulnerability have been experienced by a diverse group of countries, including some that are emerging from conflict (Democratic Republic of Congo, Djibouti, Côte d'Ivoire, Sierra Leone, Soma-

Table 2: Economic vulnerability in recent years in SSA

	EVI average SSA	# countries above value 42.0	# countries above value 44.0	# countries above value 56.0
2006	48.9	35	23	15
2009	46.8	36	23	9
2012	41.4	33	16	5

Source: Own calculations based on UN (2013).

lia), others that are small states (Cape Verde, Comoros, Equatorial Guinea, Mauritius) and the rest lacking obvious commonalities (Benin, Botswana, Ghana, Niger, Togo, Uganda). No correlation is found between economic growth and economic vulnerability for the period 2006–12. However, an observed regularity is that countries with the most rapidly growing economies are often found in the middle to higher range of economic vulnerability. This is in line with the fact that commodity export has been driving much of the recent growth and that commodity prices usually are highly volatile, and thus contribute to higher economic vulnerability.

The lowest levels of economic vulnerability are found in the SSA countries with relatively higher levels of industrialisation, such as Kenya, South Africa and Côte d'Ivoire. However, industrialisation is not all that matters. Equally industrialised countries with smaller populations and low-lying coastal areas, such as Namibia or the Seychelles, get higher vulnerability index figures.

Countries with lower average economic vulnerability are almost exclusively coastal countries, while landlocked countries almost exclusively have economic vulnerabilities above the LDC threshold of 42. The latter group of economies are mainly dominated by smallholder rain-fed agriculture, with high production uncertainties. However, many of these landlocked countries also experienced decreased economic vulnerability during the period 2006–12.

We have noted that overall economic vulnerability decreased in SSA. Still, one sub-section of the index – the measure of export concentration – went in the opposite direction. Average dependency on fewer export goods almost doubled over 20 years. This is partly explained by increasing commodity prices, because the export concentration index measures the value, and not the quantity, of exports. Nevertheless, averages do not truly reflect the structural changes that have taken place at country level. Countries with rapid increases in export concentration were not always the same as countries that experienced decreased economic vulnerability. Particularly, coastal African countries have in recent years experienced fewer and less severe external shocks.

The lower economic vulnerability that the EVI reflects does not in itself promote economic growth. There is no correlation between levels or changes in the EVI and economic growth. Rather, what the EVI measures is preconditions, which open up possibilities for future economic growth. Decreased economic vulnerability also reduces one of the important risks, namely that dependence on commodity exports may contribute to poverty traps. Lowered vulnerability would dampen the risk of the crowding out of investments.

Conclusion

The sometimes ideological debates of the 1980s and 1990s over the primacy of economic growth or social development have today developed into a discussion about how economic growth should be framed and shaped in order to lead to social development. Interlinkages between the character of growth and social development are more strongly pronounced nowadays, implying that the current character of growth in SSA countries is not sustainable. Structural change is necessary for poverty to be reduced, natural resources and climate to be preserved and growth to be long-term.

We have noted that not much of this structural change has taken place so far. The indices measured by the ACET in their Africa Transformation Index clearly show that SSA countries still have long roads to travel. Despite rapidly growing trade flows and FDI inflows, increased external exposure and linkages have not contributed much to structural change. Promoting and driving such change remains the responsibility of African governments and societies. The "policy space" of those governments has increased, but results in terms of social development seem elusive.

SSA countries have a huge opportunity in the demographic composition of their populations, with majorities being very young. When those young people reach productive age, the economy will grow if these people can find employment. As analysed per economic sector, the challenges in creating jobs in the region are immense. It has been argued that estimates presented in, for instance, the McKinsey Global Institute report "Africa at Work" are positively exaggerated. Preconditions for increased employment are less positive than portrayed.

Still, indications are that structural factors have recently improved in SSA. Despite the increases in export concentration that many African countries, and those in SSA on average, have experienced over the last decade, arguments about structural changes point in a more positive direction. A majority of countries have achieved decreased economic vulnerability over the period 2006–12. Even though the dependency on exporting a limited set of commodities has increased in several countries, and even though there are clear risks with commodity-export dependency, the wider picture is that African economies are becoming less vulnerable. Despite all the challenges African countries face in terms of employment creation, there is thus some basis for assuming that economic growth may continue in SSA.

What eventually will decide how countries in SSA manage to contend with the tremendous challenges in the areas of employment and inclusive growth is how well market-relevant institutions are functioning and how well policies will be promoted and implemented. Such issues will be discussed and debated continuously. What we have argued here is only that some important preconditions for inclusive growth have recently improved, while the major challenges remain.

References

ACET African Center for Economic Transformation (2014) *2014 African Transformation Report. Growth with Depth*. Accra: ACET.

AfDB/AU (2009) *Oil and Gas in Africa. Supplement to the African Development Report*. Oxford: Oxford University Press.

AfDB, OECD, UNDP and UNECA (2013) *African Economic Outlook – Structural Transformation and Natural Resources*. Tunis/Addis Ababa/ New York/Paris.

Africa Progress Report (2012) *Jobs, Justice and Equity - Seizing opportunities in times of global change*. Geneva: Africa Progress Panel.

Aker, J.C. and M. Mbiti (2010) "Mobile Phones and Economic Development in Africa." *Journal of Economic Perspectives* 24(3): 207–32.

Akyüs, Y. (2012) *The Staggering Rise of the South*. South Centre Research Paper 44, Geneva.

Castaldi, C., M. Cimoli, N. Correa and G. Dosi (2009) "Technological Learning, Policy Regimes and Growth: The Long-Term Patterns and Some Specificities of the 'Globalized' Economy." in Cimoli, M., G. Dosi and J.E. Stiglitz (eds) (2009) *Industrial Policy and Development. The Political Economy of Capabilities Accumulation*. Oxford and New York: Oxford University Press;

Christiaensen, L., L. Demery and J. Kuhl (2010) *The (Evolving) Role of Agriculture in Poverty Reduction – An Empirical Perspective*. Working Paper No. 36, UNU-Wider, Helsinki.

Cimoli, M., G. Dosi and J.E. Stiglitz (eds) (2009) *Industrial Policy and Development. The Political Economy of Capabilities Accumulation*. Oxford and New York: Oxford University Press.

Cornia, G.A., R. Jolly and F. Stewart (eds) (1987) *Adjustment with a Human Face, Vol 1, Protecting the Vulnerable and Promoting Growth*. New York: Oxford University Press.

Coulson, A. (2013) The End of Peasantry? Reflections based on Henry Bernstein's Class Dynamics and Agrarian Change (mimeo).

Devarajan, S. and W. Fengler (2012) "Is Africa's Recent Economic Growth Sustainable?" *Note de l'Ifri*, October, Paris/Brussels.

Easterly, W., J. Ritzan and M. Woolcock (2006) *Social Cohesion, Institutions and Growth*. CGD Working Paper No. 94, Washington DC.

Engström, L. (2013) "When Investors Leave". Nordic Africa Institute Annual Report, pp 24–5.

Eriksen, T.L. (2012) *Fattig og rik i same verden*. Oslo: FN-Sambandet.

Filmer, D and L. Fox, with K. Brooks, A. Goyal, T. Mengistae, P. Premand, D Ringold, S. Sharma and S. Zorya (2014) *Youth Employment in Sub-Saharan Africa*. Washington DC: World Bank /AFD.

Findlay, R. and M. Lundahl (1999) *Resource-Led Growth – A Long-Term Perspective. The Relevance of the 1870–1914 Experience for Today's Developing Economies*. Working Paper No. 162, UNU-Wider, Helsinki.

Fosu, A.K. (2011) "Growth, Inequality and Poverty Reduction in Developing Countries; Recent Global Evidence". Working Paper No. 1, UNU-Wider, Helsinki.

Gelb, A., C. Meyer and V. Ramachandran (2013) *Does Poor Mean Cheap? Comparative Look at Africa's Industrial Labor Costs.* Working Paper No. 325, Center for Global Development, Washington DC.

Gereffi, G., J. Humphrey and T. Sturgeon (2005) "The Governance of Global Value Chains." *Review of International Political Economy* 12(1): 78–104.

Guillaumont, P. (2009) *Caught in a Trap – Identifying the least developed countries.* Apris: Economica, p. 175.

Gylfason, T. (1999) *Natural Resources and Economic Growth: A Nordic Perspective on the Dutch Disease.* Working Paper No. 167, UNU Wider, Helsinki.

Havnevik, K. (ed.) (1987) *The IMF and the World Bank in Africa – Conditionality, Impact and Alternatives.* Uppsala: Scandinavian Institute of African Studies.

Havnevik, K. (forthcoming 2015) "The Current Afro-optimism – A Realistic Image of Africa?" In *FLEKS – Scandinavian Journal of Intercultural Theory and Practice,* Oslo and Akershus University College of Applied Sciences, Special edition in honour of Tore Linné Eriksen.

Hazell, P. (2006) "The Role of Agriculture in Pro-Poor Growth in Sub-Saharan Africa." In M. Hårsmar (ed.) *Agricultural Development in Sub-Saharan Africa.* Stockholm: EGDI, Swedish Ministry for Foreign Affairs.

Hårsmar, M. (ed.) (2006) *Agricultural Development in Sub-Saharan Africa.* Stockholm: EGDI, Swedish Ministry for Foreign Affairs.

Hårsmar, M. (2010) *Why is agriculture so important to reducing poverty?* Policy Notes No. 7, Uppsala Nordic Africa Institute.

Hårsmar, M. (2013) "Relations Key to Innovation – Peasants, Institutions and Technical Change on the Mossi Plateau in Burkina Faso." *African Journal of Science, Technology, Innovation and Development* 5(1): 5–18.

Kattel, R, J.A. Kregel and E.S. Reinert (2009) "The relevance of Ragnar Nurkse and Classical Development Economics." In Kattel, R., J.A. Kregel and E.S. Reinert (eds) *Ragnar Nurkse (1907–2007).* London: Anthem Press.

Lundstol, O., G. Raballand and F. Nyirongo (2013) *Low Government Revenue from the Mining Sector in Zambia and Tanzania: Fiscal Design, Technical Capacity or Political Will?* ICTD Working Paper No. 9, IDS, Sussex.

Magnusson, U., A. Andersson-Djurfeldt, T. Håkansson, M. Hårsmar, J. Mac-Dermott, G. Nyberg. M. Stenström, K. Vrede, E. Wredle and J. Bengtsson (2012) "A Contribution to the discussion on critical research issues for future sub-Saharan African agriculture." *Future Agriculture,* Swedish Agricultural University, Uppsala.

Matambalya, F.A.S.T. (2014) *African Industrial Development and European Union Co-operation – Reflections for a re-engineered partnership.* London and New York: Routledge.

Matondi, P., K. Havnevik and A. Beyene (eds) (2011) *Biofuel, Land Grabbing and Food Security in Africa.* London: Zed Books.

McKinsey Global Institute (2012) *Africa at Work: Job Creation and Inclusive Growth.* Seoul/San Francisco/London/Washington DC.

Mitsubishi Corporation (2006) *Sustainability Report,* Special Feature. Accessed on 13-06-08 at http://www.mitsubishicorp.com/jp/en/csr/library/pdf/06sr-07.pdf

Moore, M. (2013) *Revenue Reform and Statebuilding in Anglophone Africa.* ICTD Working Paper No. 10, IDS, Sussex.

Nelson, F., E. Sulle and E. Lekaita (2012) "Land Grabbing and Political Transformation in Tanzania." Global Land Grabbing II Conference, Cornell University, Ithaca NY.

Nyamekye. K. and N.T. Array (2012) *Ethiopian Commodity Exchange as a Model for Pan-African Commodity Exchange and other Emerging Economies.* Uppsala and Saarbrücken: Nordic Africa Institute and LAP Lambert Academic Publishing.

Oestigaard, T. (2012) *Water Scarcity and Food Security along the Nile – Politics, population increase and climate change.* Current African Issues 49. Uppsala: Nordic Africa Institute.

Olukoshi, A. (1998) *The Elusive Prince of Denmark: Structural Adjustment and the Crisis of Governance in Africa.* Research Report No. 104. Uppsala: Nordic Africa Institute.

Olukoshi, A. (2002) "Governing the African Political Space for Sustainable Development: A Reflection on NEPAD." Presentation at the African Forum for Envisioning Africa, Nairobi, 26–29 April.

Povcal.net http://research.worldbank.org/PovalNet/ accesed on 15/05/2015.

Reinert, E.S. (2008) *How Rich Countries Got Rich ... and Why Poor Countries Stay Poor.* New York: Public Affairs.

Rothstein, B. (2011) *The Quality of Government – Corruption, Social Trust and Inequality in International Perspective.* Chicago: Chicago University Press.

Sindzingre, A. (2013) "The ambivalent impact of commodities: Structural change or status quo in Sub-Saharan Africa?" *South African Journal of International Affairs* (20)1: 23–55.

Stiglitz, J.E. and B.C. Greenwald, with P. Aghion, K.J. Arrow, R.M. Solow and M. Woodford (2015) *Creating a Learning Society: A New Approach to Growth, Development and Social Progress.* New York: Columbia University Press.

Söderbom, M. and F. Teal (2004) "Size and Efficiency in African Manufacturing Firms: Evidence from Firm-Level Panel Data." *Journal of Development Economics* 73(1): 369394.

Teppo, Annika, senior researcher, Nordic Africa Institute, Uppsala, personal communication 2013.

Transparency International (2013), Corruption Perception Index. Accessed on 13-06-08 at http://cpi.transparency.org/cpi2012/results/#myAnchor1

UN, (2013) Statistics on LDC. Accessed on 08-06-2013 at http://esango.un.org/sp/ldc_data/web/StatPlanet.html,

UNCTAD/ UNIDO (2011) *Economic Development in Africa – Fostering Industrial Development in Africa in the New Global Environment.* Geneva: UNCTAD and UNIDO.

UNCTAD (2012) *World Investment Report 2012. Towards a New Generation of Investment Policies.* Geneva: UNCTAD.

UNCTAD (2014) *World Investment Report 2014. Investing in the SDGs.* Geneva: UNCTAD.

UNDP (2012) *Assessing Progress in Africa Toward the Millennium Development Goals. The MDG Report 2012.* New York: UNDP.

UNECA (2012) *Unleashing Africa's Potential as a Pole of Global Growth,* Economic Report on Africa 2012 Addis Ababa: UNECA/AU.

UNECA (2013) *Making the Most of Africa's Commodities: Industrializing for Growth, Jobs and Economic Transformation,* Economic Report on Africa 2013. Addis Ababa and New York: UNECA/UNDP.

Wade, R. (2010) "After the Crisis: Industrial Policy and the Developmental State in Low-Income Countries." *Global Policy* 1(2): 150–61.

World Development Indicators, World Bank. Accessed on accessed26-05-2015 at http://data.worldbank.org/data-catalog/world-development-indicators

Yikona, S., B. Slot, M. Geller, B. Hansen and F. el Kadiri (2011) *Ill-gotten Money and the Economy – Experiences from Malawi and Namibia.* Washington DC: World Bank.

Appendix: Economic Vulnerability Index

The EVI contains eight different indicators. Three of the indicators measure the prevalence of exogenous shocks and the remaining five indicators measure the exposure to such shocks. Each indicator is given a specific weight. The indicators add up as follows:

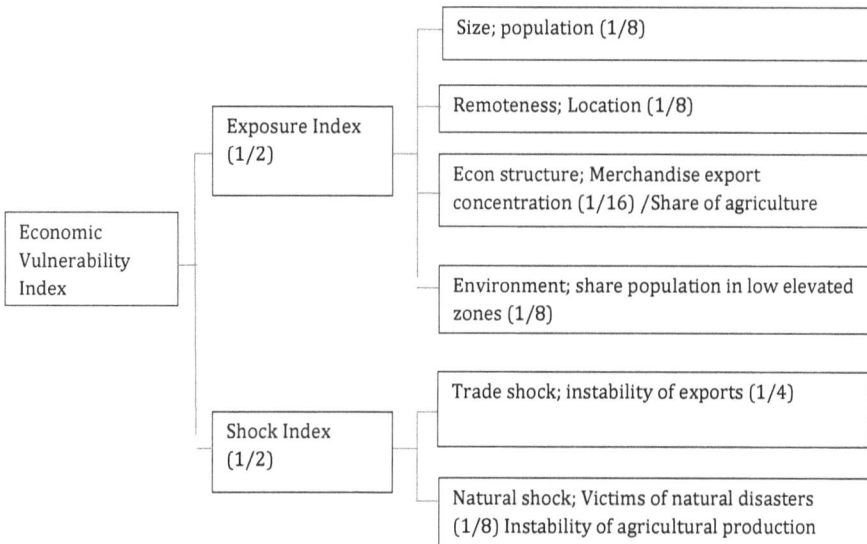

Private or customary – whither land tenure in East Africa?

Opira Otto and Michael Ståhl

Africa rising?

Is Africa rising? Over the past decade Africa has registered remarkable economic growth measured in terms of GDP (Gross Domestic Product). Some countries have achieved close to double digit growth over consecutive years. This has given rise to "Afro-optimism" among analysts, who claim that an economic transformation is imminent (*Economist* 2013). However, critics have argued that the growth is mainly in the extractive sectors, and little improvement has been noted among the rural and urban poor (Havnevik 2015; Hårsmar in this volume).

If GDP growth is to dynamically modernise African economies, then the agricultural sector must be transformed as it employs the majority of the population. More is required than handing over large land tracts to farm enterprises for producing food and fibre for export. Growth must also lift millions and millions of small-scale farming families out of poverty – but how? Agronomic, technical, sociocultural and institutional factors are involved.

This chapter discusses land tenure as a factor in agricultural development. How can land-tenure reform help smallholders secure property rights and how can it boost agricultural productivity?

Agricultural sector in East Africa

The region[1] comprises high mountains, wide plains, wetlands, sprawling towns as well as vast drylands. It is characterised by diverse ecosystems, tenures as well as agricultural and rural development potential, including small town development (Allan 1965).

Our discussion is limited to the densely settled regions including virtually all of Rwanda and Burundi, the western and central highlands of Kenya, western and southern Uganda, and the Bukoba and Kilimanjaro regions as well as parts of the northern and southern highlands of Tanzania. Here, the "land frontier" is about to close: there is very little unused land left where young farmers can establish themselves. Instead, new households are accommodated through the subdivision of parental holdings. Thus, property rights in land are a burning issue.

Agriculture in the region is rain-fed and, under suitable management, reasonably productive (Verschuren, Laird and Cumming 2000). There are great similarities in agricultural production systems, which share a similar history,

---

1.   Burundi, Kenya, Rwanda, Tanzania and Uganda.

political context and socioeconomic structure as well as comparable natural resource endowments. Over the past several decades, croplands have expanded and today virtually all cultivable land is put to some form of agricultural use. Farming is mainly small scale and subsistence-oriented, although most households also produce for markets and occasionally get paid jobs away from their farms. The typical production unit is a household-managed farm consisting of several, often scattered, fields covering a few hectares. Farm work is performed with hand tools (in some areas with oxen and ploughs). Productivity is typically low (cereal crops yield around one metric ton per hectare). As employment outside agriculture is limited, new generations of farm households have to subdivide existing plots. In the very densely populated highlands, micro-farms of less than half an hectare have emerged, and these cannot produce surpluses.

The agricultural situation in East Africa remains precarious. Food shortages persist and segments of the population occasionally face starvation. The population in all five countries almost quadrupled from 1960 to 2000 and the rate of increase remains high even today (World Bank 2011). Hence, tackling the complex issue of agricultural productivity is of the utmost importance.[2]

Large-scale land acquisitions are under way in East Africa, promoted by governments and implemented by both international and national corporations and entrepreneurs including local elites (Matondi, Havnevik and Beyene 2011). This phenomenon is, however, experienced only marginally in the very densely populated agricultural regions that are the focus of this article. Consequently, "land grabbing" is not given detailed attention. It is, however, covered extensively in several other chapters in this volume.

Multifarious tenures

Land tenure involves the relationship between users of the land and those who claim dominion over it: in other words, the institutional regime under which land use is controlled by various holders. These relations are legal and political in nature (Barrows and Roth 2008).

Land can be held under a variety of tenures.[3] African customary land tenure

---

2. Agricultural research and extension is spearheaded by regional organisations such as the Association for Strengthening Agricultural Research in Eastern and Central Africa (ASARECA), Forum for Agricultural Research in Africa (FARA), Comprehensive Africa Agricultural Development Programme (CAADP) and Consultative Group for International Agricultural Research (CGIAR). Although field trials show positive results, sustainable improvement in farm productivity has yet to be achieved.

3. The word tenure derives from the French *tenir*, to hold. In Roman law, the terms *usus*, *fructus* and *abusus* apply to ownership of land and other real estate. *Usus* is the right to use a property; *fructus* is the right to enjoy its fruits (the harvest and other benefits). The holder of *usus fructus* does not necessarily own the land. The right may be limited to a specific period, sometimes a lifetime. When a landholder also acquires the right to *abusus* (the right to dispose of the land, for instance, by selling it) the tenure takes the form of individual private property rights (Buckland 1936).

can be broadly classified as *usufructuary* rights. Land was owned in common by the clan, lineage or the like, while heads of households had the right to use the pieces of land allotted to them and to dispose of its products. Land was claimed, used and disposed of in accordance with customary regulations. These usufructuary rights were traditionally strong and gave security to landholders (Allan 1965; Huggins and Clover 2005).

European land laws were introduced during the colonial period, but did not completely displace indigenous traditions (Mamdani 1996). Statutes were enacted confirming the colonial government as the supreme land owner. European settlers who established farms and plantations were governed by statutory land laws. Their holdings became private property and were registered as individual freehold title. The same regime applied to missionary societies (Amanor 2012; Batungi 2008; Tripp 2004). However, most agricultural land remained under customary tenure and was cultivated by subsistence households organised in local communities. The colonial government also gazetted certain areas as public lands, mainly forests, rangelands and other areas not permanently settled by farmers. However, public land was used by local communities for grazing, hunting, non-permanent farming etc. This kind of land use was not recognised as true ownership by the colonial authorities.

These authorities encouraged African farmers to grow cash crops. Gradually, and especially after the Second World War, smallholder agriculture became partly commercialised. Land that was permanently used for cash crops (coffee, tea, bananas, etc.), acquired a market value and a trend emerged towards buying and selling such land. For example, in Chaggaland (Tanganyika) and in parts of Kenya individual rights were strongly asserted, and irredeemable land purchases between individuals became common during the colonial period (Allan 1965; Opio-Odongo 1992).

At independence, a variety of customary tenures grounded in local tradition and sustained by communities themselves remained (Batungi 2008). As Doyle contends (2006), postcolonial East African governments accepted the customary systems while also acknowledging and amending statutory land laws. Hence, regularising land ownership through land statutes was seen as part of modernisation and nation-building and in this process individual freehold came to be favoured at the expense of customary rules (see also Otto 2013).

Current land tenure in East Africa is thus multifarious and defies ready summary. Indigenous traditions originating long ago and further elaborated during the colonial period are still (partly) operational, while the state asserts supreme land rights and individual entitlements can be claimed. In some places, tenure relationships may be well defined and enforceable either through customary institutions or in the law courts. In others, the rules governing tenure are vague, indistinct and open to contestation (Adoko and Levine 2008).

Which tenure arrangements best serve agricultural modernisation?

There is a rich body of research investigating the relationship between various tenure arrangements, degree of tenure security enjoyed by landholders and the willingness to invest in increased production. Some analysts recommend full privatisation, while others favour strengthening individual rights through customary arrangements (Huggins and Clover 2005; Toulmin and Quan 2000; Platteau 1996; Bruce 2012). The debate on this issue is reviewed below.

Privatisation is best

The *evolutionary theory of land rights* has influenced thinking on land tenure in Africa (Lund 2001; Lund 2007; Toulmin and Quan 2000; Platteau 1996). It holds that population increases trigger competition for land. Consequently, farmers insist on formal rights in order to safeguard their holdings. Gradually, land tenure changes towards enhanced individualisation of ownership, including the option to buy and sell plots. Individual transactions may or may not be dependent on the sanction of the kinship group, village or other social community.

The related *property rights school* argues that a farmer's propensity to invest in land depends on how secure his/her control of the land is, i.e. that improved land rights facilitate investment by the land holder (Feder and Feeney 1991). A commercial interest in land emerges and land itself becomes a commodity. The proponents of commercialisation of agriculture usually claim that customary tenures act as impediments and that individualisation of land ownership is necessary for innovation and investment. The corollary is that private property is the best guarantee of security. Policy advice arising from this thinking is that the tenure regime should shift towards private property rights, because only this ensures security and thus promotes a willingness to invest labour and money in agricultural development.

An inherent assumption in the property rights school is that African farmers think of, and behave as if, their land were a commodity among other commodities and that they want to get the highest monetary value out of it. A concrete example of this thinking is the structural adjustment policies for agriculture that were implemented in Tanzania. The International Monetary Fund claimed that once the oppressive hand of African government institutions was removed from agriculture, the free market would "get the prices right." Farmers would respond to the "appropriate pricing signals" and reorient their production towards the crop mixture that gave the best prices (IMF 1986). However, farmers' actual behaviour did not significantly change after structural adjustment policies were introduced in Tanzania and the state gradually withdrew from direct control of the agricultural sector although it did not relinquish influence over land issues. The assumption proved to be erroneous, and the explanation offered was that the local societies in which farmers live and work were still permeated by values of reciprocity and redistribution rather than profit maximisation (Skarstein 2010).

Can customary systems be modernised?

The enthusiasm for wholesale introduction of private land rights waned when the costs were considered. In East Africa there are an estimated 20 million-plus small farming holdings. Farm households typically work several tiny and scattered plots. To survey, adjudicate, consolidate, register and issue title deeds to all of them would require massive amounts of expertise, sophisticated technical equipment and funds. Moreover, an all-out push to replace current tenures in favour of individual freehold would generate confusion and resistance among much of the population, including in countries that had experienced violent internal conflict. Experience from the Kenyan titling programme (see below) revealed shortcomings and limitations. Land tenure reform is, despite its seemingly technical and legal nature, a highly political issue.

Yes, they can!

As noted above, in customary land tenure land ownership is not regularised through written formal title deeds enforceable in law. In the 1990s the World Bank, the leading advocate of the individualisation of land rights, moderated its position that customary rights inhibit smallholder agricultural growth. Field research sponsored by the World Bank showed that individual private property was not necessarily the most efficient form of tenure in Africa (Migot-Adholla, Hazell, Blorel and Place 1991). Customary arrangements began to be re-evaluated with a view of modifying them and giving them legal recognition. The Bank's position since then has favoured legal registration of customary rights. This, it is argued, would be a cheaper and more acceptable approach and would gradually vest landholders with certificates conferring legal and economic rights similar to those enjoyed by private property holders. An interest arose in exploring how customary tenures could be developed, modified and administered by formal government bodies (e.g., land boards) operating at the local level (Udry 2010). Recognition of customary land rights within the overarching framework of statutory land law is now mainstream among government planners and donors involved in the agricultural sector (FAO 2010).

No, they are fraught with problems!

Customary land management and tenure have been assessed in different ways. Sometimes, they are considered to embody the wisdom and justice of traditional society in that they stress solidarity, equity and spirituality, while also being in harmony with the physical environment. Such descriptions capture important characteristics, but they may also tilt towards romanticism and ignore crucial complexities (Adoko and Levine 2008; Udry 2010).

The alternative view is that customary institutions are expressions of power and privilege and involve different actors in the community (chiefs, household heads with varying resources and degrees of influence as well as underprivileged and excluded landless individuals). Customary arrangements as we know them today emerged in the early 20th century when the colonial authorities and traditional elites (chiefs, headmen) entered into power-sharing arrangements (Mamdani 1996). Current customary land tenure principles in a community should therefore not be interpreted as the remnants of an ancient past. Although their origin is precolonial, they have evolved and are continually modified to meet challenges and opportunities and they reflect the power structure in the community (Berry 1993; Delville 2000).

Thus, any analysis of the potential of customary land tenure in modernising African agriculture depends on the point of departure. The enthusiasm about the potential of customary relations widely prevalent among non-governmental organisations, donors and planners flows from a belief that customary authority is just and protective of all members. However, if one's point of departure is based on notions of community power relations, social stratification and inequality, then one is bound to take a different view. Studies show that land tenure modernisation within a customary framework may reproduce hierarchy, favouritism, inequalities, differential access to resources and exclusion of weaker individuals and groups (women, secondary wives, youth and tenants) (Toulmin and Quang 2000).

The shortcomings of customary tenures can be expected to be most pronounced when land pressure is marked and increasing, and when few alternative income-earning possibilities (such as out-migration to industrial towns) exist. In such situations, more powerful individuals and groups may manipulate customary practices to their advantage so that land is acquired through the dispossession of individuals/households with weaker claims, with attendant disappointment and conflict within the community. In this process, the very institution of customary tenure may be questioned. Some researchers claim that customary tenures have by now eroded significantly and cause great stress among rural populations. Farmers in East Africa typically face a situation akin to "anarchy" in their use of resources: they lack the written documents to prove the land they till is their own; traditional authorities in their community have declined and cannot be trusted to support their customary rights; appointed officials assume decision-making authority; and private entrepreneurs with contacts to higher echelons encroach on their land (Kohlhagen 2011; Magharibi, Lokina and Senga 2011).

Mixed experiences in Kenya

Major land tenure reform was initiated in Kenya as the colonial era closed. The Swynnerton Plan aimed at creating a prosperous class of landed African farmers who would produce cash crops.[4] At independence, the Kenya government endorsed the plan, took over the colonial legal framework for land tenure and amended it gradually. The plan was implemented throughout the 1960s, first in the central and western highlands and subsequently in other areas, where its implementation is still under way. The first generation of post-independence Kenyan politicians, civil servants and businesspeople regarded land investment as a proper form of accumulation, either by way of agricultural production, construction or for speculation. Individualisation of land tenure provided the legal framework for the elite to build up assets (Wanjala ed. 2000a).

The essential aim of land tenure reform was the streamlining of private property rights by providing individual titles to every landholder. A short summary of the technicalities involved is given in the box.

In each area selected for implementation, a land adjudication officer was appointed and a local land committee established. Provision of title deeds proceeded as follows. An individual claimant showed the officer the plots of land cultivated by the household, which were then demarcated. The claim was open to public scrutiny for a prescribed time. Then the parcels of land were consolidated into one piece. This land was documented in the adjudication register and was thereafter entered into the land register, which was to be kept in a public office. On the basis of this documentation, the claimant (usually the household head) obtained written title.

Source: Wanjala ed. 2000a.

Settlement schemes were important in the institutionalisation of individual land rights. Backed financially by donors, the Kenyan government purchased large estates from those settlers who had decided to leave Kenya. "Million Acre Schemes" were implemented and more than a million households obtained land in this way. Some settler farms were sold directly to individuals, while others remained in settler hands for generations. Settlement scheme land was subdivided into plots (from 25 to 40 hectares). Recipients included not only landless people but also urban workers, traders, civil servants and politicians. The terms of settlement included a government loan to the recipient. Individual title deeds were granted only after the loan had been repaid. The frequent result was that poor, truly needy settlers could not repay their loans and their plots were taken over by better-to-do neighbours. Settlement schemes therefore not only provid-

---

4. The "Plan to Intensify Development of African Agriculture in Kenya" was named after the Assistant Director of Agriculture, R.J.M. Swynnerton, who drafted the programme. A detailed account of the evolution of the colonial land policies in Kenya is provided in Wanjala ed. (2000a).

ed land but also served as instruments for building-up large holdings (Wanjala ed. 2000a).

The reform measures were popular among several categories of farmers, including those who invested in cash cropping and appreciated title deeds as an insurance against other claimants. Title-holder security improved and so did title-holder status. Adjudication and titling clarified and confirmed who owned what in the community. Of course, there were winners and losers. Locally influential people with contacts among the public authorities were able to access more land than other people. The result was a far-from-even division of land. In later generations, the discrepancies in land ownership widened. Indirectly, land tenure reform promoted inequality within communities, diminished land availability for those who failed to secure title deeds and (often) disadvantaged women's land rights (Okoth Owiti and Kitevu 2000).

However, land tenure reform did not do away with customary practices. Transfers of title deeds to the descendants of the original holders have been irregular and unsystematic (Wanjala ed. 2000a). Since the 1960s, titled holdings have been subdivided, transferred, sold and bought several times over as new generations within the household come of age or through deals with outsiders. In addition, the heirs of first generation titleholders have often neglected to visit the office where the land register is kept to have their names entered into it. Hence, land records do not reflect the ownership pattern on the ground (Okoth Owiti and Kitevu 2000).

Another reason for this is that the Kenyan government has limited – and poorly coordinated – administrative capacity to systematically register and follow up on all transactions. It is also claimed that Kenyan farmers are not particularly keen to collect written evidence, as they do not always consider it necessary for security. Titleholders continue to be influenced by customary traditions (Wily 2006). A further illustration of the persistence of customary attitudes is that even though a business transaction involving a piece of land legally involves the seller and buyer alone, prospective sellers tend to consult elders or similar informal authorities in connection with the proposed sale. Hence, customary practices appear to have crept back into transfers of land (Platteau 1996; Wily 2006).

What of agricultural productivity? An oft-quoted study compared Kenyan smallholder farms with freehold titles and those without in terms of agricultural productivity and crop sales (Carter, Wiebe, Blarel and Bruce 1994). It showed that the effect of formal land title was eclipsed by other factors, mainly access to markets and size of farm. The conclusion reached was that efforts to enhance smallholder productivity via land tenure reform were likely to prove ineffective if undertaken in a vacuum. Title was less important in determining farm productivity than mediating factors such as access to markets, non-farm income and wealth.

Kenyan development strategy has involved economic diversification into industry and services. It has managed to create an economy whose size and dynamism is unmatched in the region. Nevertheless, population growth outstrips job creation. This is the background to the phenomenon of squatting. Squatters are spontaneous settlers who occupy land to which they have no legal right or even customary affiliation. The areas "invaded" can be national parks and other protected habitats, as well as large farms. The squatters are landless, unemployed people who take up squatting as a desperate means of survival. Squatting can therefore be seen as a social failure and as reflecting the breakdown of the national land tenure system (Kibwana 2000). For example, the protected forest along the Mau Escarpment has a squatter population of more than 30,000 families, of whom and only 2,000 have title deeds. There have been prolonged negotiations between the squatters and authorities, with repeated threats of forcible expulsion (The Guardian 2009).

The vast tracts of public land set aside by the colonial authorities as Crown land were transferred to the government of Kenya at independence. They include national parks, water and forest reserves, road and railway reserves, "wastelands," etc. The president has the power to make grants from public land to institutions and individuals. This prerogative has been used since the 1960s to reward political supporters. As a result, public land is constantly diminishing, while individual land possessions are increasing (Wanjala 2000b).

The following observations emerge from the Kenyan experience:

- Several million farmers have received title deeds, and have hence increased their security of tenure.
- The administrative capacity to systematically register and follow up on all transactions is limited and not well coordinated.
- Despite half a century of implementing the land titling programme, customary traditions still persist and in varying degree influence buying and selling patterns.
- There is no evidence that individualisation of title leads to increased crop yields or agricultural productivity.
- The multiplicity of tenures (customary, individual, public) has been manipulated by political elites to build up land resources for their private use.

Customary or private – does it matter for women's access to land?

It is obvious from the preceding sections that customary rights may provide a high degree of security to landholders as long as competition for land is limited and a sense of solidarity prevails in the community. However, when land is scarce and there is competition for it, customary tenure is no guarantee of security. Similarly, formal titling of land rights is very positive for the titleholder.

Nevertheless, provision of individual land titles can marginalise those household members whose names do not appear on the certificate.

We now look at land security through a gendered lens. [5]

In traditional African agriculture, household members negotiate who is in charge of specific agricultural activities (hoeing, planting, weeding, harvesting, tending livestock, growing trees, etc.) and who will control the benefits. Women are not only important in agricultural operations, but possess indispensable skills, control many production processes and can assert rights to land (Isinika in this volume). In customary tenure systems where land was plentiful, a gendered division of ownership was not an acute issue. Nevertheless, in the patriarchal agricultural societies of East Africa customary rules of inheritance favoured males (Englert and Daley 2008). Researchers are widely agreed that individualisation of land tenure tends to disadvantage women (Adoko and Levine 2008). Colonial policy strengthened male possession of land and the various tenure reforms aiming at individualisation made women's claims to land even more precarious. The household head is usually a man and he receives the certificate of ownership or the title deed when the land is surveyed, adjudicated and registered. It is far from common for husband and wife to be jointly registered as owners (Englert and Daley 2008).

Formal ownership of land as a saleable commodity thus seems to increase the right and power of the male household head. Wives tend to lose out and can be dispossessed in the event of divorce or sale of the land. Where the male head of household dies, the widow and children may be forced off the land by his relatives. Second and third wives in a household are even more insecure. Unmarried daughters are also likely to be losers (Daley and Englert 2010; Isinika and Mutabazi 2010).

The land laws enacted in East African countries in recent years reflect a consciousness of the gender imbalance and have paragraphs providing equal rights to men and women in terms of ownership of land, inheritance, decisions on sale and purchase. For example, Rwandan land law states that wife and husband have equal rights over land (Ansoms and Holvoet 2008). This is a good start, but legal recognition of women's rights to land is only the beginning. Formal land laws do not replace customary practices overnight. Adherence to the new law is not automatic and women are typically vulnerable to manipulation of the legal code. The challenge lies in how laws are implemented. This applies both to laws introducing individual private property and to laws modifying customary arrangements (Englert and Daley 2008). The official policy to encourage individual land registration as part of privatisation initiatives can intensify women's loss of rights. In circumstances of patrilineal inheritance, men can exploit their

---

5.　The article by Isinika and Kikwa, in this volume, analyses women's access to land in Tanzania.

superior status in the household and community to advance their claims to land ownership. In cases of contested family land ownership, women have limited ability to assert their rights in front of a male-dominated local decision-making body, whether customary or statutory. Examples from Uganda indicate that although most farm households report that husband and wife hold land jointly, women are less likely to be listed on the land ownership documents associated with the land policy, and are excluded in matters of land inheritance (Englert and Daley 2008).

Did yields increase?

Official policy documents in East African countries justify promotion of individual title and private property in land in terms of agricultural productivity. The argument is that customary tenures check productivity increases. For example, land tenure reforms were promoted in Uganda on the grounds that customary tenures are inefficient and generate conflict, since customary rules are imprecise and detrimental to investment (Republic of Uganda 2010).

The Kenyan individual titling programme reviewed above was motivated by assumptions that productivity would increase. The Land Use Consolidation programme in Rwanda is meant to promote efficient agriculture and boost productivity (Musahara in this volume). The official policy in Burundi is that farmers can secure their land rights by registering them under the formal titling system (Kohlhagen 2011).

While the policy statements are clear, the evidence of productivity increases related to individualisation of tenure is ambiguous. As noted above, the evidence from Kenya is mixed. In Uganda, field research reports show there is no significant difference in agricultural productivity between farms operated under customary versus freehold rights. The reason advanced is that farmers with individual titles also lack access to rural credit, agricultural inputs, etc. (Lastarria-Cornhiel 2003).

The most depressing evidence comes from Burundi, where lukewarm attempts to transform customary tenures into individual title have contributed to anarchy in land tenure and stagnant production. The formal titling system does not work. Customary land tenure arrangements are in a state of confusion since the traditional authorities (chiefs and king) have been abolished. Farmers are left in an institutional vacuum. Land disputes abound, partly due to the political situation, which encourages resettlement, and partly due to demographics. Land conflicts are becoming more violent even within households, with the older generation pitted against grown-up children and brothers and sisters set against each other (Kohlhagen 2011). Hence, the propensity to invest in land for increased productivity is not at hand.

These examples could be multiplied. It is no exaggeration to conclude that land tenure is not the sole decisive factor in agricultural development. Productivity increases can be achieved under both customary and private tenures if they provide security for landholders and are supplemented with technical improvements, marketing and credits. At the same time, nothing is more disastrous to productivity increases than land tenure systems that are vague, blurred and open to different interpretations.

How many farmers can the land feed?

Land tenure policy must also be seen from a demographic and socioeconomic perspective. Experiences from Rwanda illustrate the situation prevailing in all the densely settled agricultural regions of East Africa.

The Rwandan population grew from 1.5 million in the mid-1930s to more than 8 million in the mid-2000s. The land frontier closed in the last decades of the 20th century (only national parks and mountains were not cultivated). In the early 1960s, the family farm averaged 2 hectares, in the early 1980s it had shrunk to 1.2 hectares while another two decades later close to 60 per cent of households had farm holdings of less than 0.5 hectares (Ohlsson 1999). Until the early 1980s, food production grew at a pace slightly above population increase. Thereafter, production in absolute terms grew more slowly due to soil exhaustion and erosion, while per capita food supply decreased (Ohlsson 1999). The burgeoning population remained dependent on small-scale agriculture in the absence of a developing urban and industrial sector. Land was thus the sole means of subsistence for more than nine-tenths of the population (Musahara in this volume). Despite the fact that land was in theory state-owned, informal markets in land emerged and transactions were documented in written titles (Ansoms and Holvoet 2008). Nevertheless, land conflicts were aggravated by the extreme land scarcity resulting from the population increase. Disputes proliferated within local communities and within households, especially when young adults demanded land from their parents. Extreme fragmentation of holdings resulted in the emergence of quasi-landless households (owning less than 0.25 hectares). Many people had to turn to intermittent casual labour, petty theft or prostitution. The 1994 genocide has in part been analysed in terms of land scarcity. During the four month period when about one million people – mainly Tutsis - were murdered, often by their neighbours, the prospect of taking over Tutsi-owned farms was one of the drivers (Ohlsson 1999).

Population pressure in Burundi and in parts of Uganda, Kenya and Tanzania is approaching the level evident in Rwanda. The region is undergoing dramatic demographic change, and population growth fuels environmental change and natural resource degradation. Competition for land is on the increase and brings with it disputes and conflicts.

Summary of observations

The following issues stand out from our review:

- Privatisation of land ownership is promoted by the governments in varying degree and with varying levels of determination. Overall, individual land tenure is gaining ground while customary tenure is losing it.
- The process is driven by land scarcity and the dearth of alternative livelihood options for the rural population.
- Privatisation creates winners and losers. It is welcomed by commercially oriented farmers (including smallholders), rural entrepreneurs and agricultural corporations. The disadvantaged typically include the near landless, tenants and marginal members of the household.
- On the ground, the situation is complex. A multiplicity of tenures coexist because customary practices linger. This contributes to confusion and insecurity. It creates the opportunity for individuals to promote their land claims either through enacted law or through customary practices, or a combination of the two, depending on the local political situation.
- From landholders' perspective, the ultimate object of tenure reform is enhancement of their security against disputes and threats of dispossession through arbitrary claims. Such security can, in theory, be guaranteed by private ownership protected by law or by registration of customary claims given protection by law.
- Inefficient handling of land registration and corrupt practices diminish people's confidence in reform. Digitised technology (of land registers, etc.) managed by professionals could improve administrative performance. A different question is whether administrative measures are sufficient to improve popular confidence.
- Tenure reform establishing individual land ownership does not of itself lead to increased agricultural productivity. This requires a set of different inputs such as improved germplasm, land and water management, machinery, market information, etc., which could in theory be combined with different forms of land tenure.
- Tenure reforms that favour individual ownership are *not* a path to poverty reduction, even if they include individual smallholdings. With current population growth rates, by the 2020s many rural inhabitants in East Africa will be landless. The decisive issue is how to provide constructive livelihood opportunities for them.

Agrarian transition in East Africa?

As one looks to the future, it is useful to place the discussion of land tenure in the context of land use. Agriculture must become much more productive (both in terms of increased harvests per area unit and of increases in production per smallholder). Under what agricultural arrangements (labour, technology, inputs, infrastructure, market, ownership) can this be achieved? There are different views on which pathway agricultural change should take.[6] In the 2020s, agriculture in East Africa could in theory involve:

- millions of smallholders within an egalitarian structure, possibly featuring collective farming
- a stratified structure in which mid- and large-sized commercial farmers-led agricultural modernisation while smallholders increasingly sell off their land and work as day labourers or drift off to towns and;
- fully mechanised large-scale farm/plantation enterprises operated by specialists and employing varying numbers of seasonal labourers.

The first scenario is embraced by the ecological lobby, numerous NGOs and academics with influence in donor organisations. The second scenario used to be advocated by the World Bank, although it has moved towards the first scenario in recent years. The third scenario is advocated by national entrepreneurs, international corporations and enterprises that wish to invest in Africa for their own food and energy requirements.

Where do East African governments stand? All of them give lip service to the importance of smallholders. However, resources for peasant agriculture have mainly come from international donors rather than from national budgets. Only in Rwanda do we see a serious and systematic government-led agricultural transformation programme that incorporates a substantial number of smallholders and has resulted in drastically increased crop production (Musahara, this volume). The current trend among many African governments is to favour large-scale investments in agriculture by granting leases to international and domestic entrepreneurs. Public land has been alienated (long-term leases to corporations) and in the process customary (including pastoralist) tenures have typically been disregarded (Matondi, Havnevik and Beyene 2011). However, there is little evidence that the large-scale farming enterprises that have emerged in Africa over the past decade are the key to productivity increases. Numerous investigations show that many of these enterprises are still struggling to get started.[7]

From an agronomic/technical point of view, it is unlikely that a new generation of subsistence farming households in the 2020s, each cultivating ever smaller plots of land, could produce surpluses. Agronomic experts claim that when agricultural holdings operating with the current means of production are reduced to tiny parcels amounting to less than a hectare, bare subsistence is the most a household can hope for (Djurfeldt, Jirström and Holmen 2008). If this

6. For a review of different schools of thought on the prospects and problems of African peasant farming in the light of the Marxist debate on the "agrarian question," see Mueller (2011).

7. See articles in this volume by Beyene, Bryceson, Coulson, Holmqvist as well as Skarstein.

assumption is correct, it would indeed be an argument in favour of consolidation of holdings, selective mechanisation, crop and livestock specialisation for commercial purposes and differentiation of the agricultural workforce, including rural exodus. The policy question is: what are the exit solutions for the "surplus" population? Constructive solutions would be found in the context of structural transformation of the societies, including labour-absorptive industrialisation. If, however, the only option for the rural population remains eking out a living from low-productive agriculture or joining the urban unemployed, then disintegrative processes may set in. Hence, it is not sufficient to look for the perfect land tenure arrangement. Combinations of private and customary tenures need to be considered in the overall context of economic growth and transformation, social inclusion and political responsivity.

References

Adoko, J. and S. Levine (2008) "Falling between two stools. How women's land rights are lost between state & customary law in Apac district, Northern Uganda" in Englert, B and E. Daley (eds) *Women's Land Rights and Privatization in Eastern Africa*. London and New York: James Currey.

Allan, W. (1965) *The African Husbandman*. London: Oliver and Boyd.

Amanor, K. (2012) "Custom, Colonial Ideology and Privilege: The Land Question in Africa." In Lauer, H. and K. Anyidoho (eds) *Reclaiming the Human Sciences and Humanities through African Perspectives*. Accra: Sub Saharan Publishers.

Ansoms, A. and N. Holvoet (2008) "Women and Land Arrangements in Rwanda. A gender-based analysis of access to natural resources." In Englert, B. and E. Daley (eds) *Women's Land Rights and Privatization in Eastern Africa*. London and New York: James Currey.

Barrows R. and M. Roth (1990) "Land Tenure and Agricultural Investment in African Agriculture: Theory and Evidence." *Journal of Modern African Studies* 28(2): 265-297.

Batungi, N. (2008) *Land Reform in Uganda: towards a harmonised tenure system*: Fountain Publishers.

Benjaminsen, T. and C. Lund (eds) (2001) *Politics, Property and Production in the West African Sahel: Understanding Natural Resources Management*. Uppsala: Nordic Africa Institute.

Berry, S. (1993) *No Condition is Permanent: The Social Dynamics of Agrarian Change in Sub-Saharan Africa*. East Lansing, Michigan: The University of Wisconsin Press.

Bruce, J.W. (2012) "Simple Solutions to Complex Problems: Land Formalisation as a 'Silver Bullet'." In Otto, J.M. and A. Hoekema (eds) (2012) *Fair Land Governance. How to Legalise Land Rights for Rural Development*. Leiden: Leiden University Press.

Buckland, W.W. (1936) *Roman and Common Law – a Comparison in Outline*. Cambridge: Cambridge University Press.

Carter M., K. Wiebe, B. Blarel and J. Bruce (1994) "Tenure security for whom? Differential effects of land policy in Kenya." In Bruce, J. and S.E. Migot-Adholla (eds) *Searching for Land Tenure Security in Africa.* Dubuque: Kendall/Hunt.

Daley, E. and B. Englert (2010) "Securing land rights for women." *Journal of Eastern African Studies* 4(1): 91–113.

Delville, P.L. (2000) "Harmonising Formal Law and Customary Rights in French-Speaking West Africa." In Toulmin, C. and J. Quan (eds) *Evolving land rights, policy and tenure in Africa.* London: International Institute for Environment and Development.

Djurfeldt, G., M. Jirström and H. Holmen (2008) *Africa's Food Crisis: Does Asia's green revolution offer any lessons?* Stockholm: Royal Swedish Academy of Agriculture and Forestry.

Doyle, S.D. (2006) *Crisis and decline in Bunyoro: population and environment in western Uganda 1860–1955.* New York: James Curry.

Economist (2013) *Special Report on Africa*, 2 March.

Englert, B and E. Daley (eds) (2008), *Women's Land Rights and Privatization in Eastern Africa.* New York: James Currey.

Feder G. and D. Feeney (1991) "Land Tenure and Property Rights: theory and implications for development policy". *World Bank Economic Review.* January 1991: 135–53.

Food and Agriculture Organization of the United Nations (FAO) (2010) *Statutory Recognition of Customary Land Rights in Africa. An investigation into best practices for lawmaking and implementation.* Rome: FAO Legislative Study 105.

The Guardian (2009) *Kenya evicts thousands of forest squatters in attempt to save Rift valley* Available at www.theguardian.com/world/2009/nov/18/kenya-forest-squatters-evicted Accessed on 15 May 2015.

Havnevik, K. (forthcoming 2015) "The Current Afro-Optimism – A Realistic Image of Africa?" In *FLEKS – Scandinavian Journal of Intercultural Theory and Practice,* Oslo and Akershus University College of Applied Sciences. Special edition in honour of Tore Linné Eriksen.

Havnevik, K. and A. Isinika (eds) (2010) *Tanzania in Transition: From Nyerere to Mkapa.* Dar es Salaam: Mkuki na Nyota Publishers.

Huggins, C. and J. Clover (eds) (2005) *From the Ground up. Land Rights, Conflict and Peace in Sub-Saharan Africa.* Nairobi: African Centre for Technology Studies and Institute for Security Studies.

International Monetary Fund (IMF) (1986) "Statement by the IMF Representative." Paper presented at the meeting of the Tanzania Consultative Group, Paris 10–11 June.

Isinika, A. C. and M. Mutabazi (2010) "Gender dimension of land conflicts: Examples from Njombe and Maswa Districts in Tanzania." In Havnevik, K. and A. C. Isinika (eds) *Tanzania in Transition: From Nyerere to Mkapa.* Dar es Salaam: Mkuki na Nyota Publishers, pp. 131–57.

Kibwana, K. (2000) "Spontaneous Settlement and Environmental Management." In Wanjala, S. (ed.) *Essays on Land Law. The Reform Debate in Kenya.* Nairobi: University of Nairobi.

Kohlhagen, D. (2011) "In quest of Legitimacy: changes in land law and legal reform in Burundi" in Ansoms, A. and S. Marysse (eds) *Natural resources and local livelihoods in the Great Lakes region of Africa: a political economy perspective.* Basingstoke: Palgrave Macmillan p. 83–103.

Lastarria Cornhiel, S. (2003) *Uganda Country Brief: Property Rights and Land Markets.* University of Wisconsin-Madison, Land Tenure Center.

Lund, C. "Questioning Some Assumptions about Land Tenure." In Benjaminsen, T. and C. Lund (eds) (2001) *Politics, Property and Production in the West African Sahel: Understanding Natural Resources Management.* Uppsala: Nordic Africa Institute.

Lund, C. (2007) *Twilight institutions: Public Authority and Local Politics in Africa.* Blackwell Publishers.

Magharibi, S., R.B. Lokina and M.A. Senga (2011) *The Agrarian Question in Tanzania? A State of the Art Paper.* Current African Issues No. 45. Uppsala: Nordic Africa Institute.

Mamdani, M. (1996) *Citizen and subject: contemporary Africa and the legacy of colonialism.* Princeton: Princeton University press.

Matondi, P., K. Havnevik and A. Beyene (2011) *Biofuels, Land Grabbing and Food Security in Africa.* London/New York/Uppsala: Zed Books and Nordic Africa Institute.

Migot-Adholla, S., P. Hazell, B. Blorel and F. Place, (1991) "Indigenous Land Rights in Sub-Saharan Africa: A Constraint on Productivity?" *World Bank Economic Review,* 5.1. pp.155–175.

Mueller, B. (2011) "The agrarian question in Tanzania: Using new evidence to reconcile an old debate." *Review of African Political Economy* 38(127): 23–42.

Niemeijer, D. (1996) "The Dynamics of African Agricultural History: Is it time for a New Development Paradigm?" *Development and Change* 27(1): 87–110.

Ohlsson, L. (1999) Environment, Scarcity and Conflict: A Study of Malthusian Concerns. Department of Peace and Development Research, Gothenburg University.

Okoth Owiti, J. and R.M. Kitevu (2000) *Women's Land and Property Rights in Situations of Conflict and Reconstruction: A Case Study of the Rift Valley Province of Kenya.* Ryoichi Sasakawa Young Leaders Fellowship Fund (SYLFF) Working Paper No 14.

Opio-Odongo, J.M.A. (1992) *Designs on the land. Agricultural research in Uganda.* Nairobi: ACTS Press, African Centre for Technology Studies.

Otto, O. (2013) *Trust, Identity and Beer. Institutional arrangements for agricultural labour in Isunga village in Kiryandongo district, midwestern Uganda* (PhD dissertation). Uppsala: SLU, Acta Universitatis agriculturae Sueciae.

Otto, J.M. and A. Hoekema (eds) (2012) *Fair Land Governance. How to Legalise Land Rights for Rural Develoment.* Leiden: Leiden University Press.

Platteau, J.P. (1996) "The Evolutionary Theory of Land Rights as Applied to Sub-Saharan Africa: A Critical Assessment." *Development and Change* 27(1): 29–86.

Republic of Uganda (2010) *National Development Strategy 2010/11 – 2014/15.* Kampala.

Seppälä, P. (1998) *Diversification and accumulation in rural Tanzania: anthropological perspectives on village economies.* Uppsala: Nordic Africa Institute.

Skarstein, R. (2010) "Smallholder agriculture in Tanzania: Can economic liberalization keep its promises?" In Havnevik, K. and A.C. Isinika (eds) (2010) *Tanzania in Transition: From Nyerere to Mkapa.* Dar es Salaam: Mkuki na Nyota Publishers.

Toulmin, C. and J. Quan (2000) *Evolving land rights, policy and tenure in Africa.* London: International Institute for Environment and Development.

Tripp, A.M. (2004) "Women's movements, customary law and land rights in Africa: the case of Uganda". *African Studies Quarterly*, 7(4), 1–19.

Udry, C. (2010), "Land Tenure." In Aryeetey, E., S. Devarajan, R. Kanbur and L. Kasekende (eds) *The Oxford Companion to the Economics of Africa.* Oxford: Oxford University Press.

Van Der Molen, P. (2012) "Future Cadastres." In Otto, J.M. and A. Hoekema (eds) (2012) *Fair Land Governance. How to Legalise Land Rights for Rural Development.* Leiden: Leiden University Press.

Verschuren, D., K. R. Laird and B. F. Cumming (2000) "Rainfall and drought in equatorial East Africa during the past 1,100 years". *Nature* 403(6758), 410–414.

Wanjala, S. (ed) (2000a) *Essays on Land Law. The Reform Debate in Kenya.* Nairobi: University of Nairobi.

Wanjala, S. (2000b) "Recurrent Themes in Kenya's Land Discourse since Independence." In Wanjala, S. (ed.) *Essays on Land Law. The Reform Debate in Kenya.* Nairobi: University of Nairobi.

Wily, L.A. (2006) "Land Rights Reform and Governance in Africa. How to Make it Work in the 21st Century?" Paper presented on behalf of UNDP Drylands Development Centre and UNDP Oslo Governance Centre to the International Conference on Agrarian Reform and Rural Development (ICARRD), Porto Alegre, Brazil, 7–10 March.

World Bank (2011) *Africa Development Indicators 2011.* World Bank.

Consolidating land use in Rwanda: Inclusive and sustainable rural development and lessons from Tanzania

Herman Musahara

Introduction

Agriculture remains the mainstay of most of the population in sub-Saharan Africa. Rwanda has a predominantly agricultural economy. The preoccupation of most scholars over the decades has been analysing agriculture and rural development dynamics with the aim of uncovering the barriers to agricultural transformation, barriers that inhibit the long-term improvement of people's lives. Indeed since the achievement of independence in Africa in the 1960s, several agricultural and rural development schemes have been tried, some of them achieving admirable but short-lived successes. Large-scale agriculture promoted by the state or run by private investors with support from governments has been the most ubiquitous approach. In this chapter, one such scheme, Land Use Consolidation (LUC) in Rwanda, is revisited. It is analysed in relation to its potential to achieve food security and agricultural transformation in Rwanda. The chapter uses data from a micro-level study and secondary information to assess the concepts of inclusive and sustainable development. It also draws on the broad knowledge built up over four decades of rural development discourse in Tanzania. The question is what has the LUC achieved in Rwanda? Which micro-level indicators point to deficits in inclusive and sustainable development? How do these link to the overall inclusive and sustainable development discourse? What can LUC learn from other schemes tried elsewhere, specifically in Tanzania?

This chapter is derived from the write-up of data collected in Rwanda in 2013 and 2014. The original data sets could not be used directly as they are still the property of USAID. The findings from the study were based on feedback from 742 households from different areas in Rwanda that had experienced LUC for various crops.

The background section sets LUC within the context of Rwandan agricultural development and land dynamics. It describes the LUC scheme and the current appreciation of its contribution to agricultural transformation. The third section outlines the outcomes of LUC, while the fourth raises a number of issues with regard to inclusive and sustainable development. The following section looks at the Rwandan scenario in light of what happened in Tanzania, and the final section contains the conclusion.

Background

LUC is set in the context of Rwandan land use and political economy. Rwanda has a land area of 26,388 square kilometres and a population of over 11 million. The population density of over 430 per square kilometre is the highest in sub-Saharan Africa. Agriculture accounts for 34 per cent of GDP and 80 per cent of employment in Rwanda (GoR 2013). Agriculture is still predominantly traditional, with low productivity and limited application of technology. Unlike in other parts of Africa, agriculture can only produce greater yields through intensification and the application of modern inputs. Average land area per household in Rwanda is less than one hectare. Virtually no uncultivated areas are available in Northern and Southern Rwanda. Some uncultivated land is still available to the East such as Akagera National Park which was partially opened for settlement after 1994. The concepts of rotation farming, opening new farmland or the tropical methods of bush fallowing and shifting cultivation no longer exist in Rwanda. The major aim of agricultural intensification has been food security and also monetisation of the economy (Muhinda 2013).

In late 1980s, Rwanda, like several other African economies, was affected equally by external economic shocks and regressive reforms that affected agriculture (Storey 1999). Agricultural production declined and there were rampant food crises in most rural areas. In June 1990, Rwanda joined the ranks of those countries that were advised to adopt a Structural Adjustment Programme. The same year, in October, a civil war started. It was to last for three years and ended in the genocide of April-June 1994. The economy was shattered and agricultural production and productivity collapsed (Storey 2002). An immediate response by the state after the genocide was to conceive policy reforms that would lead to recovery. These were introduced sequentially and intensively. An important policy that had been devised earlier on paper, the Crop Intensification Programme (CIP), was put into action in 2007. CIP was seen as part of the Strategic Plan for Agricultural Transformation that operated from 2007 to 2013 (GOR 2008). The primary aim of the programme was to increase agricultural productivity, especially in relation to food crops with high potential, and to ensure that Rwanda achieved greater food security and self-sufficiency. LUC was an element of the CIP, and was introduced in 2008, although it had been mentioned as a concept in earlier land policy (GOR 2004), law (GOR 2005) and poverty-reduction strategy papers (GOR 2002; GOR 2007).

Land consolidation is a common land planning concept. However, in Rwanda it was defined in a different way and given a content that linked agriculture and land use. In principle, it was to shape settlement patterns consistent with the optimal use of scarce land. It is embodied in the land policy of 2004, land law of 2005 and revised land law of 2013. Land Law No. 08/2005 of 14 July 2005 defined LUC as "a procedure of putting together small plots of land in order to manage the land and use it in an efficient manner so that the land may give more productivity" (GoR 2005). The provision on Land Use Consolidation can be found also in Article 30 of the current revised law (GOR 2013). Unlike in other reforms, farmers retain ownership of their parcels in the consolidated land and accept advice from government experts on cultivating one crop from among the priority crops identified by the programme. Small adjoining farms are consolidated to enable economies of large-scale farming and to be able to benefit from government support for using modern farming methods. In the law, the scheme is regarded as a pathway to the commercialisation of agriculture as well.

The Ministry of Agriculture oversees the programme on behalf of the government, while the Rwanda Agricultural Board, a semi-autonomous government agency, is responsible for implementing it. Local leaders participate in site selection and in mobilising people to join the scheme. For a plot of land to be covered by LUC, it has to have a minimum of five hectares. Besides achieving economies of scale, the scheme is meant to promote efficient agricultural production; boost productivity, rural livelihoods and food security; and achieve a more equitable distribution of land resources. Priority crops include beans, maize, Irish potatoes, cassava, wheat, rice, soy and bananas. Farmers are supplied with improved seeds, subsidised fertiliser coupons, extension advice and, in some cases, post-harvest services such as storage, processing and marketing (GOR 2013). In short, LUC is part of a state-led agricultural production and transformation scheme.

LUC and changes in production and food security

LUC has ostensibly raised the yield of major food crops in Rwanda. The area under LUC has expanded from 28,016 hectares in 2008 to more than 602,000 in 2012 (Mbonigaba 2013) and the target is to cover 70 per cent of the population by 2017 (GOR 2011). As mentioned, the scheme is meant to ensure food security but is also linked to commercialisation and the resettlement of Rwandan households. So far, increases in productivity have been dramatic. From 2008 to 2013, the yield of maize increased fivefold; wheat and cassava threefold; Irish potatoes, soybeans and beans twofold; and rice by 30 per cent.

From Map 1 it is clear that LUC has been implemented variably across the provinces of Rwanda. Tables 1 and 2 imply there are still households and crops that have not been covered. However, from Figure 1 below it is clear that LUC has dramatically raised production of major food crops. According to the government, food security needs have been met by the programme (Mbonigaba 2013). What is challenging now is how to handle the surplus (Kathiresan 2012).

Taking maize as an example of one of the crops that has thrived well and has been supported extensively under LUC, Figure 1 shows the trends in output

Map 1. Hectares under LUC by province

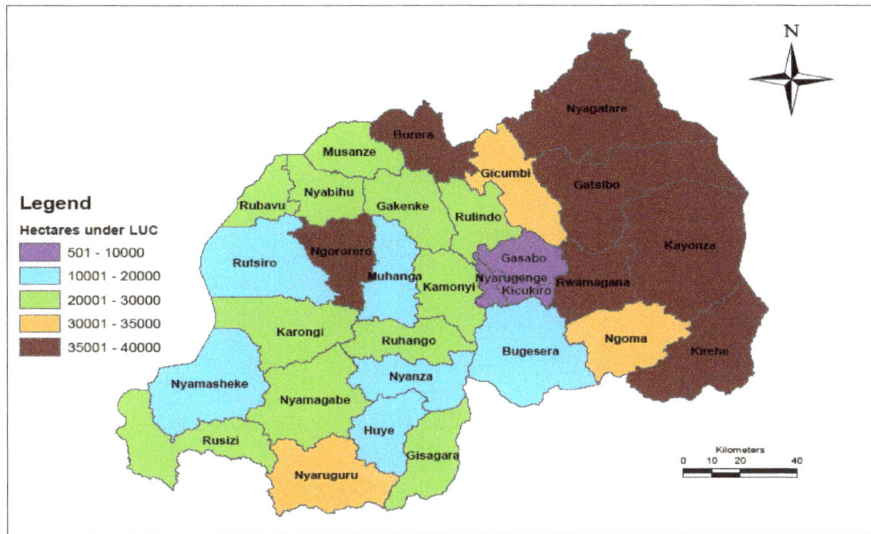

Source: Adopted from LUC/USAID report 2014.

Table 1: Topography and LUC hectares by crops

Crops	2008 A	2009 A	2010 A	2010B	2011A	2011B	Topography
Maize	17,808	35,000	83,427	29,474.29	138,490.35	83,470.70	Lowland/Uphill
Irish potato	160	5,000	36,420	2,728.71	37,183.00	60,263.00	Uphill/Lowland
Cassava	9,448	10,000	5,748	n/a	57,981.00	102,528.00	Uphill
Wheat	600	10,000	7,340	3,721.00	5,800.20	29,679.00	Uphill
Rice	0	6,000	6,703	6,900.00	8,700.00	8,500.00	Valley wetland
Soya bean	0	0	5,570	n/a	751.00	2,000.00	Uphill/lowland
Beans	0	0	105,580	n/a	254,011.00	237,745.25	Uphill/Lowland
Total	28,016	66,000	250,788	42,824.00	502,916.55	524,185.95	

Source: GOR 2013 and own classification of topography.
N.B. A refers to Season A in Rwanda which is roughly the months of September to January. B refers to Season B i.e. the period February to June.

Table 2: Coverage of LUC

	2008A	2008B	2009A	2009B	2010A	2011 B	2013A*
LUC ha.	28,000	-	66,000	-	254,448	524,186	741,817
Districts covered	8	8	17	17	24	-	30
CIP outreach by household	85,000		200,000	-	750,000	-	950,000*

Source: GOR 2013 * asterisk means estimate and Season A and B as above in Table 1.

Figure 1: Trends in maize output

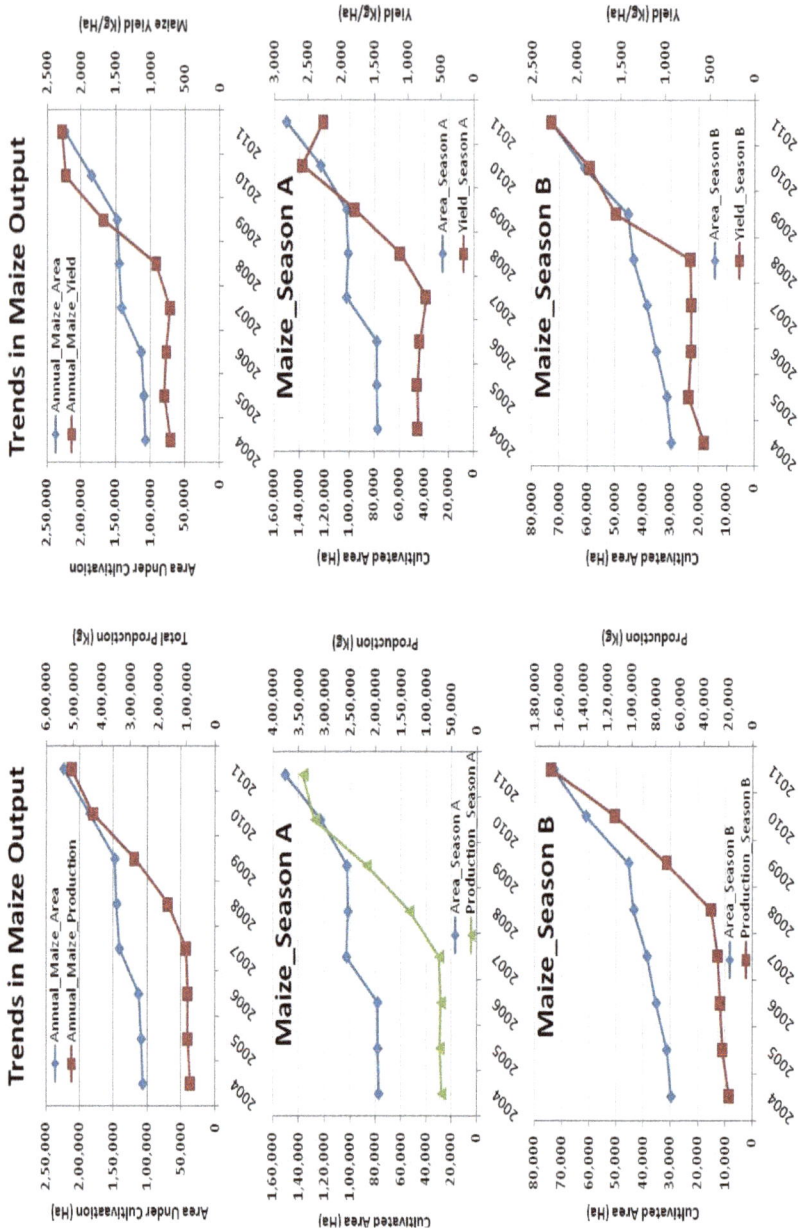

Source: Kathiresan 2011; Muhinda 2013.

and yield. The trends for the other priority crops are not very different and are also available (Kathiresan 2011). It is not difficult to note that the scheme has resulted in a remarkable change in productivity.

The discussion of the macroeconomic level outcomes that follows draws on both the quantitative and qualitative results contained in the write-up on which this chapter draws (Musahara et al. 2014).

A majority of farmers (76 per cent) stated that they joined LUC voluntarily, while 56 per cent say there was no resistance to the programme. What has been noted is that 24 per cent felt it was not voluntary and 44 per cent must have known some resistance to the programme. Some 66 per cent of respondents felt satisfied with the LUC. About 70 per cent noted that yield had risen as a result of the initiative. Asked who made the decision about LUC, 33 per cent thought it was local leaders, 39 per cent thought it was the farmers themselves, 21 per cent the Agricultural Board and 7 per cent the central government. This indicates that it is perhaps exaggerated to think that although LUC was a top down decision every decision was made at Ministerial level.

More than 63 per cent of the households perceived that LUC had improved food security. Even so, over 50 per cent of respondents had experienced food shortages seven days before the survey. About 67 per cent mentioned they had two meals a day and 23 per cent could afford one meal a day only.

Of the 742 households surveyed, 69 per cent pointed out that their living conditions had improved. Indeed, the possession of various household assets has been used as one indicator of improved earnings and livelihoods. However, there seem to be challenges in storing and processing harvested crops: about 84 per cent indicated they had no storage facilities and about 90 per cent indicated lack of processing of their harvests.

From the survey, and from other studies of Rwanda, there are many other findings related to LUC (Musahara et al. 2014). Taken together, they indicate that LUC is a success story. Yet by using existing information and the residue of the percentages reported above, it is possible to raise a number of issues regarding inclusive and sustainable development. To this we now turn.

LUC and inclusiveness and sustainability

Inclusive development

Inclusiveness is a complex term that roughly means development that does not "leave anyone behind" (UNSDSN 2015). On the other hand, there is also the question of whether it is owned by farmers and involves their participation in decision-making. Currently in development discourse, inclusive development evokes issues of pro-poor growth, poverty and inequality reduction and social inclusion (Kanbur and Reynar 2009).

LUC is based on agriculture, in which field the majority of the poor labour, so ideally it is a pro-poor programme (ATD 2015). The question is whether the poor under the programme are reduced by numbers at a greater rate than yield is increased under it. Another test would be the degree to which poor and non-poor benefit from the scheme. If non-poor households benefit more than poor farmers do, then not only does the scheme question its pro-poor growth character, but it also increases inequality between the two groups. According to our analysis below, LUC does have therefore more room to be pro-poor in promoting economic growth.

In this regard, LUC would ideally have to include all poor households and all regions. In fact, the programme involves 40 per cent of households nationally, 13 per cent of the land area and is expected to be scaled up to 70 per cent of households by 2017. Thus, the mere fact that yield has been increased and food security enhanced is not in itself a detailed enough finding, as surely there must be many more poor households that have not been touched by the windfall gains from the programme[1].

But inclusiveness entails an element of participation as well. At a theoretical level, it has been argued that large-scale consolidation hardly ever involves voluntary participation (Zhou 1999). Two responses by participants in the study mentioned above were interesting, namely whether the scheme was voluntary and whether farmers participated in the programme. About 76 per cent responded that it was voluntary and 65 per cent answered in the affirmative that it was participatory. However, some people felt there was some sort of "carrot and stick" in the process. For instance, if one did not want to participate in the scheme, then one would not get government support for fertilisers, extension services and other benefits under CIP. It is also clear that in many cases the choice of crop was based more on agronomic expertise than farmer preference. As noted previously, only 39 per cent of respondents thought the decision about LUC activities involved the farmers themselves.

In the jargon of inclusiveness, gender and youth participation is important. The question here is twofold. Women are known to play a disproportionately

---

1. Agricultural productivity can be decomposed in two different types of productivity, labour productivity and area productivity, i.e the increase in output of crops from a certain area, often denoted yields. Whereas an increase in yield signifies that production per unit of area is increasing it does not imply that labour productivity, i.e. increase in production per unit of manpower employed. In fact yields can increase without any increase in labour productivity. Labour productivity (production over labour) equals area productivity (yield, which is production over area) multiplied by the quotient area over labour. Hence increased labour productivity in agriculture, which refers to increasing surplus production in agriculture, can grow by an increase in yield only if the quotient area over labour exceeds one (see Bhaduri and Skarstein 1997). The fact that food security has been enhanced in the area implies that not only have yields increased but improvements have also taken place terms of labour productivity, implying increased food surpluses.

large role in African agriculture. There is no study yet that establishes whether the programme has succeeded in bringing about fairer participation and has improved the lot of women. Based on available documentation, no provision was made for a gender role in the programme. On the other hand, perhaps it is still too early to attempt such a determination: there is no indication that commercialisation has taken place to a level where it can provide alternative employment to the youth and rural populations. This may imply that the surplus production in LUC is still limited, in spite that yields may be improving.

Indeed, this is the major challenge. Inclusive development means a pro-poor growth pathway. The very fact that LUC is based on the agricultural sector in which most poor work better qualifies the scheme as being more inclusive than any other outside the sector. However, as has been noted in many countries, such an approach may be necessary but is not sufficient. Pro-poor growth needs to reduce poverty and inequality in addition to focusing on sectors where the poor preponderate or on activities that involve the poor themselves (Kanbur and Raynaur 2009).

The responses from the households indicated that a majority – but, importantly, not all – had moved out of poverty. In qualitative interviews, a number of households indicated that farmers have different sizes of plots under LUC and as a result increases in yield have been experienced differently across households. To obtain support by way of fertiliser and other inputs one has to have a plot of more than one hectare. In many households, plots are less than that. Informal arrangements have been adopted by farmers to pool their plots under one name in order to get the support. Nonetheless, the end result is that there is differentiation in terms of the benefits accruing to participants.

Another observation relates to the different levels of support for different crops (Musahara et al. 2014). Maize, rice and cassava seem to have been given more direct support than soybeans, potatoes and wheat. An exception is Irish potatoes, in respect of which it was noted that a significant level of commercialisation had been achieved so that farmers can afford to purchase inputs on their own.

The choice of crops and the selected areas also differed by altitude (see Table 1 above). Rice has been introduced in wetlands, maize in lowlands and valleys and most other crops have been grown on hillsides. The most successful crops are those in the lowlands. Rice and maize growers have thus benefited more from the scheme than the growers of other crops. Thus, farmers cultivating the most favoured crop are given more attention and support by government than others.

These features help to explain the problem of inclusive development. LUC, like any other large-scale agricultural scheme, can be seen to raise yields several fold. As a government-led activity, the indicators of success are quantified and visible, but in reality income and benefits vary from place to place, by categories of people and by the degree of support each element in the scheme receives. Thus, there is no doubt that the numbers indicating that food availability has been addressed by the scheme are a fair indication of success.

However, another question is whether LUC has transformed rural production techniques. First, it is still a programme that has yet to cover the whole economy, country and crop spectrum. Second, and contrary to what many people believe, the programme is still something of a side economic activity, because most cash and other crops are produced by smallholder farmers away from the consolidated land. The gain in yield has not registered as a transformative shift in the agricultural systems or the economy. The issue is perhaps not the one some tended to state when the project was started, namely supporting small farmers where they are. Rather, it is how to make the windfall gains change the livelihoods of most households and transform economic and social livelihoods. While the large-scale scheme has provided a sound basis for boosting food security, there is no evidence yet of a substantially transformed agriculture. It is perhaps too early to make any definitive judgement as the government itself had set to evaluate the entire programme after five years (Kathiresan 2011).

Sustainability

Sustainability is a fashionable word that is as loaded as inclusive development. The simplest meaning of sustainable agriculture is that it takes into consideration the environment. At that level, large-scale agricultural schemes are indeed looked at in relation to their impact on the environment (www.sustainableagriculture.org). At another level, there is the evolving discourse on climate-smart agriculture. A scheme should not just be looked at in terms of being friendly to the current ecosystem, but also be forward-looking in terms of mitigating the effects of climate change. In this section, the concept is also taken to include the ability of smallholders to continue existing and to develop on their own under market conditions and with minimum support from government.

The study from which this chapter is derived included the environment in its terms of reference. However, the outcomes were based more on the perceptions of the farmers, and these were generally positive. Farmers indicated that government intervention and support has made water more available for irrigation and fertilisers have made formerly unproductive pieces of land produce more. No water pollution is perceived. The study, however, concluded that more needs to be done on the environmental side for a number of reasons.

First, when the scheme was introduced, no base-line environmental impact assessment was undertaken. Thus it is not possible to assess the impact of LUC farming on selected environmental indicators. But secondly, environmental indicators and impacts are often quite scientific and the responses of farmers on the environment do not provide a credible answer. One particular case here is the debate on the use of chemical fertilisers. As long as water downstream still looks clear and colourless to the farmers, to them this is an indication that there is no pollution. Yet, for example, the presence of heavy metals in water as a result of the application of chemical fertilisers and runoff can only be discerned through sophisticated scientific studies, and such studies have not been undertaken in relation to LUC (Musahara et al. 2013). And this is a major point of contention in considering the sustainability of large-scale agricultural schemes.

In all known schemes of this sort, boosts in yields have been achieved by applying a greater weight of various chemical fertilisers per hectare to different types of crops. Fertilisers are commonly nitrogen-based. Nitrogen is said to be a major source of nitrous oxide, one of the greenhouse gases usually identified with climate change. The question then is how long the large-scale application of fertilisers can go on without contributing to environmental damage. The argument has been made that the amounts applied are still very low per hectare and the yield in tonnes per head low compared to other areas. Hence, it is unrealistic to expect that agriculture will be transformed and modernised without their use. Moreover, climate-smart agriculture is broader than the fertiliser debate. Large-scale agriculture can lead to forms of land degradation which in themselves are not friendly in terms of climate change.

As noted earlier LUC is a critical component of the Crop Intensification Programme (CIP). The CIP includes programmes on fertilizer and input provision, extension and marketing support and post-harvest services. CIP is part of the Strategic Plan for the Transformation of Agriculture Phase III and has among other strategic goals seed development, irrigation and water management, and agricultural mechanization. CIP and LUC are driven by the aim to shift agriculture from producing for subsistence to producing a surplus i.e. increasing the labour productivty. But it can be said that agriculture under LUC still depends on human muscular power (Kathiresan 2011). Moreover, it depends largely on family labour of which two-thirds is provided by women. Village Service Centres for technology acquisition and training have been proposed, but the survey shows that very limited application of technology has taken place. As an indication a modest allocation of less than USD 300,000 was put aside for the particular agricultural mechanisation goal alone compared to millions allocated to other goals. The strategy is to encourage Villages Service Centres to be crop related and provide required technologies such as pumps, diesel engines and equipment for irrigation and provision of equitable access to water. Technology is expected to be accelerated in post-harvest activities of drying and cleaning and storage. To the east of the country where the land is flatter the use of small tractors and drought animals has been initiated. It is noteworthy that the LUC programme encompasses a limited number of households and also a limited amount of the total household labour. About 60 per cent of the family labour is still used for subsistence agriculture outside the LUC programme. Under LUC the only difference with subsistence farming is the adjoining of the plots. The small farmers (in particular the women) continue tilling, planting, weeding and harvesting by hand.

To the farmers, however, the real problem is the availability and cost of fertilisers. So far, the government has subsidised the purchase of fertilisers and improved seeds. The challenge is whether the farmers, especially given the differentiated incomes gained from the scheme, can sustain these purchases when the government withdraws its support (Musahara et al. 2013). This may need to be studied, and it is true that this capability may vary from crop to crop and thus from area to area. The study recognised that potato growers have now realised the importance of fertiliser for yield and use part of their incomes to purchase their own chemical fertilisers, pesticides and improved seeds. Improvement can also be expected from demonstration effects and extension services. The latter have been found to be strongly correlated with expressed satisfaction with the LUC scheme.

From another angle, sustainability will depend on whether the private sector can be attracted to collaborate with farmers in the scheme. Private suppliers of fertiliser contracted by the government have shown no enthusiasm for providing their services if prices are not attractive (Musahara et al. 2013). However, the higher the price, the lower the possibility that farmers will purchase the chemicals from the market, especially the smallest farmers, whose input costs are not matched by improved profit margins.

Withdrawal by the government should not mean a change of organisation. There is the possibility that private investors can do as well in Rwanda in large-scale agriculture and crop production as in other parts of Africa. So far, government intervention under LUC has minimised this private-investor role. In one sense, LUC may not qualify as large-scale farming, since the farmers still own their small plots. However, the scale is by use, not by ownership.

One question regarding the sustainability of LUC relates to the emerging debate on its impact on food security. On one hand, the government, with a good statistical base, shows that food insecurity is no longer a problem in Rwanda. The responses of the farmers themselves supported this conclusion. On the other, there is evidence of food shortages in parts of the country at certain times. Despite macro-level indicators of food security, the study indicated that food security is still an inter- and intra-household concern (Musahara et al. 2013).

On another level, food security is a question of the availability of and access to different types of foodstuffs. While there is now national food security, there are still concerns about under- and malnutrition among infants and children. Thus, success in producing enough food crops such as cereals is no guarantee of self-sufficiency in nutrition. A bumper cassava harvest should ideally make milk and proteins more available to those vulnerable at household level.

It was also noted that food availability may be higher during some seasons than during others. Large harvests cannot be kept for long. Post-harvest services and processing are needed to stabilise food supplies over the whole year. Detailed information on food availability is needed in order to indicate in which locations there are food deficits and where food supplies are plentiful.

The question of the sustainability of LUC also has to do with change in the culture of production and consumption, the degree of technological adoption, the rate of commercialisation and the processing of agricultural produce for value addition. A good example is maize. This was grown in Rwanda mainly as an appetiser or as a treat, to be roasted on charcoal. Many households are used to bananas, beans and roots. Use of maize as porridge *(ugali)* has been common in households that have an East African background or have lived in group settings such as schools and prisons. There are no reports that bumper maize harvests in Rwanda have been consistent with higher domestic consumption of maize flour. Indeed, maize flour mills have just started to appear in Rwanda (Kathiresan 2011). A major challenge for maize production under LUC has been the high prices on the input markets and the difficulty of accessing the output markets for the sale of bumper harvests (Ekise et al. 2013). When maize mills make it possible for households to process their maize harvests, sell off the surplus and ensure that they have sufficient money to buy other goods and food enough for the rest of the year, then LUC will have improved the production and consumption capabilities of maize-producing households.

Lessons from studies on Tanzania

Rwanda and Tanzania are by any measure two different political and geographical entities. It is, however, possible to draw lessons from Tanzania that are readily applicable to Rwanda. Empirical and policy lessons applicable to both Rwanda and Tanzania do not suggest one country is doing better than the other. Unlike Rwanda, Tanzania is a large agro-ecological mass with access to the sea and a relatively peaceful background. Like Rwanda, Tanzania is agrarian and depends on agriculture for the livelihoods of a majority of its people. Both face similar challenges of agricultural transformation to bring about inclusive and sustainable development.

From the 1970s, Scandinavian scholars, and Prof. Kjell Havnevik in particular, have extensively studied rural development dynamics in Tanzania and other areas. The result is an admirable body of knowledge which, four decades later, can shed light on current questions of inclusive development and sustainability. Here, we point to a few select issues which can provide lessons and update knowledge harvesting processes in Rwanda.

There are limits to development from above. The internal and external policy environments greatly shape rural development initiatives. In Tanzania the *Ujamaa* programme (based on the vague concept of 'African socialism') greatly influenced the agricultural sector. Villagisation programmes in Tanzania and the state's attempts to induce agricultural transformation are not dissimilar to LUC in a number of ways. Both are programmes from above. LUC was set in the political economy of human settlements (*imidugudu*) and land use. One question drawn from Tanzanian experience relevant to the prospects of villagisation in Rwanda over the last two decades is the limits of development from above (Havnevik 1993). It has been noted that substantial change in different parts of the world has involved ostensible developmental state intervention. However, one of the limitations of top-to-bottom initiatives elsewhere has been their sustainability. The *Ujamaa* programme for large-scale agricultural transformation was well-intentioned but could not withstand pressure from the external environment, especially the wave of liberalisation. It failed as a forced policy, and ownership of it by ordinary farmers was easily eroded and peasants went back to small-scale household farming. Informative for Rwanda is the analysis of Rufiji District, the Stiegler's Gorge project and the overall *Ujamaa* model and the effect of liberalisation on the agricultural sector. Studies on Tanzania confirm the wisdom that development is not about growth and numbers. They also demonstrate that state intervention alone, without robust farmers' participation, is vulnerable to policy changes and often ends up, as in the case of Tanzania's *Ujamaa* collective farms, by being unsustainable.

The second lesson has been the tension between productivity and size of farm. It has been noted that there is an inverse relationship between the two. For *Ujamaa* and large-scale farms which in the *Ujamaa* model should be attained through developing large scale collective plots or by making smallholder plots contiguous in order to use advanced agricultural techniques, a major agronomic argument is large-scale economies. Yield has been shown to go up per unit of input such as fertiliser and free extension services. But these schemes, for various reasons, did not lead to transformation in production techniques and relations. In Rwanda, for example, it was noted that yields have gone up tremendously in the last five years. The question for which there are no empirical data is whether increasing yields have translated into increased surplus production and changes in household consumption dynamics. Even more challenging is how such windfall gains translate into economic transformation at the macro level.

Ujamaa and villagisation schemes in Tanzania were about the advantages of large-scale collective farms (as explained above). By the early 1980s, the *Ujamaa* rural development model was abandoned partly because of the changing global political environment, but also because of constraints related to the *Ujamaa* agricultural model which aimed for collective farming or the amalgamation of smallholder farms in contiguous large scale agricultural production. Narratives of this experience are plentiful, such as the Katoro-Buseresere village (Bryceson 2010). Individual based small-scale agricultural units, though providing no firm evidence of macro-level transformation, build on longstanding practices that take care of rural households and livelihoods. An inclusive development model should therefore not ignore the rural development dynamics based on individual farming households.

Large-scale agricultural schemes, whether in the form of *Ujamaa* in Tanzania or in other types, have serious inclusive and sustainability problems. The ending of the *Ujamaa* rural development model in Tanzania in the early 1980s was not, however, the end of the desire of the government to try launch large-scale agriculture. Such schemes have emerged in Tanzania in different ways during the last decade and mainly through private investment. While this augurs well for the open and liberal attraction of foreign investments, the important question is whether this type of agriculture has the ability to generate inclusive and sustainable development for a predominantly agrarian population. Evidence so far indicate that such large scale schemes neither contribute to food security nor provide adequate rural employment. They have not served as a viable agricultural model and have often given rise to land conflict. Indeed, another result has been land grabbing not only by foreign investors but also by local elites, who have exploited the commodification of land rights through new land markets. At times, crops for biofuels may be supported in the name of sustaining the environment, but in disregard of the food security of the rural peasantry (FAO 2013b; Abdallah, Engström, Havnevik and Salomonsson 2014).

In Rwanda, LUC cannot be said to be related to foreign direct investment. However, the provision of inputs is supposed to be by private companies. The question that arises from Tanzanian experience is whether in the long run farmers' livelihoods are improved permanently and whether the economy undergoes dynamic transformation. That said, there are studies indicating large-scale farming of biofuels (Matondi, Havnevik and Beyene 2011). Obviously there are physical limits to how much sugarcane or jatropha plantations can be grown on arable land (Huggins 2012). It is also not clear what would happen if the government ceased supporting LUC and let private large-scale investment take over. What has been witnessed in the rest of East Africa could happen even more quickly in Rwanda, given its recent record of opening up to foreign investment.

Food security is one of the basic elements of poverty reduction, but it is not the only one. Access to basic needs, social inclusion and empowerment have come forward as important elements in sustainable development. Reduction of horizontal and vertical inequality and gender imbalances are also important in an ideal sense of development (UNSDSN 2015). LUC has been shown to offer an answer to food security, even if food security is still a concern in various ways. There are seasonal variations in food availability and constraints on food security for a significant number of households. The issue of food security has implications for nutrition, especially within the household and for infants. Malnutrition is still a challenge in Rwanda, despite the dramatic rise in food crop yields (FAO 2013a).

The developmental state and the emergence of Africa are key words in the race for investment and growth. They have prompted concepts such as a "rising Africa" and "Afro-optimism" (Economist 2011). The real question from our discussion above is whether investment and growth are inclusive and sustainable. Have all the gains in production and growth resulted in similar rates of poverty reduction. If poverty reduction has been considerable, are levels of inequality in the country reduced? Above all these are quantitative and qualitative changes. Has the level of social inclusion by race, gender, religion and location improved? Now, because poverty is still a concern and rural areas are still nests of backwardness and need, inequality remains a question, as do all sorts of social exclusion. In practice, there is still a gap in the evidence on and knowledge of how to make micro- and meso-level schemes, as well as macroeconomic policy frameworks, more inclusive and sustainable.

Conclusion

Many studies on Rwanda start with post-genocide recovery. LUC is one of the post-genocide policy responses and was born of the land policy of 2004 and the land law of 2005. But the apparent success of LUC in the past six years is quite similar to the experience in other sub-Saharan countries with postcolonial efforts in agriculture. Specifically, are the recorded successes consistent with the desire to achieve inclusive and sustainable development?

There are general indicators from micro-level studies that growth from large-scale schemes such as LUC is most likely not leading to inclusive development. Rwanda has been registering admirable rates of economic growth, but apparently pro-poor growth has not reduced poverty and inequality. The end result is that there are still a large number of poor and high levels of inequality.

Sustainability is not only a question of addressing issues related to the environment. A top-down policy intervention that has not permitted participation and included the local institutional framework is not likely to last forever, no matter how good it was from an environmental point of view. This is exemplified by such as the *Ujamaa* experiment of Tanzania. Villagisation and *Ujamaa* rural development was not a voluntary scheme. LUC, like *Ujamaa*, is based on the logic that means justifying the ends and 'we must run while others walk'. The justification these days comes from the successes of East Asian developmental states. It is true that countries like Singapore and South Korea have proved that state interventionism with the right developmental ideology and discipline can make a durable change. But it is also true that state intervention fails to provide everything. It is thus important that research continues into how policies and programmes at all levels can support more inclusive and sustainable development.

References

ATD (All Together in Dignity) Fourth World (2015) *Challenge 2015.*Towards Sustainable Development that leaves no one behind. Paris.

Abdallah, J., L. Engström, K. Havnevik and L. Salomonsson (2014) "Large-scale land acquisitions in Tanzania: A Critical Analysis of Practices and Dynamics", in Kaag, M. and A. Zoomers (eds), *The Global Land Grab – Beyond the Hype*. London and New York: Zed Books.

Bhaduri, A. and R. Skarstein (1997), *Economic Development and Agricultural Productivity*. Edward Elgar Publisher.

Bryceson, D. F. (2010) "Agrarian Fundamentalism or Foresight? Revisiting Nyerere's Vision for Rural Tanzania". In Havnevik and Isinika (eds) (2010) *From Nyerere to Mkapa*. Dar es Salaam: Mkuki na Nyota.

Economist (December 2011) "Africa Rising".

Ekise, L., A. Nahayo, J.D. Mirukiro and B. Mukamugema (2013) "Impact of land use consolidation on maize production. Case study of Nyabihu districts in Western Rwanda." *Nature and Science* 11(12): 21–7.

FAO (2013a) *CAADP Rwanda. Nutrition Country Paper*. Rome: FAO.

FAO (2013b), *Trends and Impacts of Foreign Investment in Developing Country Agriculture: Evidence from Case Studies*. Rome: FAO.

GOR (Government of Rwanda) (2002) *Poverty Reduction Strategy Paper*. Kigali: Ministry of Finance.

GOR (2004) *Land Policy*. Kigali: Ministry of Land and Natural Resources.

GOR (2005) *Organic Law N° 08/2005 of 14/07/2005 Determining the Use and Management of Land In Rwanda.*Kigali.

GOR (2007) *Economic Development and Poverty Reduction Strategy, 2008-2012*. Kigali: Ministry of Finance and Economic Planning.

GOR (2008) 2007 *Annual Report. Ministry of Agriculture and Animal Resources*. Kigali: MINAGRI.

GOR (2009) *Strategic Plan for the Transformation of Agriculture in Rwanda – Phase II (PSTA II). Final Report*. Kigali: MINAGRI.

GOR (2009) *Joint Sector Review report for Agriculture*. Kigali: MINAGRI.

GOR (2011) *Strategies for sustainable crop intensification shifting focus from producing enough to producing surplus*. Kigali: MINAGRI.

GOR (2012) *Rwanda agricultural trends and outlook*. Kigali: MINAGRI http://www. minagri.gov.rw/fileadmin/user_upload/documents/RWANDA_SAKSS/Annual_ Trends_and_Outlook_Report_2012.pdf. Downloaded on 25 April 2015.

GOR (2013) *Annual Report*. Kigali: MINAGRI.

Havnevik K. (1993) *Tanzania the Limits to Development from above*. Dar es Salaam: Mkuki na Nyota.

Havnevik K. and M. Hårsmar (1999) *The diversified future. An institutional approach to rural development in Tanzania*. Uppsala: Swedish University of Agriculture.

Havnevik K. and A. Isinika (eds) (2010) *From Nyerere to Mkapa*. Dar es Salaam: Mkuki na Nyota Publishers in cooperation with the Nordic Africa Institute and Sokoine University of Agriculture, Tanzania.

Kanbur, R and G. Rauniyar (2009) *Inclusive Growth and Inclusive Development*. African Development Bank, Occasional Paper No. 8.

Kathiresan, A. (2011) *Strategies for Sustainable Crop Intensification in Rwanda. Shifting focus from producing enough to producing surplus*. Kigali: MINAGRI.

Huggins, C. (2010) *Consolidating land, consolidating control*. Land Deal Political Initiatives (LDPI) Paper, Cape Town.

Matondi, P., K. Havnevik and A. Beyene (eds) (2011) *Biofuels, land grabbing and food security in Africa*. London: Zed Books and Nordic Africa Institute.

Muhinda, J.M. (2013) *Rwanda agricultural sector and its impact on food security and economy*. Presentation on Asian lessons on agricultural transformation. Kigali.

Musahara, H. (2006) *Improving Tenure Security for the Rural Poor Rwanda – Country Case Study*. Legal Empowerment of the Poor (LEP). Food and Agriculture Organisation (FAO).

Musahara, H. (2009) *Water resource availability and use in Rwanda*. OSSREA Rwanda Chapter Monograph.

Musahara, H., T. Niyonzima, C. Bizimana and N. Birasa (2013) *LUC project reports*. USAID Land Project, Kigali.

Musahara, H., T. Niyonzima, C. Bizimana and N. Birasa (2014) "Land Use Consolidation and Poverty Reduction in Rwanda". Paper for the World Bank Conference on Land and Poverty. World Bank.

Storey, A. (1999) "Economic and ethnic conflict. Structural adjustment in Rwanda". *Development Policy Review* 17(1): 43–63.

UNSDSN (2015) Sustainable Development Solutions Network website. www.unsdsn. org.

World Bank (2011) "Rwanda Economic Update". Kigali. Available at http:// siteresources.worldbank.org/INTRWANDA/Resources/Rwanda_Economic_ Rwanda_Update_Spring_Edition_April_2011.pdf Accessed on 25 April 2015.

World Bank (2014)" Environmental and Social Systems Assessment (ESSA)". Washington accessed on 19/05/2015https://www.google.com/search?num =50&newwindow=1&rlz=1C2RNKA_enET586ET586&q=World+Bank +%282014%29+Environmental+and+Social+Systems+Assessment+%28E SSA%29.+Washington&oq=World+Bank+%282014%29+Environmental +and+Social+Systems+Assessment+%28ESSA%29.+Washington&gs_l=se rp.12...37451.37451.0.38552.1.1.0.0.0.0.730.730.6-1.1.0.msedr...0...1c.2.64. serp..1.0.0.UH-HYZEtqCc

Zhou, J.M. (1999) *How to Carry Out Land Consolidation. An International Comparison.* European University Institute, Department of Economics. Italy. http://www.iue.it/ ECO/ WP-Texts/ECO99-1.pdf. / 3.3.2002.

Large-scale land acquisitions in Tanzania and Ethiopia: A comparative perspective

Atakilte Beyene

Introduction

Both Tanzania and Ethiopia, and for that matter the whole of sub-Saharan Africa, are described as having similar patterns when it comes to current large-scale land acquisitions.

For instance, both countries have transferred extensive land resources to various actors generally labelled as investors. These include government corporations, other sovereign states and foreign and domestic investors. The agricultural policies of both Ethiopia and Tanzania emphasise the need for investment, modernisation of the agricultural sector and the utilisation of rural resources to achieve economic development. An important element in the policies is the ambition to promote Foreign Direct Investment (FDI)-driven, export-oriented, large-scale and commercial agricultural systems. These domestic policies, combined with the global surge in demand for land over the past few years, have resulted in a dramatic rise in large-scale land and water transfers to and acquisitions by big investors. Both countries are among the top 10 in Africa as sources of land for investors (Beyene and Sandström 2015).

Similarly, studies also indicate that significant numbers of the planned investments face challenges. Many do not materialise and implemented projects are few (Abdallah, Engström, Havnevik and Salomonsson 2014). In other cases, implemented projects face failure due to land conflicts (FAO 2012; De Schutter 2011; Matondi, Havnevik and Beyene 2011). This has generated "new" land dynamics at the local level as well as new sets of management issues related to the demobilisation of failed investments. These include the complexity and uncertainty of the land, property and environmental issues emerging in the aftermath of investment failures and withdrawals.

However, the two countries differ significantly in some aspects that are considered important in development and policy issues. Two such aspects that probably distinguish both countries from each other and the rest of Africa are land tenure systems and the characteristics of the state. Tanzania has been appreciated for promoting and instituting "village" and customary rights of occupancy in relation to natural resources. This characteristic probably distinguishes Tanzania from the rest of sub-Saharan Africa. On the other hand, the Ethiopian state has been characterised as highly centralised and dominant and it strongly involves itself in the governance of natural resources and the economy.

This chapter attempts to explore why, despite the marked differences in governance systems, some of the large-scale land and water acquisitions in both countries face similar challenges when implemented. Or are the challenges the same? What other common and/or differentiating attributes can be identified to explain the challenges in the current large-scale land and water acquisitions? In this regard, this chapter attempts to provide some clues beyond the generally reported challenges of large-scale land and water transfers by focusing on whether there are differences between the countries in their large-scale agricultural investment patterns. To get insights into these questions, differences between the two countries in (average) size of land allocated to investors, trends in joint foreign-domestic investments and the type/s of products (food or non-food items) covered by investment projects are explored.

The data sets used to explore the questions are drawn from the *Land Matrix* (for Ethiopia) (LM) and published data from the Land Deal Politics Initiative (for Tanzania) (LDPI). The *Land Matrix* is a comprehensive compilation, but the validity of the information is often a challenge, as the sources are diverse (NGO, government, corporate, etc.). However, the data are comprehensive, regularly updated and available online. The data compiled in the LDPI (by Locher and Sulle 2013) are updated and critically reviewed.

For the purposes of this study, only land deals by foreign investors and joint ventures involving nationals and foreigners are considered. The period for the reported land deals are 2008–2012 for Tanzania and 2008–2014 for Ethiopia.

Agriculture is the nexus

Both Tanzania and Ethiopia are dependent on agriculture and natural resources in general. In the former, agriculture accounted for 32 per cent of the GDP in 2013 and provides employment to approximately 75 per cent of all workers (World Bank 2015). For Ethiopia, the sector is even more important as it accounts for about 50 per cent of GDP and is a major source of employment for about 80 per cent of the population (GTP 2010).

In both countries, improving food security and creating decent rural employment opportunities are critical issues. The prospects of achieving these objectives depend principally on the performance of the agricultural sector. As has been widely recognised, improvement in agricultural performance remains perhaps the single most important determinant of economic growth and poverty reduction (World Bank 2007). Actualising these potentials, however, remains a serious challenge. The question of how agricultural productivity can be improved in the smallholder sector, where it is most needed continues to be critical, and smallholder farming continues to face various challenges. Among them, vulnerability to climate change, rainfall dependency as well as low levels of productivity and poor access to markets are key (AGRA 2014).

And yet, the current policy drive to promote and introduce agricultural FDI and the subsequent allocations of large-scale farmlands to companies have raised additional uncertainty about the overall relevance and contribution of large-scale investments *vis-à-vis* smallholder farmers, and the risk and potential of the investments. Two major issues with regard to the current large-scale commercial farms are that 1) the product focus of many of the such investments is on non-food commodities (e.g. biofuels) and the prospect of supplying food products to local markets is limited; and 2) the farms prefer mechanisation to increase their profit margins and the potential to create rural employment is generally very limited. Overshadowing these uncertainties is the potential for land competition and local land conflicts that the land acquisitions may generate.

The State, land and liberalisation: Brief comparative perspective

To better understand the current large-scale land acquisition deals, a brief account is given below of the role and characteristics of the Tanzanian and Ethiopian states, particularly in relation to the governance of natural resources, especially land, and their overall pursuit of liberalisation policies.

Land tenure systems

After independence, Tanzania embraced socialism as the political ideology of the country. It strove to create an indigenous socialism, commonly known as *Ujamaa,* whereby non-exploitative rural cooperatives were envisaged as the foundation of social and economic organisation (Raikes 1975). To create these institutions, resettlement and villagisation programmes were carried out across rural Tanzania. The villagisation programme was accompanied by a set of laws that implied the possibility of eliminating customary land rights (Havnevik and Hårsmar 1999).

Current land tenure systems in Tanzania are guided by the Land Act and the Village Land Act, which were adopted in 1999 (for details see Wily 2003, and, in this volume, the chapters by Bryceson and by Isinika and Kikwa). In terms of these acts, land is categorised into general land, reserve land and village land. General land mainly refers to urban areas, while reserve land refers to areas placed under environmental protection, such as forest reserves and wildlife reserves. Both these land categories are governed by the Land Act. Village land, on the other hand, refers exclusively to land falling under the jurisdiction and management of a registered village (Woldegiorgis 2015).[1] In mainland Tanzania, there are 11,165 villages (URT 2009) and most of the land in the country is village land. Each village has its own administrative unit known as the vil-

---

1.   All land in Tanzania, including village land, is public and vested in the president as a trustee for and on the behalf of all the citizens.

lage council, which is, among other things, authorised to manage, administer and define land use in respect of village land (URT 1999). Hence, each village is responsible for defining the land use categories within its boundaries, these categories being communal village land, individual and family land and reserve land (see Wily 2003).

Ethiopia's land tenure system is by comparison statist. The supreme law of the land, the Ethiopian Constitution adopted in 1995, stipulates that the "right to ownership of rural and urban lands, as well as of all natural resources, is exclusively vested in the State and in the peoples of Ethiopia" (for details see Woldegiorgis 2015). Access to land is basically considered as the right of citizens. Peasants are entitled to "have the right to obtain land without payments and the protection against eviction from their possession." Frequent land redistributions were carried out, starting with the land reform of 1975. As a result, the distribution of land holdings among sedentary smallholder farmers, often located in the highlands, is almost homogenous. The lowlands are relatively sparsely populated and pastoralism is the dominant form of livelihood. According to the constitution, pastoralists have the right to access free land for grazing and cultivation as well as the right not to be displaced from their own lands. However, while the majority of smallholders in the highlands have been given certificates of user rights, such initiatives have not been introduced in the lowlands. Consequently, in the lowlands land rights are highly problematic, particularly in areas where populations migrate over expansive territories. Such territories are described as underutilised and existing land rights may not be recognised. Many of the current large-scale agricultural investments are located in such areas.

By comparison, the Tanzanian tenure system is distinctive in Africa in terms of the state's role of "vesting authority and control over land at the local level" (Wily 2003). This condition gives Tanzanian villagers the potential to manage their land, including dis/approving land transfers and leases to investors. This has important implications for the governance of natural resources in general. For instance, if investors are to acquire village lands, village assemblies (where all registered villagers above 18 years of age are members) have to give their consent and investors have to negotiate with the village council (which is the executive organ of the village). There are cases where village assemblies and councils actively exercise their institutional power by voting against the transfer of village lands or scrutinise land deals and even reject those they feel do not meet their expectations (Beyene, Mungongo, Atteridge and Larsen 2013). However, the legal rights in land matters of village assemblies and councils are restricted to land transfers below 250 hectares. This is not, however, to suggest that the Tanzanian tenure system has reached its full potential. Villagers probably face increasing threats and insecurity in their lands. Many villages lack the financial and technical capacity to undertake the land-management required by the Land

Acts. Instead, other actors, including investors, carry out such activities on their behalf. Similarly, the government is also putting pressure on villages to identify land and transfer it to the land bank of the Tanzanian Investment Centre (TIC), a government organisation (see below). These processes can undermine village control and ownership of the planning and decision-making processes regarding village lands.

In the Ethiopian case, the state has much more institutional power to directly decide on land issues. If land is required for public and other activities that are considered significant for the nation, the government has a constitutional right to allocate such land. This could lead to violations of local land rights, as compensation is only paid for properties that are developed on the land, but not for the land itself. The government thus has the advantage of designating large areas as being available for investment. According to Rahmato, by 2011, 3.6 million hectares of land had been transferred from the regions to the federal land bank (Rahmato 2011).

Another difference between the two countries is that in Tanzania, although all investors are supposed to go through the TIC, in practice seem to have diverse entry points to access land. They can, for instance, enter into direct negotiations with village councils. In other cases, the government directly allocates land to investors, as in the case of EcoEnergy in Bagamoyo. In Ethiopia, all land deals involving more than 500 hectares go through the Ethiopian Investment Agency (EIA), which effectively means through the federal and regional governments. For allocations of less than 500 hectares, regional states are authorised to make decisions.

Economic liberalisation

As indicated above, both countries are introducing liberalisation policies and the current large-scale land acquisitions can be considered within the broader discourse on economic liberalisation.

In Tanzania, the shift from socialism to liberalisation and structural adjustment programmes started in 1983 (Green 2014). Deregulation of investment, financial and foreign exchange systems continued from 1989 to 1992. In 1990, the Investment Promotion Centre was established (now the TIC) (OECD 2013). In Ethiopia, liberalisation started in 1992 following the fall of the military regime in 1991. Gradually, the country's economy started to shift from state control to greater market orientation. Rather like the TIC, the EIA, established in 1992, promotes private investment in general and FDI in particular (EIA 2013). Both agencies aim to serve as a "one-stop shop" and facilitate FDI and the acquisition by investors of licences and land within a very short period. And both are active in the current large-scale land acquisitions. They were tasked with creating mechanisms for transferring land held under different categories of land use (including from local users) and for consolidating such land in their land banks, and finally with transferring it to potential investors.

However, liberalisation in Ethiopia appears to be selective. Investment sectors are defined in terms of who may invest in them: potential investors are identified as the Ethiopian government, Ethiopian nationals and foreigners (EIA 2013, Investment Proclamation No.769/2012). Thus, investment policy also has some protectionist strands, as it precludes foreign competition in some key economic sectors. Furthermore, liberalisation in Ethiopia does not seem to disengage the state from the economy. Indeed, the state maintains strong involvement in some economic sectors, including large-scale commercial farming. For instance, the sugar and ethanol sectors are dominated by a government corporation as a public enterprise: the government-owned Ethiopian Sugar Corporation planned to develop some 225,000 hectares of land during the period 2010-15 (EIA 2012).

These differences between the two countries indicated above in a way reflect the nature of the state. The Ethiopian state is described by some as "Africa's illiberal state-builder" (Jones, Oliveira and Verhoeven 2013), with the state making strong and centrally planned interventions. In fact, the government describes itself as a "democratic developmental state" (De Waal 2012) and argues that the state should play an active role in the economy while at the same time promoting a free market economy. This ambition also requires a mix of policies that generate incentives in every form to make success possible.

Embedded in these broad differences are also perhaps differences in state capacity and in institutional requirements to guide current land investments. It is beyond the scope of this chapter to demonstrate how the differences in the character of the states affect investments in certain ways. Now it is time to turn to the differences in the character of the land investments.

Comparison between large-scale land transfers

Land deal characteristics

In Tanzania, 24 foreign-owned and eight jointly owned companies were granted a total of 596,818 hectares of land (see Table 1 below for statistics described in this section). The proportion of land acquired by foreign companies amounted to about 80 per cent of total land transfers, while the remaining 20 per cent was allocated to joint ventures. The average size of the land allocated to foreign companies was higher (about 19,000 hectares) than to joint ventures (about 14,000 hectares). This difference is presumably due to foreign investors' superior access to capital.

Land status before acquisition is an important indicator of how land is outsourced in current land deals. In Tanzania, village land constitutes about 42 per cent of the total land transferred to investors. The second most significant source

Table 1: Characteristics of large-scale land acquisitions in Tanzania and Ethiopia

	Land acquired (ha)	Av. size of farm (ha)	Village land (ha)	Unspecified land (ha)	General Land (ha)	State land (ha)	Private land (ha)	Non-food (ha)	Food only (ha)	Both food and non-food (ha)
Tanzania										
Foreign (n=25)	481,438	19,258	221,938	142,600	81,000	35,500	400	273,709	130,229	77,500
Joint (n=8)	115,380	14,423	26,750	60,000	4,358	17,272	7,000	73,500	24,272	17,608
	596,818	18,085	248,688	202,600	85,358	52,772	7,400	347,209	154,501	95,108
Ethiopia										
Foreign (n=45)	595,562	13,235	-	-	-	595,562	-	155,800	183,463	255,800
Joint (n=13)	395,330	30,410	-	-	-	395,330	-	95,200	40,100	260,530
	990,892	17,084				99,0892		251,000	223,563	516,330

Source: Data compiled from Locher and Sulle 2013 and the Land Matrix (accessed on 18 March 2015).

of land transferred is not specified (34 per cent). General land constitutes 14 per cent. The other sources of land acquisitions include state land (9 per cent) and private land, previously under corporate control (1 per cent).

The livelihoods of village residents depend on village land. That the village lands now have become the major target of land acquisitions suggests that rural people is becoming insecure both in terms of land access and livelihoods. The term land is vague and may actually include important resource categories, such as forest areas and communally owned areas. General land is also known to include forest, including protected forest, and wildlife reserves.

In Ethiopia, 58 land deals and acquisitions were reported where the total size of the land was just below one million hectares. The proportion of land acquired by foreign companies was 60 per cent, with joint ventures accounting for the rest. The average size of the foreign and jointly acquired farms was about 13,000 hectares and 30,000 hectares respectively.

In the case of Ethiopia, the land status before acquisition is categorised as state land. Land acquisitions involve leases and concessions, and the deals are sealed between the state and the investor.

A major difference between the two countries is that in Tanzania the village land and its village constituency is recognised in the laws and constitution of the country. Thus, decisions on land transfers up to 250 hectares need village assembly approval to be valid. Whether the village assemblies and the village councils (negotiating with investors on behalf of the villages) are effective to fully utilise this legal status to their advantage is another issue. In some cases village assemblies and village councils have been successful in averting bad deals, but often they lack the insights into the consequences of the land acquisitions and the capacity to handle negotiations with investors by themselves. With an increasing size of land acquisitions the jurisdiction over land leases are shifting from villages to higher administrative levels, i.e. district government authorities, in particular the Commissioner of Land. Regarding large land acquisitions the villages and their organs tend to lose influence and control over acquisitions.

There are interesting differences between the two countries as to the prevalence of joint ventures with foreigners. As noted, while 80 per cent of the total acquired land in Tanzania was obtained by foreigners, the corresponding figure for Ethiopia was 60 per cent. In short, domestic investors in Ethiopia appear to enter into joint ventures with foreigners more often than their Tanzanian counterparts.

Products

The purpose of the land acquisitions varies by product. The distinction between food and non-food products is critical, as this can indicate whether the food security of the host countries is being considered. This information, however, does not necessarily confirm that food security is guaranteed. For instance, even if a company is recognised as food-producing, its product may not directly improve local nutrition. An example of this is tea plantations. Furthermore, whether the products are for local or global markets is not clear from the contracts.

With these limitations in mind, the proportion of land brought under food and non-food production to some extent shows the degree of consideration for local food security. In Tanzania, 58 per cent of land transferred is land allocated to non-food products. Land allocated for food production accounted for 26 per cent, while land allocated for mixed (food and non-food) products accounted for 16 per cent. In the Ethiopian case, the proportion of land allocated to mixed products is the most important, accounting for 52 per cent of total land acquisitions. The proportions of land acquired for non-food products and food products were 25 per cent and 23 per cent respectively.

Both countries show differences when it comes to investors' product preferences. The proportion of land allocated for only-food products was similar in both countries (26 per cent for Tanzania and 23 per cent for Ethiopia). The major difference between the countries is between non-food and mixed products. This could probably be due to the relatively higher prevalence of food insecurity in Ethiopia, which would prompt investors to move into food production.

Inclusion of local producers

In both cases, contract farming and out-grower schemes are very few in number. In Ethiopia, only two of the 58 investments involved contract farming (for vegetable production), while in Tanzania a few sugarcane investments indicated the possibility of out-grower schemes. This suggests that current investment patterns pay little attention to local farmers' production and marketing preferences. It is therefore unlikely that FDI will bring technological change that can lead to meaningful employment and hence such investments have a limited potential to improve the food security of local communities.

Geopolitical aspects

Some of the land allocations in Ethiopia have geopolitical dimensions. The country is situated in a region where resource interdependence has historically been considered a political liability. Over the last few years, however, the country has been actively employing its territorial and transboundary resources to create regional economic opportunities. Notable initiatives are expanded hydropower production and export and the targeted allocation of large-scale lands to downstream countries. An example is Egypt, which has acquired land in Ethiopia. In general, according to the *Land Matrix* database, the Arab countries are actively investing in Ethiopia.

Conclusion

Ethiopia and Tanzania face many similar conditions. Both countries are highly dependent on agriculture and face huge challenges in building their rural economies, including addressing food security and providing decent rural employment opportunities. Both countries have championed agricultural FDI and have striven to facilitate such investments, which often result in large-scale land acquisitions. To this end, the governments of both countries have committed themselves to providing land for investors and both governments play key, however somewhat different roles in current land acquisitions and their associated land deals.

In these processes, smallholders in both countries are facing increasing insecurity related to their land access and food security. In the case of Tanzania, village institutions have by law the potential to decide on and influence the terms land acquisitions up to 250 hectares. However lack of information about the consequences of land acquisitions and village councils' limited legal, technical and financial capacities have undermined the scope of village institutions to realise the full potential of the institutional land rights vested in them (as stipulated in the Village Land Act and the Land Acts of 1999). In the case of Ethiopia, lack of clear rights of communities to land, particularly in sparsely populated areas, is a source of insecurity.

In the Ethiopian case, as in Tanzania, land is state property. Identification, designation and allocation of land to investors are done by the Ethiopian government and associated land deals are concluded solely by the government and investors with no involvement by local authorities. Land acquisitions and deals in Ethiopia are highly centralised and rural communities do not have a similar possibility as in Tanzania to influence land acquisitions up to 250 hectares. This allows the Ethiopian state to deliver land to investors more effectively than in Tanzania.

In the case of Tanzania, land is also owned by the state, but land management is institutionalised across different administrative layers, among which the village organs (the village assembly and council) have important roles to play in terms of local land governance, in particular as to land acquisitions up to 250 hectares. In Tanzania village organs according to law have a space to influence and determine land identification, allocation and agreements with investors and in particular so if there already exists an official land use plan.

However, complexities regarding technical issues and details of land allocations, investment benefits and legal capacity tend to overtax the village councils, as representatives of the village, and undermine the potential of villages to attain land deals with long term benefits to themselves. As land acquisitions have increased with the expansion of large scale land investments over the last decade, higher administrative levels are acting on behalf of the government in these activities, often with poor consultations with villages from which the land is transferred to investors. As a result, villages tend to lose control of the land acquisitions.

The activities and interventions of Tanzanian Investment Centre and subsequent acquisitions of land from villages to the land bank administered by the TIC show how the government has become an increasingly important actor in land acquisitions and associated land deals. While Tanzania appears to have a more decentralised system of land governance in place compared to that of Ethiopia, the central government is becoming increasingly involved in land deals as they have increased in size.

As Green (2014: 13) points out, the Tanzanian state continues to "implement development through its relations with citizens as village beneficiaries." Strengthening local institutions and creating more space for village organs to make autonomous decisions regarding land acquisition even beyond the current 250 hectares restrictions, would constitute important elements. In this regard, educating and informing villagers about the content and potential consequences of the land acquisitions would provide a better foundation for village assembly decisions to transfer village land to external investors. Strengthening village council financial and technical capacity to thoroughly analyse investment proposals and their consequences[2] would be vital to protect village land rights and livelihoods.

---

2.   Land transfers in Tanzania involve six stages: physical planning, valuation and compensation, preparation of detail plan, plot surveying, land allocation and title registration (URT 2009).

The Ethiopian government has the capacity to mobilise and swiftly allocate land to investors, but it is crucial that it critically assesses the existing status and uses of the land and whether and how the allocation of land to investors impacts current users. This is particularly important in pastoralist areas, where most of the current large-scale land allocations are taking place and where land rights are particularly complex.

References

Abdallah, J., L. Engström, K. Havnevik and L. Salomonsson (2014) "Large-scale land acquisitions in Tanzania: A critical analysis of practices and dynamics." In Kaag, M. and A. Zoomers (eds) *The global land grab: Beyond the hype*. London: Zed Books, pp. 36–53.

AGRA (Alliance for a Green Revolution in Africa) (2014) *African agriculture status report: Climate change and smallholder agriculture in sub-Sahara Africa*. Nairobi.

Beyene, A. and E. Sandström (2015) "Emerging water frontiers in large-scale land acquisitions and implications for food security in Africa". In Tvedt, T. and T. Oestigaard (eds) *A History of Water*, Series 3, Vol. 3. *Water and Food: From hunter-gatherers to global production in Africa*. London: I.B. Tauris. In press.

Beyene, A., C. Mungongo, A. Atteridge and R. Larsen (2013) *Biofuel production and its impacts on local livelihoods in Tanzania*. Working Paper No. 3, Stockholm Environment Institute.

De Schutter, O. (2011) "How not to think of land-grabbing: Three critiques of large-scale investments in farmland." *Journal of Peasant Studies* 38(2): 249–79.

De Waal, A. (2012) "The theory and practice of Meles Zenawi" (review article). *African Affairs* 112 (446): 148–55.

EIA (Ethiopian Investment Agency) (2012) *Investment opportunity profile for sugarcane plantation and processing in Ethiopia*. Addis Ababa: EIA.

EIA (2013) *Ethiopian Investment Guide*. Addis Ababa: Ethiopia. Available at http://www.ethemb.se/TEXT%20files/InvestmentGuide%202013.pdf Accessed on 15 April 2015.

FAO (2012) *Trends and Impacts of foreign investment in developing country agriculture: Evidence from case studies*. Available at the Food and Agriculture Organization of the United Nations, Rome.

Green, M. (2014) *The development state: Aid, culture and civil society in Tanzania*. London: James Currey.

GTP (Growth and Transformation Plan) (2010) *Growth and Transformation Plan 2010/11-2014/15*. Addis Ababa: Ministry of Finance and Economic Development.

Havnevik, K. and M. Hårsmar (1999) *Diversified future: An institutional approach to rural development in Tanzania*. Stockholm: Almqvist and Wiksell.

Jones, W., R. Oliveira, and H. Verhoeven (2013) *Africa's illiberal state-builders.* Refugee Studies Centre, Working Paper NO. 89, Oxford Department of International Development, University of Oxford. http://www.rsc.ox.ac.uk/files/publications/working-paper-series/wp89-africas-illiberal-state-builders-2013.pdf, accessed on March 12, 2015.

Land Matrix (2014). *The Online Public Database on Land Deals.* Available at http://www.landmatrix.org/en/. Accessed on 18 March 2015.

Locher, M. and E. Sulle (2013) "Foreign land deals in Tanzania: An update and critical view on the challenges of data (re)production". *Land Deal Politics Initiative*, Working Paper 31. Available at http://www.iss.nl/fileadmin/ASSETS/iss/Research_and_projects/Research_networks/LDPI/LDPI_WP_31_revised.pdf . Accessed on 10 February 2015.

Matondi, P., K. Havnevik.and A. Beyene (eds) (2011) *Biofuels, land grabbing and food security in Africa.* London: Zed Books.

OECD (2013) *Overview of progress and policy challenges in Tanzania.* OECD Investment Policy Reviews: Tanzania. Paris: OECD Publishing. Available at http://dx.doi.org/10.1787/9789264204348-6-en . Accessed on 15 April 2015.

Rahmato, D. (2011) *Land to investors: Large-scale land transfers in Ethiopia.* Addis Ababa: Forum for Social Studies.

Raikes, P. (1975) "Ujamaa and rural socialism". *Review of African Political Economy* 2(3): 33-52.

URT (United Republic of Tanzania) (1999) *Village Land Act (of Tanzania) 1999.* Dar es Salaam: Ministry of Lands, Housing and Urban Development.

URT (2009) *Basic facts and figures on human settlements: Tanzania mainland.* National Bureau of Statistics. Dar es Salaam: Ministry of Finance.

World Bank (2007) *World Development Report: Agriculture for Development* 2008. Washington DC: World Bank.

World Bank (2015) *Tanzania overview.* Available at http://www.worldbank.org/en/country/tanzania/overview. Accessed on 20 February 2015.

Wily, L. (2003) *Community-based land tenure management.* Issue Paper No. 120, International Institute for Environment and Development (IIED).

Woldegiorgis, B. (2015) *Land laws and proclamations in Tanzania and Ethiopia.* Occasional Paper. Uppsala: Nordic Africa Institute.

Witchcraft, witch killings and Christianity: The works of religion and parallel cosmologies in Tanzania

Terje Oestigaard[1]

Introduction

According to one statistical survey, 60 per cent of the population of Tanzania is Christian, 36 per cent Muslim and 4 per cent subscribes to another or no religion. What is more striking about this survey is that 93 per cent of Tanzanians believe in witchcraft (Christians 94 per cent, Muslims 92 per cent) and traditional African religious beliefs and practices are prevalent among 62 per cent of the population (Pew Forum on Religion and Public Life 2010: 34, 64, 178). Although one should be cautious about these statistics, they may nevertheless indicate the ubiquity of witchcraft in Tanzania and the prevalence of traditional beliefs among even Christians and Muslims. The figure of 93 per cent regarding belief in witchcraft is remarkable, if accurate, and implies that witchcraft beliefs are far more common in Tanzania than in other countries. Even if the actual percentage is considerably lower, it would seem that witchcraft is widespread.

The Sukuma group, numbering about five million, mainly live along the southern shores of Lake Victoria in Tanzania. For more than a century, they have been integrated into the global world, but in varying degree, and missionaries have been spreading the Gospel and Christianising the Sukuma since the 1880s. Traditionally, the society was culturally and cosmologically structured around the chief and rainmaking. Everything depended on the rain. The chief was responsible for providing the life-giving rains believed to heal the land, a power that afforded him legitimacy as ruler. Both chieftainship and rainmaking have now disappeared, while at the same time Christianity is spreading and both witchcraft and witch killings are flourishing (with more than 500 alleged witches killed annually in Tanzania, predominantly among the Sukuma). Similarly, the role of the ancestors has diminished and tradition is no longer as important in culture and cosmology. In a religious context, rainmaking is perceived as not working anymore and the role of ancestors is declining. Thus, the overall questions are: Is the declining role of ancestors enabling *both* the spread of Christianity and the increase in witchcraft? How and why are witchcraft and

---

1. This chapter was presented as a paper at the Satterthwaite Colloquium in Grasmere, the Lake District, England in 2014, and builds on T. Oestigaard (2014) *Religion at Work in Globalised Traditions. Rainmaking, Witchcraft and Christianity in Tanzania*. Newcastle: Cambridge Scholars Press.

Christianity as religious practices seemingly working perfectly together? What are the consequences when traditions disappear and how are society and cosmology being restructured? These questions will be analysed through an approach that emphasises the work and works of religion.

How religions work – beyond structural functionalism

Notwithstanding exegesis, dogma and theology, religions are always concerned with practical human problems in some way. "Our approach is not concerned with the origins of religions so much as their *functions*. We relate and explain the force of religious ideas by reference to the needs of individuals in their everyday lives, not to society and its forms," Reynolds and Tanner argue. They continue: "We have become convinced by the evidence worldwide that *the function of religions is to respond to human needs*, to help people at times of personal crises (e.g., at funerals), or when they are undergoing a change of status (e.g., at weddings), or generally in relation to everyday strains of normal life. Ours is thus a *functional approach*" (Reynolds and Tanner 1995:15). Moreover, "religion caters to needs at all levels, but perhaps mostly at the more basic level … However … the concept of need … is not sufficient to explain what religions appear to be doing in the world" (Reynolds and Tanner 1995:305).

By emphasising that religion functions and works, it is necessary to clarify my meaning in the term *religions work*. Concepts such as "work" and in particular "function" have, as part of the criticism of structural functionalism, gained negative connotations in the history of anthropological thought. In *Ritual and religion in the making of humanity,* Roy Rappaport asserted that "neither religion 'as a whole' nor its elements will, in the account offered to them, be reduced to functional or adaptive terms." He continued: "An account of religion framed, *a priori*, in terms of adaptation, function or other utilitarian assumptions or theory would … paradoxically, defeat any possibility of discovering whatever utilitarian significance it might have by transforming the entire inquiry into a comprehensive tautology" (Rappaport 2001:2). This example suffices for me to make my point: I do *not* perceive religion in adaptive terms.

Rather, allow me to approach religion from the perspective of the divine realm (or, at least, how it is perceived and presented by believers), and start with Christianity and its Jewish antecedents. Christianity *works* and very much so, if we are to believe Christians. In Hebrew myth, there is creation from nothing: "And God said. 'Let there be light'; and there was light" (Gen. 1:3). By the word alone, God created the cosmos and the world and all within it in only six days. This is the kind of work I refer to when I say religions *work*. Importantly, in Christianity there is a fundamental doctrine that "God works in mysterious ways." Thus, humans may or may not know how and why God works, but that does not matter. Even if humans have only partial knowledge of this, they have sufficient to adhere to the cosmic laws given by God. And here God works again. Jesus was crucified and by taking on human sin, he ensured salvation for all. As a consequence, if one follows the rules, one may attain eternal life in heaven. This is a huge promise and a durable work of a God – what more can a devotee wish for? Miracles are another way of illustrating that religion works, and in this particular case, the Christian God works. Believers truly believe that miracles take place, that prayers and wishes are suddenly fulfilled, and that sometimes miracles happen without human requests. These are simply the works of God originating in and fulfilled through his own plans. However, for sinners, that is, those who act against God and his will, and this is also a sign of free will (Hertz 1996), God has worked in other ways to prepare a rather unpleasant destiny for eternity, hell in its various elaborations throughout history.

However, in emphasising the function and work of gods, one must also address questions of time and scale. Gods may once have worked in a primordial era, but may not do so anymore. This does not alter the ontological status of the gods as existing: in a cosmic perspective, humans are not in a position to demand that gods work for them (indeed, in Christianity this is seen as heresy). The Supreme Being among the Sukuma is one such god. It is impossible to reach him through sacrifices and prayers and he is so remote that he does not interfere in the fate of individuals. He is not working any longer because he has done his job. What he created, exists and has never changed, and therefore he has withdrawn (Cory 1960:15). If there were no such conception of gods, cosmic principles or divinities working on a grand scale, including the Buddhist conceptions of karma, there would be no religion as broadly defined. In practice, a kind of Western atheism would prevail.

Thus, I am not concerned here with the origins or existence as such of religion. My approach is the believers' approach in practice: God, gods and the ancestors exist, including various malignant forces such as the devil, roaming ghosts, etc. But they do not merely exist in another sphere: in varying measure, they influence this world. From this and the believer's perspective, what are the beliefs about how the spirits and divinities of the other world, which are superior to humans, function and work in this world? How do they intervene and in which realms do different religions (defined broadly) impact worldly matters? This approach also emphasises which rituals are performed and how people can approach their gods, divinities and ancestors with a view to changing daily life in this world. As I will argue, Christianity and the world of the ancestors, including the practice of witchcraft, operate on different premises and affect this world in substantially different ways. Precisely because of this, they can coexist and work hand in hand.

A common feature of many African cosmologies is the division of the world into two distinct realms. One is the visible or the manifest world, which is "ob-

vious" to all, and the other is the invisible or unseen world, which is nevertheless as real as the visible world. Indeed, it is more real in that it structures and
defines the premises of this world. The visible world is the everyday world of
living – farming, collecting water and fuel, political and economic matters, etc.
The invisible world comprises the ancestors, God and the realm of witchcraft
and the occult, among other spiritual forces. These two realms are intrinsically
linked and the invisible forces largely determine outcomes in the visible world.
The visible world is therefore shaped by a deeper, "more real" reality, and consequently, it is of utmost importance to control the spiritual and occult forces
that would otherwise harm society (Sanders 2001:169). In many cosmologies,
humans facing problems turn to the ancestors or gods. Religion works and may
have practical consequences here and now.

On the other hand, Christianity, in practice, works quite differently. The
here and now is largely omitted from the realm of this religion. Whether people starve or die, plagues haunt society and diseases kill animals, women are
debarred and life-giving rains do not come at the right time, there is a double
perception at work. On one hand, these misfortunes are not believed to be the
Christian God's work. Although in principle the Christian God can control
these events and processes, since he is believed to be almighty, it is also believed
that such mundane problems are not the concerns of God in his daily and practical work. Or rather, although mitigating worldly problems *may* be a concern of
God, usually he does not solve them here and now. Rather, these misfortunes are
placed within the larger cosmological framework in which God works. Thus, on
the other hand, such misfortune is also commonly and in varying degree seen
as God's penalty for sin. Throughout Christian history, God is believed to have
punished sinners and unbelievers collectively with plagues, droughts and floods.
In other words, it is not for God to solve the problems he has brought down on
sinners and misbelievers. That is for humans to do, cosmologically through obe-
dience and repentance and practically by surviving as best they can.

This does not imply the Christian God does not work (in all senses of the
term, including penalising humans). To the contrary, he does very much work,
with eternal consequences for humanity, if one is to believe Christianity. However, his main active engagement in the cosmos is after humans die. The grace
of God may send some to heaven for eternity, whereas others may be doomed to
hell. Indeed, this is a very powerful way of having an active god at work, and was
ultimately used by missionaries as *the* main argument why one should convert
to Christianity.

Apart from eschatology and what may happen after death, the ways in which
the Christian God works as compared to the ancestors point to a crucial aspect
in one's attempts to understand religion and how it works in society. There are
two main differences. First, Christianity mainly works in the other world and

the hereafter, whereas ancestors work in the here and now in society. Thus, the religions resolve different problems in different realms. Christianity may promise an eternal life in heaven, but cannot (or at least does not) procure the life-giving rains upon which people are utterly dependent for life and well-being or solve any other acute problems here and now. The ancestors can resolve the latter problem. This brings us to the second difference: the ancestors are active and can be contacted and requested to solve current problems. Thus, *the ancestors can be activated, or, in other words, humans may manipulate the divine world for their own betterment*. This is also in the interests of the ancestors, since the descendants are their heirs and family. An approach such as this is not possible in Christianity. There is no way humans can manipulate God to secure health and wealth through ritual and sacrifice. One may pray, but the outcomes are highly uncertain. Miracles are believed to take place in Christianity, but where, when and why is a mystery. Even Christians acknowledge that miracles to solve problems in this world happen rarely. The rule of the game is that humans have to solve their problems themselves. The ways and means by which humans engage in the world and solve their problems are, however, judged after death, and include severe penalties for eternity.

This has created a space for different religious practices to operate on different scales by different means. Wisjen and Tanner state that "the Sukuma see religion in terms of the options it provides rather than the obligations it creates. They have periodic problems and their religious practices tend to be periodic" (Wijsen and Tanner 2000:30). Thus, conversion to Christianity is not a straightforward displacement of one religion by another. Instead, it is a process of syncretism or parallel cosmologies. The different religious systems offer different possibilities and solutions to various problems. The benefits of Christianity are also largely its main shortcoming – it does not solve the most acute problems here and now, the problems that *have* to be resolved. Consequently, religious solutions are sought elsewhere. This highlights the premises on which the Sukuma world works. "Causation in their thinking is animate rather than inanimate. An event, particularly an unfortunate one, has to be caused by someone or something, living or dead, with malevolent intentions toward the sufferer. There are no pure accidents in Usukuma" (Wijsen and Tanner 2000:47). As will be discussed, this is the realm in which belief in witchcraft flourishes.

Although it was held that one could achieve much the same results by propitiating the ancestors, there was a sense that in the modern world it is better to use the modern way and not approach the ancestors. They are connected with the past and tradition, but witchcraft is connected to the challenges of today and tomorrow. Thus, witchcraft has to some extent replaced the role of ancestors and is perceived as a way of being modern.

Witchcraft and witch killings

According to the 2002 Tanzania Witchcraft Act (Cap. 18 [R.E.2002]), witchcraft is defined as "sorcery, enchantment, bewitching, the use of instrument of witchcraft, the purported exercise of any occult power and purported possession of any occult knowledge" (Tanzania Human Rights Report 2011: 33). All acts of witchcraft are punishable if murders are committed, and in January 2009 Prime Minister Misengo Pinda stated that those caught in the act of murdering albinos should be killed on the spot (Bryceson et al. 2010: 374).

A phenomenon peculiar to the Sukuma in Tanzania has been the intensity of witch killing, although such killings also occur in other regions. Since the 1960s, witch killings have increased significantly in Sukumaland (Abrahams 1994:15). According to Tanner in the 1950s, old men could still remember that before the Germans occupied the country witchcraft was rare (Tanner 1956a: 443). Similarly, in the 1960s witchcraft incidents were rare (Per Brandström personal com.). Still, the problem of witchcraft was acknowledged by the British and the territory's high court produced a table of murder statistics in mid-1944 (Mesaki 1993: 64).

Table 1: Murder cases in Sukumaland 1935–1943

Year	Murder cases	Witch-related
1935	35	5
1936	20	4
1937	39	4
1938	40	7
1939	26	3
1940	41	5
1941	30	3
1942	35	4
1943	56	11

Source: Mesaki 1993.

There are, of course, uncertainties about the actual number of witch killings and many killings may not have been reported to the authorities. In any case, even if the actual number was two or five or even ten times higher, it would nevertheless have been modest compared to the rate from the 1970s onwards. In short, there seems to have been a dramatic increase in murders associated with witchcraft.

Importantly, statistics in Tanzania are highly unreliable, and there are serious methodological obstacles regarding witch killings. Apart from the fact that the statistics are not published and are largely based on second- or third-hand observations (for example, anonymous police sources largely impossible to check), it is also unclear how witch killings are documented, or what is categorised as a "witch killing." Witchcraft may also be used as a local term for violent death and police officers often use it loosely (Stroeken 2010: 199). Thus, the actual numbers may be higher or lower than the figures presented here.

The killing of suspected witches became gradually more noticeable in the 1960s and notoriously so by the mid-1970s. By the end of the 1980s, the situation seemed to be out of control and the government instituted the Mongela Commission on witchcraft in 1988 to investigate the phenomenon. The commission's conclusions were alarming (Mesaki 2009: 72-3) Between 1970 and 1984, 3,693 suspected witches were killed – 1,407 men and 2,286 women (Mesaki 1993: 98). Here it is important to add a comment on the statistics, since the number of killed witches is 3,693 whereas the number of witch-related cases was 3,333. Mesaki explains: "It should be noted that the number of cases does not necessarily match the number of those killed because a single case can lead to several deaths while in other cases no murders occur" (Mesaki 1993: 99).

Table 2: Witch killings in Tanzania 1970–1984

Year	Cases	Men	Women
1970	106	31	84
1971	181	50	133
1972	133	49	106
1973	308	135	192
1974	216	74	156
1975	242	87	168
1976	219	68	175
1977	189	94	131
1978	164	41	172
1979	225	81	163
1980	220	116	119
1981	294	199	158
1982	221	97	151
1983	324	144	212
1984	291	141	163
Total	3,333	1,407	2,286

Source: Mesaki 1993.

Mwanza and Shinyanga regions accounted for no fewer than 2,246 of these witch killings, and in the following period, from 1985-88, a further 826 were killed in Sukumaland, for a total of 3,072 in this area between 1970 and 1988. The statistics on the killings from 1970–84 were broken down on a regional basis by Mesaki (1993: 99).

Thus, the killing of witches has mainly been a Sukuma phenomenon and among the 2,246 Sukuma killings before 1984, 1,869 were women and 377

Table 3: Regional distribution of witch killings 1970–1984

Region	Cases	Men	Women
Iringa	132	120	16
Kagera	82	77	70
Kigoma	17	10	7
Mara	3	2	1
Mbeya	13	13	-
Morogoro	1	1	-
Mtwara	1	6	-
Mwanza	1,098	269	927
Pwani	2	1	1
Ruvuma	4	3	1
Singida	731	675	185
Shinyanga	1,022	108	942
Tabora	227	122	133
Total	3,333	1,407	2,286

Source: Mesaki 1993.

were men aged over 15 years, a ratio of 5 to 1. Of the women victims, 62 per cent were 41 and older, that is, post-menopausal. On a monthly basis, some 10-12 people were killed for suspected witchcraft among the Sukuma (Wijsen and Tanner 2002: 135), with an average of 160 deaths a year in Mwanza and Shinyanga regions. For Tanzania as a whole, there were 246 killings per year on average.

From 1984 to 1993 there are no reliable figures for killings of alleged witches. A newspaper reported in 1998 that 325 people had been killed in Shinyanga region from 1996 to 1998: 133 in 1996, 102 in 1997, and 90 between January and October 1998. Another survey conducted by TAMWA (Tanzania Media Women's Association) revealed that between 1993 and 1998 in Mwanza region alone, 318 elderly people had been killed. According to a police official in Shinyanga region, however, when other innocents who are killed in remote villages are taken into account, murder would be seen to occur more or less daily in Shinyanga and Mwanza regions (Mesaki 2009:73), although not all these deaths are related to witchcraft. A leaked Ministry of Home Affairs report indicated that 5,000 people had been killed between 1994 and 1998 (Duff 2005), although not all these deaths were necessarily related to witchcraft.

Prime Minister Pinda told parliament in late January 2009 that 2,866 elderly people accused of being witches had been murdered in the past five years, for an average of 573 a year (Banda 2009). The police in Mwanza reported in February 2009 that more than 2,585 old women had been killed in eight (of 21) mainland regions of Tanzania over the previous five years (Tanzania Human Rights Report 2009: 21).

Table 4: Witch killings in 8 regions 2004–2008

Region	Deaths in the five years prior to February 2009	Average deaths per year/region
Mwanza	698	140
Shinyanga	522	105
Tabora	508	102
Iringa	256	52
Mbeya	192	39
Kagera	186	37
Singida	120	24
Rukuwa	103	21
Total (eight districts)	2,585	517

Source: Tanzania Human Rights Report 2009.

Based on these numbers, every third day an old woman accused of being a witch was killed in Mwanza region, and every fourth day in Shinyanga. The actual number of killings of suspected witches was believed to be higher, because not all such killings are reported to the police. As one respondent from Shinyanga put it: "It's risky to inquire of the police about a relative killed due to witchcraft … because you will be regarded as an accomplice. And they might end up taking your life as well" (Tanzania Human Rights Report 2009: 21).

The number of witch killings may total more than 1,000 a year. In a newspaper interview in 2005, Simeon Mesaki asserted that in Shinyanga region a minimum of 300 witch killings take place annually, and the total was most likely the same in Mwanza. According to an official who wanted to remain anonymous: "The government figures are very low, not accurate. I know a much higher number, and even that is not the full situation" (Duff 2005).

Official statistics and statements suggest that in the period 1970–84 an average of 246 people were killed as witches, whereas today almost 600 people are killed annually. In each year from 1970 to 1988, an average of 160 persons were murdered in Mwanza and Shinyanga region, whereas this number has now increased to 245. In Tabora region, the annual average has increased from 17 killings to 102. However, according to the Tanzania Human Rights Report 2010, in that year about 50 people were killed in Tanzania because of witchcraft accusations. Although this number is provisional, compared to previous years there has been a significant decrease (Tanzania Human Rights Report 2010:57). In 2011, however, the national figures were higher according to the Tanzania Human Rights Report:

Between 2005 and 2011, about 3,000 people were lynched to death by fearful neighbours who believed them to be witches. This suggests that an average of 500 elderly people, old women … in particular [are] killed [on] suspicion of being witches annually all over Tanzania. For instance, 242 people were killed due to witchcraft beliefs in Shinyanga alone from January 2010 to June 2011 … [P] olice statistics [also show] the growing trend of killings due to witchcraft beliefs from 579 in 2010 to 642 in 2011 (Tanzania Human Rights Report 2011:34).

The discrepancy between the numbers given in the 2010 report and the 2011 report was explained by new data provided by the police in a letter. In the *Tanzania Human Rights Report 2012* it is reported that 630 persons were killed as alleged witches (Tanzania Human Rights Report 2012: 31). In the *Tanzania Human Rights Report 2013* it is written that witchcraft related killings claimed the lives of 765 people – 505 women and 260 men (Tanzania Human Rights Report 2013: 36). In 2013, a new form of abuse was encountered, with many people being buried alive for various alleged misdemeanours, often including suspicions of witchcraft. In sum, despite gaps in official statistics and the shortcomings of other surveys, the conclusion appears to be unequivocal: the killing of accused witches has increased dramatically.

As a comparison, in the whole of Europe there were about 90,000 prosecutions of witches and some 45,000 executions during the 300 years the main witch craze lasted (Levack 2006:23). If the rate of witch killings in Tanzania is 500 per year or more, then there will be more witch killings in Tanzania in only a century than there were during Europe's much longer witch craze. The estimates may be too high, but even if only 150 witches are killed each year in Tanzania, this is equal to the rate of executions throughout Europe. Indeed, the witch craze seems to be spiralling out of control, as evidenced by, inter alia, the killing of albinos and the even more recent trend to kill people for their wealth.

Albino killings and the mining industry

Albinos have traditionally been stigmatised and discriminated against in society and there are numerous rumours that albino children have been killed at birth as 'mercy killings." In agro-pastoral communities, albino babies have also been placed in the cattle kraal gateway and trampled to death, but those who survived were allowed to live. Births have been reported as stillbirths and albinos have often been called *zeruzeru*, which is believed to refer to *zero,* an archaic term for ghost-like creatures, probably referring to the lack of pigment and denial of personhood (Bryceson, Jønsson and Herrington 2010: 367–8). In the past, giving birth to an albino was seen as a bad omen. The whole family was stigmatised. Other villagers were not allowed to marry the albino, but people were also reluctant to marry any other member of that family for fear that their own children would be albinos. Albinos were stigmatised in the same way as people with leprosy. Even a visit by an albino was seen as a bad omen and people refused to eat and share food with them.

Today, however, this has in principle changed, and people marry members of families with albinos. Even so, the lives of albinos have gone from bad to worse.

When albinos are born, men often accuse their wives of unfaithfulness with the devil or white people, and there are also widespread beliefs that children born with albinism are punishment for an ancestor's wrongdoing or for having sex during menstruation (Ackley 2010: 44). The sexual connotations of albinism have taken new form in recent years, the most disturbing being the belief that sex with an albino may cure HIV/AIDS (Baker, Lund, Taylor and Nyathi 2010: 177). Albino women are even raped because of this belief (Alum, Gomez and Ruis 2009: 8–9).

Albino killings in Tanzania began in 2006, but there were also earlier reports. From 2000 to 2009, the number of albinos killed was 68 (Tanzania Human Rights Report 2011: 36). However, from 2007 to 2009 alone 59 albinos were killed (six in 2007, 37 in 2008 and 16 in 2009) and nine were mutilated. In 2010 and 2011, there were no reports of albinos being killed (Tanzania Human Rights Report 2010: 58–9), whereas one albino was killed in 2012.

The killing of albinos among the Sukuma is a recent phenomenon and seemed to "come from nowhere" (Bryceson, Jønsson and Herrington 2010: 368, 379 fn. 10). In the 1980s and 1990s, there were rumours that bald people would bring prosperity and as a consequence such people were reported decapitated and their heads used in magic potions. Thus, apart from witch killings, there are indications that people were killed and used for various purposes among the Sukuma, although these practices would also be part of the world of ancestors. Still, the killing of albinos is new. Why albinos and why as part of witchcraft?

According to the Tanzanian government, there are about 1.5 million artisanal miners out of a total population of some 40 million, and Mwanza and Shinyanga have seen more mineral rushes than other regions (Bryceson, Jønsson and Herrington 2010: 379). The work is dangerous and the miners have no medical insurance, so many of them believe they need powerful witchcraft protection. Moreover, if they have money, there is always the danger it might be stolen. They also believe they need good luck to find the minerals. Thus, there is a double need for witchcraft: protection and good fortune.

It is impossible to know which parts of an albino's body will be used, but often it is the legs from below the knees. It is believed that one cannot start working in the mines without first going to a traditional healer, and success or failure depends on the effectiveness of the medicines. And even if a man has no place or mine where he can start digging, if he has consulted a traditional healer he can start searching anywhere, even outside the mines, and achieve success and riches. The miner does not pay the healer in advance. However, after the miner has struck gold or diamonds, he will return to the traditional healer, who will instruct him on how to use his finds. In many cases, the traditional healer will claim the first find as payment for providing good luck, and the next find of gold or diamonds will belong to the miner. Consequently, many traditional healers are exceedingly rich, at least by local standards. If a miner does not return to the healer with his share, it is believed that all of his haul will magically disappear and the miner will be left with nothing.

Some believe the origin of albino killings has its roots in macabre Nigerian movies, which are popular among the miners when they have time off. One police officer allegedly commented that "an influx of Nigerian movies, which play up witchcraft, might have something to do with it, along with rising food prices that were making people more desperate." According to other Tanzanian policemen, the value of a killed albino, including all four limbs, genitals, ears, nose and tongue, may amount to USD 75,000 (Ackley 2010). Others believe albinos are killed because they are not useful and will not be missed in society, while another explanation is the analogy between the rare occurrence of gold and the rareness of albino charms. How this practice began will most likely remain hidden, but it is undoubtedly propagated by the *waganga* (medical practitioners). Even though nobody really knows why and how albino charms work, the belief that they do keeps such beliefs and practices alive (Bryceson, Jønsson and Herrington 2010: 368–9, 371).

The use of body parts in medicines is based on the assumption that it is possible to appropriate another person's life-force literally through the consumption of that person. It is also believed that the acquired life-power is much greater if the body parts are removed while the victim is still alive (Vincent 2008:43). This has other implications: "The albino fetish has become the most expensive because it is perceived as harnessing spirits that are far more powerful than any plant or animal charm that *waganga* could otherwise offer" (Bryceson, Jønsson and Herrington 2010: 371). As a consequence, there has also been a transition from healers to dealers (Bryceson, Jønsson and Herrington 2010: 364).

Although it is often claimed that the use of body parts in witchcraft is recent, this is only partly correct. In Tanzania, among the Sukuma, for instance, there were practices in the past involving such uses. These were, however, very limited. Recent ritual innovation has led to an increase in such practices and to their incorporation into spheres where previously there were no such traditions. In this sense, current witchcraft practices build on and continue older worldviews and practices, which are reinterpreted and more widely adopted.

Chief Charles Kafipa of Bukumbi chiefdom explained past traditions of using body parts in medicines and how they worked (personal communication). The killing of albinos and use of their body parts in medicines is not part of tradition and, indeed, the chief argued strongly that it was against tradition. Moreover, according to him, those who kill albinos and use this type of medicine will not be successful in their endeavours: killing people for medicine is murder and has no ritual effects, and such killings are seen by all as truly horrible.

Still, according to the chief, the bodies of chiefs and albinos are very important and powerful traditional medicines if they are properly handled by qualified healers. Albino bodies are only effective as medicines if their owners die naturally. The extraordinary power of such medicines derives from the belief that albinos are composed of something different on account of their complexion: it was believed there is something missing or something extra in their composition. Traditionally, albinos were buried beneath the interior mud floors of their homes, with only the nearest family at the funeral. Thus, a healer could only get body parts with the consent of family members. This practice was both legal and had superior ritual potential. There were also beliefs that albinos are somehow alive after death, and it is this that gives the medicines their special power. Today, with cement floors in modern houses, albinos are buried in outside graves. This has resulted in the looting of albino body parts. Even where the albino died naturally, such stolen parts are ineffective as medicine, because they were taken without family consent. Thus, the agreement of relatives is necessary if the medicines are to be effective, and the other practices now escalating do not even work as ritual, the chief said.

Religions at work

The poignant question then becomes why both witchcraft *and* Christianity are on the increase in Africa? What kinds of solutions do the different religious systems offer, and how do they differ, since Christians also use witchcraft? The short answer is simple: witchcraft is believed to be more efficient than Christianity. More importantly, witchcraft is believed to work in this world, solving mundane and practical problems here and now and creating health, wealth and prosperity. It is generally agreed that the Christian God, although omnipotent, does not bother about these trivial matters. His ambitions for humanity are more fundamental, namely the ultimate destiny of humans in heaven or hell. Still, for poor people without food and water or facing other miseries, the mundane is far from trivial. Consequently, the problems of the mundane have to be solved in one way or other. The Christian God is utterly silent in providing help or solutions and uninvolved in daily life and the miseries of common people. Thus, the parallel religious cosmologies work perfectly well together: one solves the problems of this world and the other the problems of the next.

One may therefore say that Christianity has once again created a devil, although not intentionally. By strongly opposing ancestral tradition for more than a century, the church has largely undermined this tradition, but has also created a cultural and religious vacuum. But no such vacuums can persist. The miseries and problems the ancestors were believed to resolve continue, and may have become more acute with increased poverty. Christianity as a religion is basically not intended to resolve current miseries such as these, but witchcraft can do so perfectly here and now, it is believed.

Regarding how God works within Pentecostal Christianity, or at least in the preaching, I draw on two complementary examples. First, there were the two American Pentecostal missionaries I met struggling to convert people. They were frustrated by what they called the lack of self-sacrifice among the Sukuma. One of the missionaries had refused to bless a congregant because he had not paid his weekly dues to the church. According to the missionary, converts had to follow the same principles as they themselves did and make sacrifices to God. The missionaries had paid their air-tickets to Tanzania with their own money, and each week they donated money to the church. These missionaries stated that the person denied the blessing had once given money at the altar, and they concluded he had money, or had to find it somewhere and prioritise God! As they put it, what good are excuses that they had to support their family and not the church when they face God on Doomsday?

This example highlights the emphasis on godly matters and their interaction with worldly concerns. From these missionaries' perspective, the world hereafter is the sole reference point: what happens after death and the consequences of being judged on Doomsday. However, worldly matters *do* matter to the people. Children need school uniforms and fees have to be paid, the family needs food on the table and medical bills have to be met. In the missionaries' overall cosmic framework, these are mere excuses.

Second, the charismatic founder of the successful Pentecostal International Central Gospel Church in Accra, Rev. Mensa Otabil, gave some illuminating insights into the ways God is believed to work in one of his many fire-and-brimstone sermons. While blaming the sad state of affairs on African politicians, he said: "But you can't claim anyone's money by faith – it's illegal. If you want to have money, there is only one way: work … I prayed to God to prosper, but we have to change economic structures and social structures. If I don't have that opportunity, I can pray all I want and I'll still be poor … You can pray all you want, but it won't help … unless we start looking at the structures of our nations" (Van Dijk 2004: 178–9). In other words, you can pray all you want in church for food and money, it will not help: this is not the way God works. He is not uninterested in his children and human suffering, but he has a bigger and more important issue to deal with, the devil. Or something else.

A further example of how Christianity is generally believed to work can be seen in the old woman I met during the drought of 2011 in Sukumaland, one of the three worst droughts she had experienced in her whole life. She argued strenuously in favour of rainmaking – rainmaking worked and provided prosperity to the community. However, the tradition had been lost, which she regretted, and now all had become Christians. During the drought of 2011, they went to the church and prayed to God for rain and food, but as she said, nothing happened and they left the church even hungrier. The Christian God does not solve problems here and now and does not provide food on the table when it is really needed.

From this perspective, Christianity, missionaries and evangelisation have been highly successful in eradicating ancestral tradition as religious practice, but have largely failed to replace the role of the ancestors with the Christian God: these are basically different entities or realms working at different scales within and among humans. God belongs to the other world, and so do the ancestors, but whereas the ancestors, properly propitiated, help the living in their daily lives, God does not intervene in this world among his children. Christianity has therefore created one cosmology, but also left a whole cosmology ripe for reinvention. It has replaced the role of the ancestors in the world beyond with God, but not fully displaced the role of ancestors in this world and their abilities to solve problems for the living. Christianity has diminished that role in this world, but not the logic of how the ancestors work. And that logic of causation has proved more durable than the power of the ancestors themselves: this is point of departure for witchcraft. It provides the means to manipulate or approach the forces of the otherworld for the betterment of this world.

Whereas Christianity is immune from criticism about what happens in the otherworldly realm (and on this side), this is where witchcraft is superior. Witchcraft can, or at least is believed to, resolve any kind of problem in this world: it is the source of wealth and success and can deprive others of the same riches and resources and ultimately cause their deaths. The outcomes are possible to measure and adjudge in a world where poverty increases while some become exceedingly rich. The precise ways in which witchcraft works are impossible to know, but the mere fact that someone, somehow has gained immense wealth whereas others suffer more and even die, is all the evidence needed that witchcraft works, and is at work.

Accidents and misfortunes still happen and this is where witchcraft as logic and religious system has its supreme force. Whereas in the ancestral cult such misfortune could be explained in terms of the ancestors not solving the problems, a failing that over time could challenge the rationale of such beliefs, in witchcraft there are always others to blame. Somebody else has employed stronger and more effective medicines. Misery and evil, or the success of others in becoming wealthy and powerful, becomes the ultimate evidence of why a person's own medicines and witchcraft did not work. This circular, self-referential evidence is complete, and the only way to break out of this vicious circle is by employing even stronger and more dangerous medicines, ultimately by using human body parts. The very logic of how witchcraft works is also the source of its increase. The consequences of witchcraft can only be combated by employing more witchcraft.

Conclusion

The burden of evidence in Christianity, in which it is strictly impossible to prove the existence or effectiveness in this world of the Christian God, favours the spread of witchcraft. Witchcraft also works in mysterious, albeit more mystical and magical, ways. Although there are many unknowns, witchcraft is still more tangible both as regards how and why the rituals work and the outcomes of the rituals. The healer makes medicines, using whatever ingredients, which may include human body parts; he propitiates and incorporates the ancestors, the other worldly realm well known in the community's culture; and the client physically employs the medicines either by ingestion, or by applying it to the body or sprinkling it. The materiality of witchcraft and its operation on existing cultural premises and horizons of understanding strengthens the beliefs. Everything is here and now – from the healers and his medicines to the partaker and his problems. And it continues the logic of causation on which the ancestral tradition was based: it is possible to actively interfere with the spirits to improve conditions in this world.

Explaining why witchcraft increases, based on a religious logic that religions work although nobody can know for sure how, why and when, seems somehow straightforward. People seek refuge in the magical world given the premise that religion works. This is a world in which changing the premises and the outcomes of daily life and affairs is believed to be possible. The church may also promise this, but very rarely are the outcomes explicitly evident. The church does not promise a one-to-one relationship between prayer and good health, successful work, prosperous marriage or excellent exam results. Witchcraft does or is believed to do so. Whether this happens is another question, but then within this logic there are sufficient ad-hoc explanations legitimising the cosmological system and its effectiveness, even when it fails. Explaining why witches are being killed, and at a seemingly accelerating rate, is more difficult, because an increase in witchcraft does not necessarily imply intensified witch killing.

In a cross-cultural perspective, human sacrifice is at the pinnacle of any sacrificial system, but it is difficult to pinpoint the exact reasons for, or cultural patterns behind, the prevalence among the Sukuma of human killing within a ritual framework. Rainmaking rituals have historically included human sacrifice, as for instance in ancient Egyptian, Mayan and Aztec civilisations. However, sacrifices carried out in this manner require a sacred person to consecrate the offerings. The sacrificial victim incarnates the society as a whole and therefore human sacrifices can be made only for the benefit of the collectivity (e.g. Valeri 1985:49). Strictly speaking, the killing of albinos for personal wealth in the mining industry is at odds with current sacrificial theory. Since the empirical data are not wrong and these theories are based on other data, it would appear that something peculiar and particular is going on in Tanzania. From a purely logical perspective, human sacrifice is understandable given certain premises regarding how gods and the cosmos are perceived to work. From a human perspective though, it is harder to understand how anyone can believe in such practices, let alone carry them out.

References

Abrahams, R. (1987) "Sungusungu: Village Vigilante Groups in Tanzania." *African Affairs* 86(343): 179–96.

Ackley, C. (2010) "The Fetishization of Albinos in Tanzania." University of Chicago, p. 44. Available at http://www.underthesamesun.com/sites/default/files/The%20 Fetishization% 20of%20Albinos%20in20Tanzania.pdf (Accessed on 2 June 2015).

Alum, A., M. Gomez and E. Ruis (2009) *Hocus pocus, witchcraft, and murder: The plight of Tanzanian albinos.* International Team Report 2009 – Tanzania. Available at http://www.underthesamesun.com/node/7 (Accessed on 2 June 2015).

Baker, C., P. Lund, J. Taylor and R. Nyathi (2010) "The myths surrounding people with albinism in South Africa and Zimbabwe." *Journal of African Cultural Studies* 22(2): 169-81.

Banda, S. (2009) "Tanzania: PM cries over albino killings." *Africa News,* 1 February. Available at Africahttp://www.africanews.com/site/Tanzania_PM_cries_over_ albino_killings/list_messages/22930 (Accessed 25 May 2011).

Bryceson, D.F., J.B Jønsson and R. Herrington (2010) "Miners' magic: Artisanal mining, the albino fetish and murder in Tanzania." *Journal of Modern African Studies* 48(3): 353–82.

Cory, H. (1960) "Religious beliefs and practices of the Sukuma-Nyamwezi tribal group." *Tanzania Notes and Records* 54: 14–26.

Duff, O. (2005) "Tanzania suffers rise of witchcraft hysteria." *The Independent,* 28 November. Available at http://www.independent.co.uk/news/world/africa/tanzania-suffers-rise-of-witchcraft-hysteria-517157.html (Accessed 25 May 2011).

Hertz, R. (1996) *Sin and expiation in primitive societies.* Occasional Papers No. 2. British Centre for Durkheimian Studies, Oxford.

Levack, B.P. (2006) *The Witch-Hunt in Early Modern Europe.* Third edition. London: Longman.

Mesaki, S. (1993) Witchcraft and witch-killings in Tanzania. PhD thesis, University of Minnesota.

Mesaki, S. (2009) The Tragedy of Ageing: Witch Killings and Poor Governance among Sukuma. In Haram, L. and B. Yamba (eds) *Dealing with Uncertainty in Contemporary African Lives.* Uppsala: Nordic Africa Institute, pp. 42–90.

Pew Forum on Religion and Public Life (2010) *Tolerance and Christianity in Sub-Saharan Africa.* Washington DC: Pew Research Center.

Rappaport, R.A. (2001) *Ritual and religion in the making of humanity*. Cambridge: Cambridge University Press.

Reynolds, V. and R. Tanner (1995) *The Social Ecology of Religion*. Oxford: Oxford University Press.

Sanders, T. (2001) "Save our skins. Structural adjustment, morality and the occult in Tanzania." In Moore, H. and T. Sanders (eds) *Magical Interpretation, Material Realities: Modernity, Witchcraft and the Occult in Postcolonial Africa*. London: Routledge, pp. 160–83.

Stroeken, K. (2010) *Moral Power. The Magic of Witchcraft*. Oxford: Berghahn.

Tanner, R.E.S. (1956) "The Sorcerer in Northern Sukumaland, Tanganyika." *Southwestern Journal of Anthropology* 12(4): 437–43.

Tanzania Human Rights Report 2010. Dar es Salaam: Legal and Human Rights.

Tanzania Human Rights Report 2011. Dar es Salaam: Legal and Human Rights.

Tanzania Human Rights Report 2012. Dar es Salaam: Legal and Human Rights.

Tanzania Human Rights Report 2013. Dar es Salaam: Legal and Human Rights.

Valeri, V. (1985) *Kingship and sacrifice. Ritual and Society in Ancient Hawaii*. Chicago: University Press of Chicago.

Van Dijk, R. (2004) "'Beyond the rivers of Ethiopia': Pentecostal pan-Africanism and Ghanaian identities in the transnational domain." In van Binsbergenand, W. and R. van Dijk (eds) *Situating Globality. African Agency in the Appropriation of Global Culture*. Leiden: Brill, 163–89.

Vincent, L. (2008) "New Magic for New Times: Muti Murder in Democratic South Africa." *Tribes and Tribals*, Special Volume No. 2: 43–53.

Wijsen, F. and R. Tanner (2000) *Seeking a good life. Religion and society in Usukuma, Tanzania*. Nairobi: Paulines Publications Africa.

Wijsen, F. and R. Tanner (2002) *"I am just a Sukuma". Globalization and Identity Construction in Northwest Tanzania*. Amsterdam: Rodopi.

Language, knowledge, development and the framing of common destiny in contemporary Ethiopia: some reflections

Tekeste Negash

Though resource-poor, Ethiopia is now ranked as one of the fastest growing economies on the African continent. Addis Ababa and the regional capitals are visible demonstrations of this growth. It is true that most of the funding for growth is either borrowed or donated by powerful states with a strong interest in security and stability in the region. Remittances and the growing interaction between the diaspora and home country are also of considerable significance.

The economic upswing has brought with it an acute and extreme inequality between the few rich and the poor, who constitute the absolute majority of the population. Bridging the gap through an equitable system of distribution and social protection is one of the challenges facing the government and state.

It is important to note that the economic growth/recovery that the country has experienced since the downfall of official communism has very little to do with the performance of the education system. Education is a crucial factor, but it is neither the most important nor the only factor in economic development. Economic policies, as well as the international alignment of Ethiopia with the Western world and the favourable international climate, are primarily responsible for growth. This does not mean that education is not important, but we need to be very clear about what the educational sub-sector can do in promoting development.

It is difficult to discuss the role of education in development until we deconstruct and/or disaggregate the following concepts: education, knowledge, development and the state as main provider. So what is education and how does it become a factor in the development of the country in the wider sense of the term?

One of the most important myths to dismantle is the equation of education (irrespective of quality and relevance) with the wellbeing of the nation. A related myth is the equation of knowledge with education.

There is an unwarranted belief, promoted by the education industry, that knowledge not mediated through and by the formal education sector is worthless (Negash 2006). I believe it is time for this belief to be rejected for the good of the education sector itself. Formal education can be useless or a pure waste of resources if it does not meet the requirements of quality and relevance. Of course, it can be argued that an education programme deficient in quality and relevance is better than no education at all. This position can be strongly argued when it relates to an individual. But an education service is provided by a state that is constantly constrained by resource challenges and entrusted with creating and maintaining an education system that enables it to meet the challenges of survival and sustainable growth.

However, it is important to note that the education system now in place is the source of some knowledge that is good for those who go through the system and the society of which these students are part, but not of all relevant knowledge. What we learn outside school from parents, peers, formal and informal institutions and by using our brains is, I would argue, of far greater importance. It is the knowledge we acquire outside school that enables us and society to meet the challenges we face as individuals or as members of that society. Although the relationship between knowledge we acquire as individuals and the knowledge that we get through formal schooling needs to be looked at closely, it is important to remember that we humans have the capacity to create usable knowledge.

Here it is worthwhile to define the concept of knowledge itself: knowledge is the interpretation of information. In other words, knowledge is information (about any subject or phenomenon) that is processed and internalised. It is in this context that one can argue that a society such as Ethiopia could move ahead (not all the way, of course, but a long way) even if it has an educational system that produces more failed students than otherwise – or, to put it more starkly, even if it has an education system that is on the verge of collapse or has collapsed. The human brain is not just the product and reflection of a number of years of formal schooling. Rather, the human brain, judging from its social expressions (beliefs, quantifiable skills, etc.), has the capacity to reflect, interact and interpret its condition. An educational system that functions well brings the added value of enhancing the power of reflection on the construction of the future.

What is development and how does it relate to Education?

The shortest definition of development is the rational and cumulative exploitation of human and natural resources (cf., Wolf 2004). We need to bear in mind the key indicators that define the concept of development. Rationality involves choice and priorities. The cumulative aspect of development implies continuity over time. Exploitation in turn implies mobilisation and effective use of people and resources. By defining development in this manner, I am prepared to argue that tropical African societies in general, and Ethiopian society in particular, are oppressed but not exploited. I go further and maintain that the greatest problem facing societies such as Ethiopia is that they are underexploited. Neither the material nor the human resources are exploited so as to lead towards development as I have defined it. There is a huge difference between oppression and the rational and cumulative exploitation of both people and resources. Whereas oppression stifles initiative and breeds resistance, rational and cumulative exploitation leads to the benefit of society as a whole.

In spite of the globalisation hype, development takes place within national frontiers. The capacity of some countries (judged by their governments' ability to rationally exploit the human and material resources within their territories) to go beyond their national economies in search of cheap raw materials and labour is what is really called globalisation. The revolution in communication technologies has only accelerated the process of expansion that started centuries ago.

Insofar as we can learn from the logic of development as it has been applied in Western Europe, there are three things of crucial importance to launching and sustaining development. These are a strong state based on law; a judicial system that upholds laws and regulations; and an educational system that spreads values of common destiny that are shared by the majority of the citizens of the nation.

There are basic differences between strategies of survival and strategies of development. Most human societies would continue to survive using the information flows (and hence the knowledge they possess) that they daily acquire while engaged in the sheer logic of keeping alive. Strategies of development, on the other hand, are based on a qualitatively different way of organised life in which the constant search for renewal and improvement is the guiding principle for the state and its citizens. Reflexivity (the collective ability to reframe the present on the basis of lessons learned) is the crucial difference between strategies of survival and strategies of development. One may, of course, criticise the obsession with development for the sake of development that at times varies with needs and wellbeing of citizens at the cost of huge damage to the environment, but that is another question.

If we were to rank the crucial factors for development, the rule of law put in place by the state would be the most important followed by a strong state and a functioning education system. Here it is worth noting that education's most important role is not the transfer of skills but the transfer of values that bind together the citizens of the country. In developed countries, this role of education was quite well recognised about a century and half ago, but has now receded as some of education's functions have been taken over by television and other media. Moreover, education as a transformative value is much less needed in national states than in multicultural or multinational states such as Ethiopia.

So how is the education system serving development in Ethiopia?

Some years ago, I argued that the Ethiopian education system was on the brink of collapse mainly due to the use of English as a medium of instruction and the expansion of the education sector without adequate financing (Negash 2006). The national learning assessments for grades 4, 8, 10 and 12 revealed that less than 40 per cent of students scored a passing grade. The majority of those who passed the tests scored slightly more than 50 per cent. An educational system that fails the great majority of enrolees is a failed system. The main purpose of a well functioning system is not to fail students but to make sure that all of them get the support they need to pass. The problem does not lie with the students, but with the system itself. In short, the school is either not ready to create conditions for all students to complete the programme of studies successfully or is incapable of doing so. The psychological impact of being told that one has failed to complete one's studies is indeed huge. The greatest problem facing the school-age generation is not learning difficulties but language difficulties, especially in secondary school and beyond, a challenge complicated further by huge classes, poorly trained teachers and the virtual absence of educational materials.

How bad is the Ethiopian education system?

Our state of knowledge on the various subsectors is not as we wish it to be. Whereas we have some studies on the conditions in the primary and secondary subsectors, we have virtually no studies on higher education. I think it would be a challenge to the university community to get its act together and to find ways and means of examining itself. Unfortunately, higher education can only be studied by those who are in it, unless one asks the World Bank to do the job. The bank certainly would do it, but would definitely lose sight of the key issues along the way.

According to a number of studies carried out by various joint USAID and Ministry of Education (MOE) taskforces, the situation in primary and secondary schools is very bad. The most recent study on reading among second and third grade students revealed that the majority either cannot read or do not understand what they read (USAID/Ethiopia 2010). These are students taught in languages spoken at home. The USAID and MOE study on early grade reading concluded that at least 80 per cent of the students in the eight regions studied were not reading at the expected fluency rate (USAID/Ethiopia 2010). And when it comes to reading comprehension, the USAID study concluded that more than 50 per cent of the children in most regions were unable to answer a simple question (USAID/Ethiopia 2010). The USAID study was carried out in 2010. More than 300 schools and more than 13,000 students participated. In ten years, many of those who participated in the study will come knocking at the doors of universities and colleges, including Addis Ababa University. Judging from this single, but important, study it is hard not to conclude that the Ethiopian education sector faces huge crises.

In my earlier writings (Negash 2006), I argued that Plasma education (televised lectures) has compounded the crisis in secondary schools. I identified English as the medium of instruction as the main obstacle. To a large extent this has been corroborated by a recent (2013) World Bank study entitled *Secondary Education in Ethiopia: Supporting Growth and Transformation*. The bank, after noting that 61 per cent of those who sat the Grade 12 national exams scored less than 50 per cent, concluded: "It is clear that the poor quality of education in Ethiopia which results in low levels of student learning is compromising the further development of the education system" (World Bank 2013: 35-6). The study further notes that the secondary school curriculum promotes the learning of factual data rather than the understanding of underlying concepts, leaving learners little or no time to practise and develop meta-cognitive skills, that is, the ability to think and the ability to use learning as an instrument for auto-education. According to the World Bank study, Ethiopian secondary school education is designed to identify and encourage fast learners rather than to help the greatest number of students. This is a great tragedy.

The World Bank study does not even attempt to link this aspect of the curriculum to the constraints that English as a medium of instruction imposes on everybody engaged in the sector. The study notes that the switch from home language to English in Grade 9 creates learning problems, but offers no remedies. This is not surprising because the World Bank does not encourage developing countries to abandon English as medium of instruction. Of course, the World Bank is wrong. Ethiopian students, like all students elsewhere, do not have learning difficulties, but only difficulties directly related to a foreign language as medium of learning. The problem lies in the language.

Before I conclude this brief review of the World Bank study, I would like to mention two interesting insights. The first is about Plasma technology. The introduction of Plasma education was technology-driven without any evidence that it would improve learning. And according to the World Bank study, the results of Plasma can only be seen as disappointing. The second insightful conclusion of the World Bank study is that 70 per cent of secondary school students in grades 11 and 12 are boys and that the rural population and ethnic minorities are discriminated against. In Addis Ababa, more girls attend secondary school than boys. The conclusion I draw from this is that the secondary education sector now caters to the rich in urban areas. I am sure this is not the intention of government but is rather the consequence of a policy environment that stresses the expansion of the sector without due reflection.

How is education related to the maintenance and enhancement of a common destiny?

Nobody can tell what the future holds. However, immense strides have been made in analysing the making of the future in which education has a very important role to play. We know how the present is made. It is a fusion of yesterday and our reactions to it today. I am aware that I am over-generalising and abstracting, but let this be for the purposes of this discussion. Unprecedented events such a serious environmental disaster may call for a rapid and radical adjustment, followed by diverse solutions. Not everything can be planned to keep the future under control. But the development of the culture of reflexivity (learning from past lessons and planning for all scenarios) appears to offer the hope of taming the future for the wellbeing of citizens. It is in promoting common values as well as the capacity for reflexivity that education becomes an important instrument. The primary goal of education, as I mentioned earlier, is the transmission of values that bind a society. But it has to be made clear that this huge and important task cannot be managed by an education sector alone. The education sector of any given country is an outcome of policy. Education is not an independent variable that can propel a society towards development. The sector functions when it is closely tied to politics and policy.

How can education serve Ethiopia's development and social cohesion?

Perhaps the starting point is the bitter realisation that Ethiopia behaves, by fault or design, in the same manner as a former colony. The widespread belief that Ethiopia is the only country not colonised by a European power is a truth that demands considerable qualification. Ethiopian education does not in any way reflect the fact that Ethiopia has always been independent. So although true, the narrative of Ethiopian independence has rhetorical value but very little content. The best demonstration is the country's reluctance to privilege its languages and cultures as the medium of instruction throughout the education sector.

I subscribe to the view of many African scholars before me that it is only by replacing English with Ethiopian languages as the medium of instruction that Ethiopia can achieve sustained development and social cohesion. It is worthwhile mentioning briefly two authors who perceived the link between development (as I have defined it above) and the enhancement of indigenous languages. Ngugi (1986) argued repeatedly that there could be no African university that does not enhance African languages. Secondly, Kwesi Prah has consistently maintained (2013) that the only way for African states (including Ethiopia) to deal with their inferiority complexes is to switch from European to African languages.

I want to make it clear that English would remain as very important language as it is par excellence the source of most of the knowledge available in the world today. As many people as possible ought to be encouraged to master it so as to participate in the flow of knowledge and information. My argument is that Ethiopia cannot and ought not to attempt to educate its citizens through the medium of English for two reasons. First, English is not even a second language in Ethiopia. Teachers are unable to teach in English, students end up being uneducated and the country loses the added value of a population able to understand concepts very much needed for development and social cohesion.

The success of Ethiopia will depend on the quality of its people. There is sufficient reason to give credit to Martin Wolf (2004) for arguing for a causal relationship between the economic success of any state and the quality of its people. The latter is measured through two principal indicators, health and education. A country that does not pay attention to the health of its people (by making food cheap and accessible) will not be able to get the best out its population. Likewise, a nation that fails to institute an education system that does not encourage learners to reflect on what they are learning will fail to get the best out of its population. And a well-functioning education system, in tune with its cultural base, can produce citizens who would enhance the quality of the state and economy. However, despite the enormous investment in education, Ethiopia is not deriving the benefits (in terms of creating citizens of quality) due to the uncritical adoption of curricula and English as the medium of instruction.

The second reason is that the status of English in the Ethiopian society as whole is diminishing, partly due to the growth of Amharic and other Ethiopian languages.

There is one country in Africa that has devoted adequate attention to the damaging effects of English as the medium of instruction, South Africa. Since 2009, South African institutions of higher learning have intensified their efforts to introduce the home language of learners either as a learning support to the main (English) medium of instruction or as an alternative language of education. The South African case is interesting for several reasons. English is a native language for several million South Africans (Wildsmith-Cromarty 2014). Yet, there are many South Africans whose native language is other than English and who find it difficult to follow their studies in that language. It is indeed commendable that these South African institutions have understood that the main problem was not learning difficulties but language difficulties. I believe that Ethiopia can learn much from the South African experience. And I do hope that the Department of Comparative Education that is being established at Addis Ababa University will give more attention to trends and developments in the middle-income countries of the South rather than to the traditions of countries in the European Union and North America.

Can one abandon English and provide education that contributes to development and social cohesion? Whose responsibility is it?

For all intents and purposes, English is no longer the medium of instruction. True, textbooks are in English and exams as well. Code switching – the practice of using other Ethiopian languages alongside English – is widespread at secondary schools and quite common at universities as well. In my view, it is possible and highly desirable to abandon English in favour of a maximum of two Ethiopian languages, with the caveat that the transition be planned well ahead of time. The responsibility for such transformation rests with the state.

The transition from English to Ethiopian languages, complex as it might appear, is doable. Earlier, I have argued that Amharic and Oromiffa ought to be developed as the medium of instruction for the whole country (Negash 2006). While the position of Amharic is given (it is already the language of government), the argument for the introduction of Oromiffa is based on numbers. The Oromo are the largest single ethnic group in Ethiopia, comprising nearly 30 million people.

A point of great importance is the decision by the Southern Nations, Nationalities and Peoples region, commonly called the South, to use Amharic as the language of communication. This region is highly diversified, possessing more than 45 ethnic groups. Moreover, it was by far the most oppressed part of the Ethiopian empire from its incorporation in the mid-19th century until the mid-20th century. At the risk of digressing, I wish to place on record that the role of the South in the evolution and development of social cohesion in this country has been an inestimable blessing.

What does the future hold for education and its role in development?

In conclusion, I limit myself to two scenarios. But I would first like to say few words on the survival capacity of the Ethiopian state. I believe that in spite of the politicisation of ethnicity, Ethiopia is more united now than it was a couple of decades ago. I do not need to dwell on the dispersal of human and material resources caused by ethnicity politics and I believe that the government will soon redefine its policy. Ethiopia is still rural and the mentality of the rural will continue to shape the strategies of survival.

The first scenario for the future is continuing along the same lines in the hope that the education system will produce the manpower needed by the society. This would work despite the weaknesses of the education system. As I mentioned earlier, the formal education system does not have a monopoly as regards the creation and transmission of knowledge. However, continuity may allow the society to survive, but not to embark on development strategies that allow for the rational and cumulative exploitation of human and material resources.

The second future scenario is for Ethiopia to redefine its relationship with its citizens in terms of resources to be fully exploited for their own good and for the wellbeing of society. In addition to food, the education sector has to be the focus of such redefinition. The introduction of Amharic and Oromiffa would, I believe, be the most daunting challenge, but in the long run the most rewarding. There is no better alternative than the second scenario if Ethiopia is to make the best use of its population.

Such a radical reframing with a focus on education would certainly require a roadmap. The main point of departure for the roadmap is the realisation that the use of English cannot enhance Ethiopia's capacity for a rational and cumulative exploitation of its human and material resources. It would be futile to discuss a roadmap without consensus about the problem of the use of English in the Ethiopian school system. However, assuming there is such consensus, then a roadmap for the reorganisation of Ethiopian education could contain two principal phases.

The first phase is building consensus among all sectors of society on the reasons for the change of language of instruction. It is important that enough time (up to five years) be given for consensus building. It is also important that the Ethiopian state resists the temptation to manufacture consensus, the difference being that consensus building is participatory whereas consensus manufacturing appears to be but in fact is not.

The second phase could be planning and implementing the actual shift from English to Amharic and Oromiffa. This phase could very well demand the establishment of language and translation academies and could take up to 20 years to accomplish. This may sound long, but such a timeframe is quite short compared to Ethiopia's past and its future.

References

Negash, T. (2006) *Education in Ethiopia: From Crisis to the Brink of Collapse.* Uppsala: Nordic Africa Institute.

Ngugi Wa Thiongo (1986) *Decolonising the Mind: The Politics of Language in African Literature.* Nairobi: East Africa Education Publishers.

Prah, K. (2013) "No country can make progress on the basis of borrowed language." *eLearning Africa.*

USAID/Ethiopia (2010) *Ethiopia Early Grade Reading Assessment.* Addis Ababa: USAID.

Wildsmith-Cromarty, R. (2014) "Challenges to the Implementation of bilingual/multilingual language policies at tertiary institutions in South Africa (1995–2012)." *Language Matters* 45(3): 295–312.

Wolf, M. (2004) *Why Globalization Works.* New Haven: Yale University Press.

World Bank (2013) *Secondary Education in Ethiopia: Supporting Growth and Transformation.* Washington DC: World Bank.

Land reform, natural resources governance and food security: Message from and to Africa and beyond

Prosper B. Matondi

Introduction

I have been a student, mentee and colleague of Kjell Havnevik for some 17 years. In those close to two decades of professional relationship, we have shared many thoughts on land reform, natural resource governance and food security in Africa. He has been a top scholar and Africanist who believes that these subjects are of such importance they should be part of the world's scholarship, policy and practical discourse. His contribution as a teacher for many generations has been outstanding, and I am both fortunate and privileged to have been one of his close students – even now, mid-career, when I am trying to make a contribution and a difference. I work in the same area, not by coincidence, but because I believe there have to be some ideological shifts on these matters.

For Kjell, the underlying questions and issues include *what type(s) of governance institutions and mechanisms will lead to improved livelihood outcomes and environmental sustainability in rural Africa?* It is this my chapter seeks to address. This is not an easy question to answer, yet it must be answered in several ways. First, by understanding the local knowledge and capital base, and opportunities for collective action/institutional development for strengthening the productive capacity of fractured households and communities. Second, by enhancing the adaptive capacity of communities to climate change and emerging market opportunities and risks (technical, technological, climatic and social aspects). Third, by examining the impact of land grabbing on livelihood strategies and rural dynamics (labour shortage for agriculture, impact on access to and use of natural resources, on gender, on property rights of affected segments and on family and social values and safety nets). Fourth, natural resource governance must achieve a balance between rural life improvement and environmental sustainability. Fifth, production and markets (formal and informal) must be governed to achieve rural improvement (labour productivity, technology, innovations, institutions, pro-poor market development). Sixth, governance mechanisms should be in place to promote African agency (promoting sound policies and institutions at all levels, countering ill-devised policies and mitigating the negative impacts of globalisation on rural livelihoods and on the management of natural resources).

Kjell has a passion for global justice and the rights of smallholder farmers in Africa, and it is in that spirit that this chapter tackles the above issues. Within the ambit of governance, there has been much confusion, misunderstanding and contestation over what governance implies in Africa in relation to access to and use of natural resources in general and the position of agriculture in food security. These are the matters this chapter seeks to unpack against the backdrop of two contested realities. Governance is used by powerful global forces as a basis for market expansion, whereby African states are conditioned to be accountable and transparent, while allowing Foreign Direct Investments (FDIs). In contrast, smallholders, civil society actors and development academics such as Kjell view governance through the lens of justice and equity for the poor.

Africa's image and the central role of smallholder agriculture

This snapshot of Africa provides the premise upon which Kjell devoted his professional and intellectual career. The image of Africa globally is one of poverty, underdevelopment and with a population with no answers of their own to the challenges they face. Africa is the most underdeveloped continent; it has the largest population dependent on external relief; civil war – whether externally instigated, promoted by a dissatisfied military with an appetite for power or due to incumbent leaders resisting leadership renewal – is the norm; African economies continue to under-perform and attract very little investment; rural areas remain underdeveloped, with high levels of illiteracy, malnutrition and food shortage; women and youths are trapped in poverty, with high risks ranging from vulnerability to marginalisation. The images on Western television of drought-stricken animals or people wasting away from hunger seem to reveal a continent still in the Dark Ages.

Yet, there is a need to understand Africa better, and Kjell has contributed enormously to this through his research on agriculture and smallholder farmers. Agriculture remains the main source of livelihood for the majority of the rural poor, and farming in Africa is dominated by smallholders. Given this, the sector is laden with challenges that continue to undermine its potential to contribute to economic growth and development and at the same time drive vulnerable smallholders deeper into poverty and insecurity. There is therefore, a critical need to focus on the role of agriculture and rural production in averting poverty and promoting economic growth. Further, while some African countries have registered such growth over the last decade, a larger number still grapple with high poverty levels, particularly among the rural poor and women. I have often engaged with Kjell and others interested in Africa in an effort to understand, critique and deliberate on the many challenges that African smallholders and rural producers face.

The instability in communal areas can be traced to population growth and relative scarcity of land, resulting in conflicts and social tensions. Communal tenure has proven to be unstable and insecure, leading to an unwillingness to invest in land improvement. This has had a deleterious effect on production and led to economic stagnation and land degradation, since weak property rights mean that farmers do not benefit from long-term investment in land. However, land scarcity encourages private ownership in place of communal property and the emergence of institutions that facilitate the recognition and regulation of property rights. Stable property rights across the societal strata (large- and small-scale farming areas) facilitate the further development of agriculture by creating suitable environments for investment in land and for credit and risk markets that use land as security and collateral. Property rights emerge when individuals are willing to invest to gain stable and recognised rights in land and when the benefit of this investment are considered to outweigh the costs. Land markets, stable property rights and institutions that monitor these emerge when the costs of creating them are lower than the gains to productive investment in land.

The choices of what works best for Africa can be divided into two. First, there is the model of smallholder livelihoods, which, when well backed by government at policy level, and the private sector through value chain and market support, can help achieve food security and income earning for families. Second, the development of large-scale farming through displacement based on land acquisitions and leasing from authorities makes smallholders food vulnerable, and as they become workers on estates they then depend on the markets for their food needs. In much of Africa this is happening at a wider scale with the dominant assumption being that large-scale leads to lower prices, sustained production, better quality of produce, etc. Our argument has always been that smallholder farmers should primarily benefit from public investment and be prioritised by public policies. These should provide measures, incentives and infrastructure that support smallholders' investments, secure their access to natural resources and enhance their access to local and domestic markets. Smallholders in Africa are the central productive units whose productivity can readily be enhanced through better connections to the global market, better integration into global value chains and improved technologies.

The paradox of land and Africa's social inequities

Access to land and tenure security are the primary means to secure livelihoods in Africa, although achieving them often pits markets against the state, and indigenous communities become either victims of state inaction or market offensives. Often, the narrative trajectory has been associated with access to and uses of land and natural resources. We have had numerous debates about resolving problems of access to land, and agree that though much has been said, little has been achieved. Various types of land reform have been implemented across Africa, but they have been inadequate to resolving the contested demands for land and security of tenure and in achieving favourable agrarian outcomes. Access by

Africans to land, water and other resources and the rights to own, use and transfer these resources remain weak. International and local policy-makers, though paying attention to these challenges, are still far from providing solutions that move the majority of Africans out of poverty and underdevelopment.

The land problems of Africa, particularly sub-Saharan Africa, relate to the skewed distribution that is a result of colonial history. From the 1950s, in order to deal with these challenges, many countries in Africa needed sophisticated policy-making to get public resettlement programmes going. At the same time they needed to balance social needs with the technical restructuring of their economies. But balancing conflicts based on race, class and ethnicity to lay the foundations for creating equity meant that governments had to make hard choices, change social policy priorities and redress inherited imbalances (Cliffe 2000; Herbst 1990; Palmer 1990). The racial connotations meant that the socio-demographic features, including population, wealth, income and employment patterns, favoured farmers of settler origin against blacks. That chasm in race was defined in terms of superiority and inferiority in the colonial period, and privileges were allotted accordingly. The result in former settler colonies is that wealth and income were concentrated in one minority racial group, which benefited far more from economic development in a region where the majorities were poor and had weak tenure rights.

Land reform in former settler colonies became political, simply because the colonial "project" had resulted in the displacement of blacks from the most productive land. In addition, land ceilings were imposed on people who were pushed on to marginal land, and a host of regulations were issued as to what could and could not be done with the land. The colonial land reform programme was racist and was aimed at subjugating black people (Mamdani 1996). Therefore, the communal areas with high population densities were a colonial creation and not the result of natural forces (Matondi 2001). Colonial states, when they conceived of the communal areas, saw the dangers of population increase for the environment and the potential political consequences of mass poverty.

The dominant problems facing land reforms can be summarised as follows: i) *Unequal land ownership:* A large percentage of productive land is in the hands of a few large farmers in Namibia, Zimbabwe and South Africa. In Mozambique and Zambia, there is increasing foreign land ownership, with foreigners owning disproportionately large holdings. There is also the issue of underutilisation by large farmers and foreign landowners amidst growing landlessness due to "land grabbing" through secretly negotiated government-to-government agreements; ii) *Tenure problems:* Some enjoy freehold tenure while most communal farmers owned their land on the basis of customary law. Customary ownership is replete with rules and regulations enforced by multiple competing institutions (traditional and government), all of which make the land unattractive for private financing. The result is that customary areas have weak connections to commercial services (banks, agricultural service contractors, offshore finance, etc.); iii) *land administration problems:* In much of Africa land management is a key challenge, because it is highly centralised, with lower structures at times making decisions without reference to national structures and vice versa. For instance, traditional leaders have been known to grant concessions to land to external investors without the knowledge of the central government. Information flows and data on land ownership and access tend to be weak; iv) *legal problems*: Redress for land-related conflicts is not only expensive, particularly for the poor, but also complex, since the justice system is too elitist, making it inaccessible; v) *land-use planning problems:* Planning systems tend to focus on the short term and to be uncoordinated. For example, ministries of agriculture, the environment, and fisheries may have different plans for the same area, at times confusing local people. These current paradoxes in Africa are products of the past, are constructions formed by social relations of domination and resistance.

In terms of solutions, various instruments have been tried over several decades. The three most important are firstly, the *willing seller - willing buyer* instrument. The central argument in land reform is that it must lead to poverty alleviation (World Bank 2003) while also ensuring economic growth and social stability. Yet, curiously, from the 1950s to 1970s, the bank argued for land registration and titling, invoking a market instrument and the associated willing seller and willing buyer principle as the alpha and omega of reform. The basic argument for this instrument was the protection of acquired land rights through market control of land pricing beyond what government and ordinary people are willing and able to pay.

Secondly, a *market-led or market-assisted* approach was promoted by the World Bank for resolving land conflicts. It was believed at the time that markets were non-political and would be juster and fairer than the state. However, as we have found out, free markets will not deliver a just agrarian system in Africa. Leaving markets alone is a myth, as one leading African thinker on social policy, Professor Thandika Mkandawire, has pointed out: "Markets are created and markets can be shaped" (Mkandawire 2001). The World Bank has over the years tried to argue for a lesser state role in land distribution. Instead, they have argued for "market-assisted land reform." The neoliberal agenda for land redistribution is based on market-led land reform. The basis for land reform is seen in the context of cooperation by large landowners through their voluntary willingness to sell. The market approach prefers land taxation to land ceilings as a way of forcing large landowners to relinquish land they are not fully utilising. Large landowners subvert this reform process by subdividing their farms and only releasing the worst portions, and by engaging in legal battles to slow the redistribution of land. Moreover, the approach has the potential to promote land speculation. The issue of compensation to large landowners has been raised as a major deterrent to compulsory acquisition. There is a view that the compensation offered to large landowners in state-run land redistribution schemes is usually below the market value of land, and this provokes landowner resistance to reform.

In free markets for land there is little reference to notions of social equality and justice. Market transfers work in a context of land abundance relative to land demand. The major problem with market transfers is that they perpetuate the *status quo* of land inequity. Market approaches are usually resistant to the equity that may be established through transfers. In practice, market land transfers do not result in redistributive reforms through public resettlement programmes. Indeed, as has been seen in South Africa and Zimbabwe, this approach results in escalation of land prices through land speculation. By contrast, state land-acquisition programmes concentrate on redistribution to address political pressures. Very little emphasis is placed on the productive use of the land. The end result is that either land speculators or resistant large landowners win the game by holding on to the land, or the state wins at the cost of productive land going to waste. Is there a potential for a middle reform path that can work for the people to address political, social and economic issues, not least poverty?

Thirdly, there is *state-enforced redistribution* whereby land reform is achieved through the forced or negotiated acquisition of land and its redistribution to disadvantaged groups. Such reforms are principally aimed not just at security of tenure but also have political dimensions. The main instrument in state land-reform programmes is compulsory acquisition, referred to in some contexts as expropriation. It may be seen more extremely as nationalisation of private land for public purposes. To achieve this, the state largely depends on control of the legal instruments to ensure the success of its programme of land transfers for the purposes of achieving social equity (including gender equity), breaking the monopoly of large farmers and reducing poverty. Yet in practice the state may use land redistribution to build political capital without necessarily changing the circumstances of the poor. Indeed, state redistribution is usually seen as inefficient and driven by political rather than economic imperatives. Productive farms are subdivided into smaller efficient farms.

The beneficiaries of this programme are frequently elites, not poor households without the capacity to farm the land efficiently. The implementation of state-led reform is frequently top-down and associated with rent-seeking activities, not with land distribution on the basis of need, particularly where land is expropriated at below market price. This prevents the most efficient farmers from acquiring land, and discourages the development of an agricultural credit sector releasing loans against land collateral. It is further argued that expropriation of large landowners drives capital from the farm sector, and that land ceilings and prohibition on sales and rentals by farmers awarded land discourages the development of a land market that would promote collateral. This also discourages external investors from entering the agricultural sector (Deininger 1999). State administration of land has frequently resulted in greater inequity and land concentration as people in positions of economic power take advantage of the less powerful. This has often encouraged land speculation rather than investment in land (Bruce 1993).

If we take the case of Zimbabwe, there was consensus on the need for land reform to redress unjust colonial imbalances. However, there were differences about the strategy and approach to implementing land reform. It has been diffi-cult for Zimbabweans to oppose something they agree on in principle but differ on regarding implementation. The politics of land reform demonstrate that it is easier to fight against the "what" you do not agree with than against the "what" all agree with, except in terms of the "how." Even so, given that land in Africa is a highly valued resource, contests over who takes what land are endemic.

International land grabs: the new elephant in the room

A major issue in global development discourse relates to the nature of the For-eign Direct Investment African agriculture requires (Matondi and Mutopo 2011). In view of increasing food insecurity and reliance on food imports amid decreasing crop and livestock productivity, many countries on the continent re-quire FDIs. Furthermore, with most African nations struggling to attract inter-national investment, the energy industry has shown continued interest in invest-ing in farmland for biofuel production. The book I edited with Kjell (Matondi, Havnevik and Beyene 2011) alluded to a dominant but misleading view that Africa has abundant under-utilised land, which can be used for biofuel feed-stock production. Yet amid such views, many Africans, facing food insecurity, are struggling to gain access to land or secure their rights. Arguments have been made that Africa needs to industrialise on the model of Western and emerging Asian nations. In this view, FDIs are a basis for stimulating economic growth through employment and foreign currency injection. While FDIs are necessary and industrialisation itself is good for Africa, they have to be considered in terms of Africa's evolving culture and the rights of Africans.

The current global food system is dependent on major companies making large-scale land investments for cash crop production, controlling the value chain and operating mostly in the international market (Hall 2011). The supply of investment resources by the private sector is often considered the solution, in terms of reversing agricultural disinvestment and enabling required change. This brings us to two contradictory visions of agricultural development: one with smallholders at the centre, with their own rights and autonomy in design-ing systems that better benefit them; the other with smallholders serving the corporates, with a strong focus on profit that often undermines the potential for livelihoods and food security.

Land grabs in Africa are premised on agribusiness corporations' capitalising not only on land but also on the wealth produced by peasant families, as they become protégés of the main processing and contracting companies. In the end, firms that industrialise and commercialise peasant crops capture the majority of the wealth. Yet at times they introduce crops such as jatropha or convert sugarcane into ethanol into areas where they were not produced before. In countries such as Ethiopia, the expansion of cut flower production has displaced traditional agro-food production systems and converted indigenous people into workers. These processes intensify inequalities by deepening wealth concentrations, further enabling corporate control over territories and technologies and reinforcing corporate subordination of indigenous people. They also lead to devastated environments, where nature is transformed and people lose their autonomy. For advocates of FDI in agriculture, the monopolisation of technology, the rural exodus, and territorial concentration are part of a "natural" process of agricultural modernisation. For analysts of the agrarian question, however, such violent and destructive outcomes could be minimised if the state intervened with policies to control the excesses of corporate agriculture.

The impact large-scale private investments are having on smallholder families and communities has to be considered when we take a stand of which vision to support and promote. At this time, many smallholders, women and indigenous people are being driven off their land, deprived of the control and use of their resource base, are victims of human rights abuses and are forced into a life without a house, food or dignity. When they are integrated into new farming systems as a result of contracts with large companies, they often become wage workers whose labour rights are not respected and whose livelihoods and prospects are not improved. In many cases, large tracts of land are sold or leased to private and foreign investors, thereby depriving communities of their resource base in return for unfulfilled promises and dramatic livelihood changes. Women are often the most severely affected.

Food security the foundation of Africa's development

Kjell was passionate about food (in)security in Africa, and this dovetails with agriculture, land and water and broadly with the natural resource management discussed next. To him, poverty is largely expressed through lack of food and more poignantly through lack of access to food by Africans in a world where there is abundant food, which often has to be thrown away in some countries. He spent a lot of his time researching and speaking publicly on this matter, while teaching future generations. To me, the connection of food (in)security to poverty is a clear indication of the failure of the world's institutional and policy systems, despite the grandeur with which these policies are announced.

Therefore, the complexities of agricultural and rural production and livelihood systems represent profound challenges for interventions and support aiming to enhance agricultural productivity, natural resource management and broad-based development. Over the last three decades, strategies by nation states, international financial institutions and donors have failed to unlock the potential of sub-Saharan agricultural and rural production, and/or have worsened conditions and deepened exclusion and marginalisation. Why are strategies and policies to reduce rural poverty and enhance agricultural productivity failing? Are they constrained by lack of knowledge or undue emphasis on certain interests or factions, or are the capacities to conceptualise and the methods at hand unequal to the complexities being faced? How can interventions and their effects be productively analysed and understood? How can land and tenure reforms be designed in a manner that will address poverty rather than accentuate it?

Underlying analytical messages: structure and agency

Kjell's strong arguments at a workshop in Harare in November of 2006[1] were that no country could prosper without state structures to effectively manage the development process. This goes beyond the moral case for tackling poverty, with all its inequality and dehumanisation. Through the lens of structure and agency, we can better appreciate how development evolves in Africa and its contestation. Yet, in reality this is not a new approach, because structure and agency have long formed the basic framework of the land governance debate, even though understandings of the paradigmatic nature of the struggle have changed as the institutional identity of participants has been transformed over time. More often than not, the poor in Africa have not been served by dominant state structures and agencies. There are exceptions though, where countries such as Zimbabwe have moved to support indigenous people for various reasons, and where shifting politics and power forced the state to align with the poor.

In general, marginalised classes in Africa have tried to strengthen their control over land, only to find the state aligned against them in alliance with powerful elites. The indigenous people have hardly ever risen up against the imposition of laws that displaced them, and instead civil society organisations and academics have, in the interests of the poor, provided information on and questioned structure and agency. Yet, the issues of structure and agency lie in the detail. Agencies are at times powerful actors in decision-making on land,

1. Conference on "Livelihoods, natural resource governance and environmental sustainability in East and Southern Africa" organised by NAI in cooperation with the Institute of Environmental Studies, the University of Zimbabwe.

food security, natural resources management and so on. However, often they are not. This is because in most of Africa political power is central to decisions, not socioeconomic issues that affect the majority of actors. Thus, the structures of the state fail to perform their functions.

For example, land administration systems in Africa are beset by a number of problems, including desuetude, bureaucratic complexity, managerial opacity, inefficiency and high transaction costs (Okoth-Ogendo 2007). Desuetude is most evident in the juridical and cadastral functions of land administration (Okoth-Ogendo 2007). In most jurisdictions in Africa, land delivery, demarcation and survey, registration and records-keeping, and cadastral mapping procedures and processes are not computerised and storage facilities and support services are often inadequate and under-funded. The result is inaccuracies and management lapses. Even simple, routine information is often hidden in "confidential" or "secret" files, while transactional procedures are often couched in undecipherable legalese that might defeat even the most adept lawyer. In turn, this leads to operational inefficiency as well as high transaction costs. This is particularly true of state-maintained land-administrations, which insist on complex and precise procedures.

Interdisciplinary approaches: the key to better appreciation of rural development

In the many years I have known Kjell, a multidisciplinary approach has been central to his understanding of the complexity of Africa's rural development problems. He has worked with a wide network of students and researchers in disentangling the issue. For instance, his take on governance emphasised institutions that address land rights, land redistribution, tenure reform and policies and drew on the work of many eminent researchers (Bruce and Migot-Adholla 1994; Platteau 1995; Okoth-Ogendo, 1991; Lund 1998; Toulmin and Quan 2000; Barros et al. 2002; Hammar and Raftopoulos 2003). The same is true of his work on the management of common pool resources (Ostrom 1990 and 1999; Agrawal 2001; and McKean and Ostrom 2005) and the institutional preconditions for their sustainable management. Also of relevance in this area is his analysis of the implications of the decentralisation and/or devolution evident in most African countries.

He argues that most of the studies mentioned above show the limited institutionalisation of sustainable management and governance regimes. Rather, what seems to emerge in Africa is a dynamic diversification of livelihoods among communities and households, including the landless, landowners and the female-headed households, in response to subsistence needs, commercialisation, population growth and government interventions. This diversification is part

of the struggle for survival but may result in land and natural resource degradation. Yet, an integral strand in many of the studies associated with him has
been the attempt to improve, adjust or develop new approaches and theories in
addressing the sociocultural, institutional, economic and political complexities
of rural Africa. Linkages between politics, institutions and sustainability issues
in sub-Saharan Africa have been given added weight through related research
by his many students at doctoral level (Larsson Lidén 2000; Matondi 2001;
Nemarundwe 2003; Belaineh 2003; Habtemariam 2003; Beyene, 2003; Kowero et al. 2003; Hårsmar, 2004; Gunnarsdotter, 2005; Arora-Jonsson, 2005;
Lindahl, 2008; Sandström 2008). While many of these studies remain discon-
nected, there has been a tendency for each theoretical strand to broaden and for
a more comprehensive approach to be adopted. To me this is Kjell style, he leaves
a legacy for multi-disciplinarity, rural development and his vision of picking not
just students, but niche areas of knowledge generation of which I have been a
prime beneficiary.

Africa's development future

This was perhaps the starting point for Kjell, when as a young student he wrote
on Tanzania. During his student days, he was confronted by the harsh realities of Africa's underdevelopment as seen in Tanzania. He was to make this
country not only his second home, but a place in which to carefully dissect and
understand Africa's development problems and how best the continent could
define its future. The global community is at a crossroads in terms of how best
to respond to Africa's supposed "rising" or its economic growth of 5-6 per cent.
It is pertinent to celebrate growth that addresses poverty, yet one needs also to
differentiate those who in the past grew their economies without concern for
the ecological footprint of that growth. My point is that Africa must desist from
"revenge" growth, but undertake growth that does not jeopardise the future
of current and ensuing generations. This means that Africa will need to make
choices and political decisions.

Political mobilisation is now key to addressing the issues this chapter identi-
fies. The message is clear that communities and organisations need to mobilise
around the defence of their natural resources and the development of spaces and
abilities to define their own development path. Better appreciation of natural
resource governance and the role of the poor provides scope for social and political mobilisation so that governance becomes consistent with the normative
values of the poor globally. People need to engage in land and natural resource
management as a priority and as citizens with real control over their resources.

Given Kjell's background as an educationist, this includes mobilising learning resources so that the people are better informed and better able to inform

– in short, to be heard and to hear. The development agenda requires income above subsistence, so that individuals are liberated from the everyday toil that prevents them from enjoying broader engagement in the world.

This leads us to question some of the received wisdom used by dominant powers. Concepts such as "stakeholder" consultation have been abused by power gatekeepers, and are used in "charm offensives" rather than as an avenue for substantive engagement of the people most affected by natural resource attrition. Beyond the simple acknowledgement that "stakeholders" are all parties with a claim or interest and therefore entitled to participate, there is no clear delineation of stakeholder or the validity of their stake in community development. How are stakeholders validated, by whom and why? These are complex questions that Kjell leaves us to find answers for or forms of engagement with. In doing so, we must muster the courage to question how participation and stakeholder discourse are used to obfuscate the complex power relations that exist between interests to perpetuate relations of domination.

Conclusion

In all our discussions with Kjell over the years, we strongly felt that the land question in Africa was of paramount importance. The last encounter on this subject was when he designed a programme at the Nordic Africa Institute aimed at unpacking the land question in the Great Lakes region, with lessons drawn from countries such as Zimbabwe. Though he was not able to see through this proposed project, he felt there was a need for a regional focus to demonstrate not just the issues, but also the complexities and possibilities of finding solutions to this nagging question.

The land question in Africa is multifaceted and complex, and speaks to a whole range of governance-related issues, because most resources that are accessed and used by people are found on the land. Land redistribution and tenure reform are pressing matters, but so too are natural resource rights, land use and planning and land administration, production and so on. Given that land reform encompasses a gamut of issues that touch upon the welfare of Africans, it directly affects their economies and life, their social welfare, cultures and relations. Therefore, the politics of land control cannot be easily separated from the life of Africans. International development trends have tended to put the land issue on the back-burner, yet the economic progress of Africa cannot be achieved without examining land and its meaning for African people.

In 2006, we attempted a workshop in Harare to discuss climate debates. This initiative was prescient, for climate has become a key defining feature of global governance in terms of rights, equity, roles and responsibilities. Climate change, biofuels, land and resource degradation, poverty and underdevelopment connect with Africa's land question(s) in complex ways. Yet, we did not follow-up on climate change as thoroughly as we did the other matters discussed in this chapter. My hope is that the current generation of scholars, in which Kjell has invested so much of his intellectual life, will pick up this subject with much greater determination. I would say the climate discourse raises fundamental questions of the rights of the poor to development, and there is pressure on Africans to mitigate or adapt in exchange for economic benefits. This in itself is problematic, because the dominance of markets places greater pressure on communities to preserve resources.

In many contexts, the rights of communities are being rapidly eroded through, for instance, land grabbing for biofuels, mining and tourism and through a complex mix of green growth that hides the important usurpation of local community rights. I certainly believe that Kjell would agree with me that the rights of communities are being reduced, extinguished or modified given the massive power imbalances and structurally entrenched inequities.

References

Agarwal, B. (1995) "Women's legal rights in agricultural land in India". *Economic and Political Weekly*, March.

Agarwal, B. (2001) "Common Property Institutions and Governing the Commons". *World Development* Vol. 29, No. 10, pp. 1649–1672.

Arora-Jonsson, S. (2005) *Unsettling the Order. Gendered Subjects and Grassroots Activism in Two Forest Communities*. PhD dissertation No. 2005:70. Uppsala: SLU.

Barros, F., S. Sérgio Sauer and S. Schwartzman (eds) (2003) *Brasilia – The Negative Impacts of World Bank Market Based Land Reform*. Rede Brasil.

Belaineh L. (2003). *Risk Management Strategies of Smallholder Farmers in the Eastern Highlands of Ethiopia*. PhD dissertation. Department of Rural Development Studies. Uppsala: SLU.

Beyene A. (2003) "Soil Conservation, Land Use and Property Rights in Northern Ethiopia. Understanding Environmental Change in a Smallholder Farming System". *Agraria* 395. Uppsala: SLU.

Binswanger, H. P. and K. Deininger (1997). "Explaining Agricultural and Agrarian Policies in Developing Countries". *Journal of Economic Literature* 35(4): 1958–2005.

Bruce, J. W. and S.E. Migot-Adholla (eds) (1994) *Searching for Land Tenure Security in Africa*. Dubuque: Kendall/Hunt Publishing Company.

Bruce, J.W. (1993) "Do Indigenous Tenure Systems Constrain Agricultural Development?" in Basset, T.J. and D.E. Crummey (eds) *Land in African Agrarian Systems*. Madison: University of Wisconsin Press.

Cliffe, L. (1988) "The Prospects for Agricultural Transformation in Zimbabwe" in Stoneman, C. (ed.) *Zimbabwe's Prospects*. Basingstoke: Macmillan.

Cliffe, L. (2000) "Land Reform in South Africa". *Review of African Political Economy*, No. 84, 273–286.

Conyers, C. (undated) *Whose Elephants are they? Decentralization of Control over Wildlife Management through the Campfire Program in Binga District, Zimbabwe*. Mimeo.

Deininger, K. (1999) "Making negotiated land reform work: Initial evidence from Colombia, Brazil, and South Africa." *World Development* 27(4): 651–72.

Deininger, K. (2003) "Land Markets in Developing and Transition Economies: Impact of Liberalization and Implications for Future Reform." *American Journal of Agricultural Economics* 85(5): 1217–22.

Deininger, K. and H. Binswanger (1999) "The Evolution of the World Bank's Land Policy: Principles, Experience, and Future Challenges." *World Bank Research Observer* 14(2), 247–76.

Gunnarsdotter, Y. (2005) *Från arbetsgemenskap till fritidsgemenskap. Den svenska landsbygdens omvandling ur Locknevis perspektiv*. (In Swedish) PhD dissertation No. 2005:3. Uppsala: SLU.

Habtemariam K. B. (2003) "Livestock and livelihood security in the Harar highlands of Ethiopia. PhD dissertation (sammanfattning/summary). *Acta Universitatis agriculturae Sueciae*. Uppsala: SLU.

Hammar, A and B. Raftopoulos (2003) Zimbabwe's Unfinished Business: Rethinking land, state and nation" in Hammar, A., B. Raftopoulos and S. Jensen (eds) *Zimbabwe's Unfinished Business: Rethinking Land, State and Nation in the Context of Crisis*. Weaver Press.

Havnevik, K., T. Negash and A. Beyene (2006) *Of Global Concern- Rural Livelihood Dynamics and Natural Resource Governance*, Sida Studies No. 16. Stockholm: Sida.

Havnevik, K., D. Bryceson, L-E. Birgegård, P. Matondi, and A. Beyene (eds) 2008. African Agriculture and the World Bank: Development or Impoverishment? Uppsala: Nordic Africa Institute.

Hårsmar M. (2004) *Heavy Clouds but No Rain – Agricultural Growth Theories and Peasant Strategies on the Mossi Plateau, Burkina Faso. Agraria* 439. Uppsala:SLU.

Herbst, J. (1990) *State Politics in Zimbabwe*. Harare: University of Zimbabwe Press.

Kinsey, B.H. (1999) "Land Reform, Growth and Equity: Emerging Evidence from Zimbabwe's Resettlement Programme". *Journal of Southern African Studies* 25(2):173–96.

Kowero G., M. Bruce, M. Campbell and U. R. Sumaila, (2003) *Policies and Governance Structures in Woodlands of Southern Africa*. CIFOR, Indonesia.

Larsson Lidén L. (2000) *Democracy Grassroots Movements and Rural Development – Case studies from Zimbabwe, Zambia and Kerala. Agraria* 230. Uppsala: SLU.

Lindahl K. (2008) *Frame Analysis, Place Perceptions and the Politics of Natural Resource Management – Exploring a Forest Policy Controversy in Sweden*. PhD dissertation, Department of Rural Development Studies 2008:60. Uppsala: SLU.

Lund, C. (1998) *Law, Power and Politics in Niger. Land Struggles and the Rural Code*. LIT Verlag/Transaction Publishers.

Mamdani, M. (1996) *Citizen and Subject: Contemporary Africa and the Legacy of Late Colonialism*. Princeton: Princeton University Press.

Matondi, P.B. (1998) "A Review of the Land Reform Programme in Zimbabwe". Unpublished report. Uppsala: SLU.

Matondi, P.B. (2000) "A Critical Evaluation of Access to Land and Water Resources in Zimbabwe's Rural Environments." In Moyo, S. and D. Tevera (eds) *Environmental Security in Southern Africa*. Harare: Sapes Books.

Matondi, P.B. (2001) *The Struggle for Access to Land and Water Resources in Zimbabwe: The Case of Shamva District*. PhD dissertation, Department of Rural Development Studies. Uppsala: SLU.

Matondi, P.B. (2006) "Institutional and Policy Context for Social Protection in Zimbabwe: RHVP Regional Evidence-Building Agenda (REBA)." Unpublished paper.

Matondi, P.B. (2008) *The question of tenure and land rights in the resettled areas in Mazowe district in Zimbabwe. Zimbabwe*. Lands and Livelihoods Programme, CRD, Harare. Mimeo.

Matondi, P.B. and M. Munyuki-Hungwe (2006) "The Evolution of Agricultural Policy: 1990–2004." In Rukuni, M., P. Tawonezvi, and C. Eicher with M. Munyuki-Hungwe and P.B. Matondi (eds) *Zimbabwe's Agricultural Revolution* (2nd edition). Harare: University of Zimbabwe Publications.

Matondi P. B. and P. Mutopo (2011) "Attracting Foreign Direct Investment in Africa in the Context of Land Outsourcing for Biofuels and Food Security" in Matondi, P. B., K. Havnevik and A. Beyene (eds) *Biofuels, Land Grabbing and Food Security in Africa*. London: ZED Books.

Matondi, P. B., K. Havnevik and A. Beyene (2011) *Biofuels, Land Grabbing and Food Security in Africa, London*. London: ZED Books.

McKean, M. A. and E. Ostrom (1995). "Common property regimes in the forest: just a relic from the past?" *Unasylva* 46(1):3–15.

Mkandawire, T. (1995) "Fiscal Structure, State Contraction and Political Responses in Africa" in Mkandawire, T. and A. Olukoshi (eds) *Between Liberalisation and Oppression: The Politics of Structural Adjustment in Africa*. Dakar: Codesria.

Mkandawire, T. (2001) "Thinking about Developmental States in Africa", *Cambridge Journal of Economics*, Vol. 25, 289–3.

Nemarundwe, N. (2003) *Negotiating Resource Access, Institutional Arrangements for Woodlands and Water Use in Southern Zimbabwe*, PhD dissertation, Department of Rural Development Studies. Uppsala: SLU.

Okoth-Ogendo H. W. O. (1991) *Tenants of the Crown, Evolution of Agrarian Law and Institutions in Kenya*. Nairobi: African Centre for Technology Studies.

Okoth-Ogendo, H. W. O. (2007) *The last colonial question: an essay in the pathology of land administration systems in Africa*. Keynote presentation at a workshop on Norwegian land tools relevant to Africa. Oslo: 3–4 May.

Ostrom, E. (1990) *Governing the commons: the evolution of institutions for collective action*. New York: Cambridge University Press.

Ostrom, E. (1999) "Coping with tragedies of the commons". *Annual Review of Political Science*, Vol. 2: 493-535.

Palmer, R. (1990) "Land Reform in Zimbabwe, 1980–1990". *African Affairs* 89, April.

Platteau, J. P. (1995) *Reforming Land Rights in Sub-Saharan Africa: Issues of Efficiency and Equity*. Geneva: United Nations Research Institute for Social Development.

Rukuni, M. and C. Eicher (eds) (1994) *Zimbabwe Agricultural Revolution*. Harare: University of Zimbabwe Publications.

Sandström E. (2008) *Reinventing the Commons. Analysis of the Emergence of Natural Resource Management Arrangements*. PhD dissertation. Department of Rural Development Studies. Uppsala: SLU.

Scott, J. (1985) *Weapons of the Weak: Everyday Forms of Peasant Resistance*. New Haven: Yale University Press.

Shivji, I., S. Moyo, W. Ncube and D. Gunby (1998) "Draft National Land Policy for the Government of Zimbabwe" Discussion Paper. Harare: Ministry of Land and Agriculture.

Skälnes, T. (1995) *The Politics of Economic Reform in Zimbabwe: Continuity and Change in Development*. London: Macmillan.

Stoneman C. and L. Cliffe (1989) *Zimbabwe: Politics, economics and society*. London: Pinter.

Toulmin, C. and J. Quan (2000) *Evolving Land Rights, Tenure and Policy in sub-Saharan Africa*. London: International Institute for Environment and Development.

Van Zyl, J., J. Kirsten and H. P. Binswanger (1996) *Agricultural Land Reform in South Africa*. Cape Town: Oxford University Press.

Von Blackenburg, P. (1992) "The Situation of Zimbabwe's Large Commercial Farmers in a Period of Structural Change". Working Paper AEE. Department of Agricultural Economics and Extension, University of Zimbabwe.

World Bank (2008) *World Development Report: Agriculture for Development*. Washington DC: World Bank.

About the contributors

Atakilte Beyene is a senior researcher at the Nordic Africa Institute. He holds a PhD from the Swedish University of Agricultural Sciences and has worked in universities and research institutes in Sweden and Ethiopia. His research focuses on agrarian and rural institutions, natural resource management, food security and gender studies. He has conducted extensive field studies in Ethiopia and Tanzania. He has both coordinated and worked as part of interdisciplinary research projects in Nordic and African countries. His current research includes large-scale agricultural investments in Africa and their implications for local economies. Atakilte worked with Kjell Havnevik as a research student.

Deborah Fahy Bryceson received her BA and MA in geography from the University of Dar es Salaam and her DPhil in sociology from Oxford University. Her research interests have spanned food insecurity, agrarian development, rural transport, gender, structural adjustment and income diversification, artisanal mining, urbanisation and transnational families. Changing labour patterns in relation to processes of deagrarianisation and mineralisation in Africa has been her central concern since 2000. Her most recent publication (2014) is an edited collection entitled *Mining and Social Transformation in Africa: Mineralising and Democratizing Trends in Artisanal Production*, published by Routledge Studies in Development and Society.

Andrew Coulson graduated in economics from Cambridge University in 1967 and was posted as an ODI Fellow to the Ministry of Agriculture in Dar es Salaam, Tanzania. After four years there, and four more teaching in the Department of Economics at the University of Dar es Salaam, he lectured at the Project Planning Centre for Developing Countries in Bradford, England, where he wrote books and articles about Tanzania and supervised Kjell Havnevik's doctoral thesis on agriculture in the Rufiji Valley. At the Institute of Local Government Studies at the University of Birmingham, he worked on matters relating to local government in Britain. After his retirement in 2009, he started visiting Tanzania again and writing about Tanzanian political economy and agriculture. He remains an Associate of the Institute of Local Government Studies.

Stig Holmqvist is an author and documentary film producer. He works internationally and has produced 50 films and TV series, among them documentaries about Dag Hammarskjöld, the Swedish explorers Sten Bergman and Sven Hedin, as well as about life in Dadaab, the world's largest refugee camp, located in northern Kenya. He has written books of fiction as well as specialist literature, mainly dealing with Africa, where he has followed and documented the life of the Barabaig pastoralists of Tanzania for more than 30 years. He has also had consultancies for international organisations such as UNICEF and UNHCR.

Mats Hårsmar is programme manager at the Swedish Expert Group for Aid Studies (EBA), as well as a researcher associated with the Stockholm International Water Institute (SIWI). Previously he held positions as researcher, research leader and temporary director at the Nordic Africa Institute and as chief analyst for development policies at the Swedish Ministry for Foreign Affairs. He has also served as head secretary for the Expert Group for Development Issues (EGDI) in the same ministry. Hårsmar earned his PhD at the Swedish University of Agricultural Sciences in 2004. His research interests include technical change in small-scale African agriculture, poverty issues as well as wider issues of social and economic development in sub-Saharan Africa.

Aida C. Isinika is a professor of agricultural economics at the Institute of Continuing Education (ICE), Sokoine University of Agriculture in Tanzania. She has over 40 years of working experience in the fields of agriculture and rural development and as an academic. She is editor of the *Journal of Continuing Education and Extension*. She has been district agricultural officer and in 2008-10 coordinated an agricultural value chain development project for Oxfam (GB) Tanzania. Her publications have focused on production, productivity and resource-use efficiency. Her other interests include efficiency in land administration, land markets and gender.

Anna Kikwa has a background as teacher and banker and has since 2004 been working as an activist and as head of programmes and administration at the Tanzania Gender Network Programme (TGNP), a local NGO working on gender issues. She also facilitates training programmes designed to empower grassroots members of TGNP to become effective in pursuing their rights, including land rights. She has participated in seminars and advocacy activities focusing on land and gender issues.

Prosper B. Matondi is the executive director of the Ruzivo Trust, a not-for-profit organisation based in Harare, Zimbabwe. He holds a PhD in rural development from the Swedish University of Agricultural Sciences in Uppsala. He has more than 20 years of experience researching issues related to land, natural resource management, and environmental policy and planning in Zimbabwe, and, since 2008, on renewable energy. He has published numerous book chapters, and his latest publication is *Zimbabwe's Fast Track Land Reform*, published in London by Zed Books (2012). Prosper has been a policy advisor to the private sector, civil society and local authorities.

Herman Musahara is the executive director of OSSREA (the Organisation for Social Science Research in Eastern and Southern Africa). He holds an MA in economics from the University of Dar es Salaam and PhD in development studies from University of the Western Cape. He is a former dean of Faculty of

Economics and Management and acting vice-rector (academics) at the former National University of Rwanda. He has taught at postgraduate level, conducted research, undertaken consultancies and published in several social science fields. He was for many years a research assistant to Kjell Havnevik in Tanzania.

Tekeste Negash is professor emeritus. He has lived and worked in Eritrea, Ethiopia, Italy, Great Britain and Sweden. He has written numerous articles and books on Italian colonialism, Eritrean and Ethiopian social and political history, and on education policies, especially in Ethiopia. He is the author of *Italian Colonialism in Eritrea* (1987)**;** *Eritrea and Ethiopia: The Federal Experience*, (1997); *Brothers at War: Making Sense of the Eritrean-Ethiopian War,* with Kjetil Tronvoll (2000); *LÉtiopia entra nel terzo millennio: Saggio di storia sociale e politiche dell'istruzione* (2009).

Bertil Odén has a Master's degree in social sciences from Stockholm University and a Ph. Licenciate degree from the Department of Peace and Development Research, Gothenburg University. He has worked for the Swedish International Development Cooperation Agency as an economist, evaluator and advisor. He has been advisor to the Ministry of Planning in Mozambique and the Ministry of Finance in Tanzania. He was deputy secretary to the Swedish Parliamentary Commission on Development Cooperation. He headed a research and policy analysis programme on Southern Africa at the Nordic Africa Institute and was secretary to the Expert Group on Development Issues (EGDI) at the Ministry for Foreign Affairs. He has written and contributed to a large number of academic and popular science publications, mainly on Southern Africa's political economy and on development cooperation issues.

Terje Oestigaard (Dr. art) is a senior researcher and leader of the Rural and Agrarian Change, Property and Resources programme cluster at the Nordic Africa Institute, and docent in archaeology at Uppsala University. He has conducted fieldwork in Bangladesh, Egypt, Ethiopia, Greece, India, Jordan, Nepal, Palestine, Tanzania and Uganda. His recent books include *Religion at Work in Globalised Traditions – Rainmaking, Witchcraft and Christianity in Tanzania* (2014); *A History of Water: Water and Urbanization,* series III, vol. 1 (2014), co-edited with Terje Tvedt; *Water, Christianity and the Rise of Capitalism* (2013); and, together with Gedef Abawa Firew, *The Source of the Blue Nile – Water Rituals and Traditions in the Lake Tana Region* (2013).

Opira Otto works as a lecturer at the Department of Urban and Rural Development, Swedish University of Agricultural Sciences (SLU) – Uppsala. He earned his PhD in Rural Development from SLU in 2013 for his research on understanding the role and influence of social institutions on labour transactions in crop farming in Midwestern Uganda. Hence, Opira's research interests revolve around analyses of institutional intervention for resolving policy and livelihoods challenges in the context of uncertainties, including climate change. His current research interest is on land rights and the future of food and farming in the drier areas of north-eastern Uganda. His particular focus however, shall be on exploring the potentials of edible insects for improved food security and adaptation to climate change.

Rune Skarstein is associate professor emeritus at the Department of Economics, Norwegian University of Science and Technology (NTNU), Dragvoll campus, Trondheim, and associate at the Nordic Africa Institute, Uppsala. His primary research focus is development economics and macroeconomics. He has spent long periods doing research in Tanzania and has been a visiting researcher at universities and research institutes in Argentina, India, Mexico, Germany and Austria.

Michael Ståhl holds a PhD in political science from Uppsala University and a docent degree in Water Management Studies at Linköping University. He has 40 years of experience in research and development cooperation in Africa. He was director at the Nordic Africa Institute in the early 1980s and thereafter held management positions at the Swedish Agency for Research Cooperation (SAREC) and the Swedish International Development Cooperation Agency (Sida). In the 1990s, he was director of a regional environmental programme in East Africa and then head of the Swedish development cooperation programme in Ethiopia. Between 2002 and 2010 he was director of the International Foundation for Science. He has published extensively on natural resource management issues in Africa.

Kjell Havnevik – curriculum vitae and major publications

Born September 1948 in Aalesund, Norway

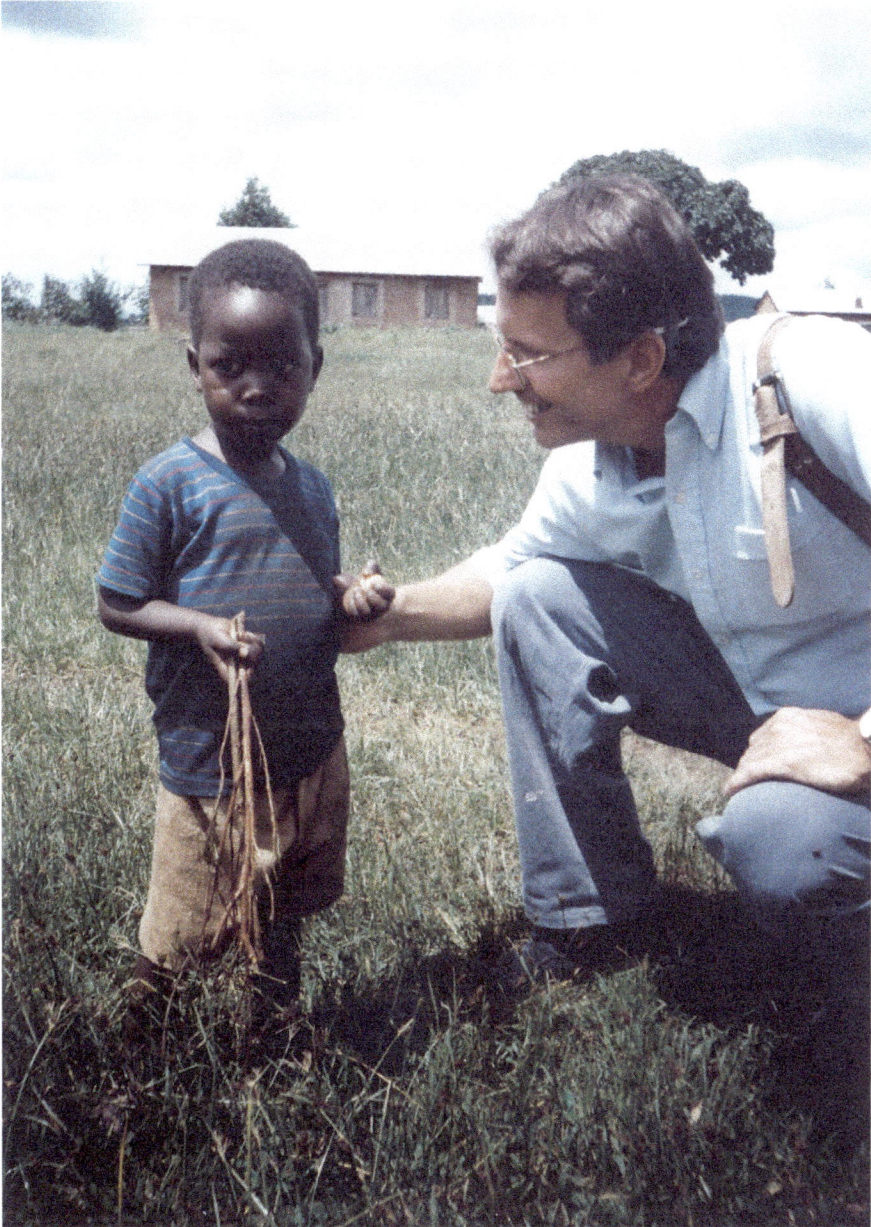

Village visit in Iringa Region, Tanzania, January 1993.

Academic qualifications

1970–1974   Norwegian School of Business Administration and Economics (Civilekonom), Bergen.

1984–1988   PhD, Postgraduate School of Studies in Planning, University of Bradford, UK: *State Intervention and Peasant Response in Tanzania* (principal supervisor: A. Coulson).

Professional positions

1975–85   Researcher and Senior Researcher – Chr. Michelsen Institute, CMI, Bergen.

1978–80   Research Fellow – Bureau of Resource Assessment and Land Use Planning, BRALUP, University of Dar es Salaam (currently Institute of Resource Assessment, IRA), Tanzania.

1985–87   Research Fellow – Nordic Africa Institute, Uppsala.

1987–88   Senior Researcher – Centre for Development Studies, University of Bergen, Bergen.

1988–1992   Head of Nordic Research Group – Nordic Africa Institute, Uppsala.

1992–1996   Independent researcher, advisor and part time lecturer at Agder University College, Agder.

1996–2005   Professor of Rural Development – Department for Rural Development Studies (currently the Department of Urban and Rural Studies), Swedish University of Agricultural Sciences, SLU, Uppsala.

2005–2008   Adjunct Professor – Department for Rural Development Studies, SLU, Uppsala.

2005–2015   Senior Researcher and Head of Agrarian Research Cluster (until 2013) – Nordic Africa Institute, Uppsala.

2005–present Adjunct Professor in Development Studies – Agder University, Agder.

Academic committees and reviews

Discussant and examiner of PhD dissertations and assessment of honorary doctorates at various universities:

Norwegian University of Life Sciences (NMBU); Norwegian Technical and Natural Science University, NTNU; Gothenburg University; Uppsala University; Swedish University of Agricultural Sciences (SLU); Linköping University; Stockholm University; Lund University; The School of Architecture and the Built Environment, KTH, Stockholm; Roskilde University Centre; University of Oxford; The Warsaw School of Economics; and The University of Dar es Salaam.

Committees for evaluation, reorganisation and creation of development related research and education:

The University of Bergen; The Norwegian Technical and Natural Science University (NTNU); Uppsala University; The Swedish University of Agricultural Sciences (SLU); Centre for Environment and Development (CEMUS), Uppsala University; University of Oslo; NOKUT, Oslo; The Volkswagen Foundation, Hannover; the Master's programme in Development Research and Practice, MADRAT, SLU; the Nordic Research School on Local Dynamics, NOLD (cooperation of five Nordic universities); The Research School at the Centre for Development and Environment (SUM) University of Oslo; The National Rural Development Master's Programme, Vietnam.

Reviews and evaluations for research councils and national and international organisations, NGOs, networks and editorial councils;

UN Habitat, Nairobi; UN Development Programme (UNDP) New York; UN Food and Agricultural Organization (FAO) Rome; International Foundation for Agricultural Development (IFAD), Rome; International Foundation for Science (IFS) Stockholm; The Swedish Agency for Research Cooperation (SAREC) Stockholm; The Swedish Research Council, Stockholm; The Swedish Bank Centenary Foundation, Stockholm; The Swedish International Development Cooperation Agency (Sida); The Swedish Ministry for Foreign Affairs, Stockholm; The Swedish FAO Committee; The Swedish International Agricultural Network Initiative (SIANI); The Hammarskjöld Foundation, Uppsala; The Africa Groups in Sweden; Vi Agroforestry Programme, Stockholm; the Norwegian Research Council (Development Paths in the South and FRIMUF); the Norwegian Agency for International Development (NORAD); The Ministry for Development Cooperation, Norway; Forum for Development Studies (editorial committee), Oslo; Vardöger (editorial council), Trondheim; Fellesrådet for det sörlige Afrika, Norway; the Danish International Development Agency (Danida) Copenhagen; The Small Industry Development Organization and The Tanzanian Ministry for Industries and Trade, Dar es Salaam.

Principal supervisor of Doctoral theses at the Swedish University of Agricultural Sciences (SLU):

2000. Lisbeth Larsson Lidén *Democracy, Grassroots Movements and Rural Development – Case Studies from Zimbabwe, Zambia and Kerala.* Agraria 230, SLU.

2001. Prosper B. Matondi, *The Struggles for Access to Land and Water Resources in Zimbabwe – The Case of Shamva District.* Agraria 297, SLU.

2003. Melaku Bekele, *Forest Property Rights, the Role of the State and Institutional Exigency: The Ethiopian Experience*. Agraria 409, SLU.

2003. Atakilte Beyene, *Soil Conservation, Land Use and Property Rights in Northern Ethiopia. Understanding Environmental Change in Smallholder Farming Systems*. Agraria 395, SLU.

2003. Nontokozo Nemarundwe, *Negotiating Resource Access – Institutional Arrangements for Woodlands and Water Use in Southern Zimbabwe*. Agraria 408, SLU.

2004. Mats Hårsmar, *Heavy Clouds But No Rain - Agricultural Growth Theories and Peasant Strategies on the Mossi Plateau, Burkina Faso*. Agraria 439, SLU.

2005. Seema Arora-Jonsson, *Unsettling the Order. Gendered Subjects and Grassroots Activism in Two Forest Communities*. Doctoral Thesis No. 2005:48, SLU.

2005. Yvonne Gunnarsdotter, *Från arbetsgemenskap till fritidsgemenskap. Den svenska landsbygdens omvandling ur Locknevis perspektiv*. Doctoral Thesis No. 2005:3, SLU.

2008. Karin Beland Lindahl, *Frame Analysis, Place Perceptions and the Politics of Natural Resource Management – Exploring a forest policy controversy in Sweden*. Doctoral Thesis No. 2008:60, SLU.

2008. Emil Sandström, *Reinventing the Commons – Exploring the Emergence of Local Natural Resource Management Arrangements*. Doctoral Thesis No. 2008:48, SLU.

2009. Sen Hoang Thi, *Gains and Losses: Devolution of Forestry Land and Natural Forest. A study of forest allocation in North Central Coast, Vietnam*. Doctoral Thesis No. 2009:72, SLU, Uppsala (supervision during the early phase of thesis).

2013. Deborah Duveskog, *Farmer Field Schools as a transformative learning space in the rural African setting*. Doctoral Thesis No. 2013:47, SLU (supervision during funding and the early phase of thesis).

2013. Opira Otto, *Trust, Identity and Beer – Institutional Arrangements for Agricultural Labour in Isunga village in Kiryandongo District, Midwestern Uganda*. Doctoral Thesis No. 2013:76, SLU (supervision during funding and the early phase of thesis).

Publications of books, articles, major studies and evaluations over time

2015. Havnevik, K., T. Oestigaard, E. Tobisson and T. Virtanen (eds) *Framing African Development – Challenging Concepts*. Leiden and Boston: Brill.

2015. "Framing African Development – Challenging Concepts." In Havnevik et al. (eds) *Framing African Development – Challenging Concepts*. Leiden and Boston: Brill.

2015. "From Food Security to Food Sovereignty." In Havnevik et al. (eds) *Framing African Development – Challenging Concepts*. Leiden and Boston: Brill.

2015   (forthcoming). "The Current Afro-Optimism – A Realistic Image of Africa?" In *FLEKS – Scandinavian Journal of Intercultural Theory and Practice*, Oslo and Akershus University College of Applied Sciences. Special edition in honour of Tore Linné Eriksen.

2014.   Abdallah, J., L. Engström, K. Havnevik and L. Salomonsson "Large Scale Land Acquisitions in Tanzania." In Kaag, M. and A. Zoomers, *Land Grabbing – beyond the hype*. London and New York: ZED Books pp. 36–54.

2014.   *Responsible agricultural investments in developing countries - how to make principles and guidelines effective*. Study conducted for the Swedish FAO Committee. Stockholm: Publication Series 9, Swedish FAO Committee and Swedish Ministry of Rural Affairs.

2014.   "Bannlys alla politiska beslut som ger mer klimatutsläpp." (in Swedish). Authored by 23 researchers based in Sweden in *DN Debatt, Dagens Nyheter*, May 10.

2014.   Havnevik, K. and B.M. Fernandes (coordinators),"Inquiry into alternative sustainable global development models and the role of agriculture and rural development: an interdisciplinary comparative study across three continents." Application for international research network submitted to the Swedish Research Council in April 2014 by universities and research institutes in Colombia, Bolivia, Brazil, Tanzania, Mocambique, Norway and Sweden. Appendix A summary, 8 pages.

2013.   " 'Science for science' or 'science for social relevance?' Some observations and reflections on African environment." In Berge, L. and I. Taddia (eds) *Themes in Modern African History and Culture. Festschrift for Tekeste Negash*. Libreria universitaria.it edizioni, Italy, pp. 257–263.

2013.   Havnevik, K. and L. Engström "Inclusive growth through agricultural development." Memorandum prepared for the Nordic-African Foreign Ministers' Conference, Finland, June 15–16, 2013. Uppsala: Nordic Africa Institute.

2013.   "Afro-optimismen en falsk bild." (in Swedish) *UNT Debatt, Upsala Nya Tidning*, 24 June.

2012.   "Varför brister politikerna när det gäller miljömålen?" (in Swedish). Authored by 19 researchers based in Sweden in *DN Debatt, Dagens Nyheter*, 27 December.

2012.   "Färre fattiga, men fler hungriga." (in Swedish) *UNT Debatt, Upsala Nya Tidning*, 12 September.

2011.   Dietz, T., K. Havnevik, M. Kaag and T. Oestigaard (eds) *African Engagements. Africa Negotiating an Emerging Multipolar World*. Leiden and Boston: Brill. 388 p.

2011.   "African engagements: on whose terms?" In Dietz et al. (eds), pp. 1–35.

2011.   Matondi, P., K. Havnevik and A. Beyene (eds) *Biofuels, Land Grabbing and Food Security in Africa*. London and New York: Zed Books. 230 p.

2011.   Matondi, P., K. Havnevik and A. Beyene "Introduction: biofuels, food security and land grabbing in Africa." In Matondi et al. (eds) 2011, pp. 1–20.

2011. "Grabbing of African lands for energy and food: implications for land rights, food security and smallholders", in Matondi et al. (eds) 2011, Chapter 1, pp. 20–44.

2011. Havnevik, K. and H. Haaland "Biofuel, land and environmental issues: the case of SEKAB's biofuel plans in Tanzania." In Matondi et al. (eds), chapter 6, pp. 106–134.

2011. Matondi, P., K. Havnevik and A. Beyene "Conclusions: land grabbing, smallholder farmers and the meaning of agro-investor-driven agrarian change in Africa." In Matondi et al. (eds), pp. 176–196.

2011. Havnevik, K. and E. Yglesias "Community forestry in Babati, Tanzania". Production of a research-based DVD. Uppsala: Nordic Africa Institute and Sokoine University of Agriculture, Tanzania.

2010. Havnevik, K. and A. Isinika (eds) *Tanzania in Transition – from Nyerere to Mkapa.* Dar es Salaam: Mkuki na Nyota Publishers in cooperation with the Nordic Africa Institute and Sokoine University of Agriculture, Tanzania. 276 p.

2010. Havnevik, K. and A. Isinika "Tanzania in Transition – To What?" In Havnevik and Isinika (eds), pp. 1–19.

2010. "A Historical Framework for Analysing Current Tanzanian Transitions: The Post-Independence Model. Nyerere's Ideas and Some Interpretations." In Havnevik and Isinika (eds), pp. 19–57.

2010. "Postscript: Tanzania in Transition – Summary and Trends 2005–2010." In Havnevik and Isinika (eds), pp. 265–279.

2010. Adams, W., C. Brun and K. Havnevik, "Doctoral Thesis. Mattias Tagseth 2010. Studies of the Waterscape of Kilimanjaro, Tanzania: Water Management in Hill Furrow Irrigation", *In Norwegian Journal of Geography* Vol. 64, pp. 172–173.

2010. Trang Thi Huy Nhat, L. Chiwona-Karltun, K. Havnevik and B. Ogle, "Tackling Household Food Insecurity: The Experience of Vietnam." In *Asian Journal of Agriculture and Development,* Vol. 5, issue 2, pp. 41–56.

2009. Korsnes, O., A. Rabo, K. Havnevik and I.S. Gilhus *"Evaluation of Unifob Global."* Bergen: University of Bergen.

2008. "The Research Programme 'Globalisation and Marginalisation – Development Paths in the South': Some Reflections." In *Forum for Development Studies,* Norwegian Institute for Foreign Affairs, NUPI, June.

2008. *Establishment of an Agro-Forestry Academy in East Africa.* Study conducted for Vi Agro-forestry, Stockholm and Kisumu.

2007. Havnevik, K., D. Bryceson, L.-E. Birgegård, P. Matondi and A. Beyene (eds) *African Agriculture and the World Bank.* Uppsala: Nordic Africa Institute, Policy Dialogue No. 1, 75 pages.

2007. "The Suledo Forest and the Burunge Wildlife Management Area: Natural Resource Management Interventions in the Land Management Programme (LAMP) 2002–2007". Study conducted for ORGUT, Stockholm.

2006. Havnevik, K., T. Negash and A. Beyene (eds) *Of Global Concern – Rural Livelihood Dynamics and Natural Resource Governance*. Stockholm: Sida Studies no. 16. 258 p.

2006. Havnevik, K., T. Negash and A. Beyene "Introduction to Rural Livelihood and Governance Issues." In Havnevik et al. eds, pp. 11–31.

2006. "Successful Community- Based Forest Management in Northern Tanzania: Reflections and Theoretical Implications." In Havnevik et al. (eds), pp. 165–196.

2006. "Dubbelt svek drabbar Afrikas bönder" (in Swedish) *UNT Debatt, Upsala Nya Tidning*, March 9.

2005. Nemarundwe, N., K. Havnevik et al. *Access to Natural Resources for Sustainable Livelihoods: A synthesis of lessons learned from three case studies in southern Zimbabwe.* Study presented to the International Development Research Centre, IDRC, Canada.

2005. "Experiences with Community Based Forest Management in Babati District, Tanzania." In *Currents* No. 31/32, October, pp. 37–42. Uppsala: SLU.

2005. Bryceson, I., K. Havnevik et al. *Mid-Term Review of Natural Resource Management Programme, Tanzania.* Dar es Salaam: NORAD/Norwegian Embassy.

2005. *Sustainability Analysis of the VI-Agroforestry Programme in Kenya, Uganda and Tanzania.* Study conducted for Vi Agroforestry Programme, Stockholm.

2005. "Alternativ modell för Vietnam?" (in Swedish) *UNT Debatt, Upsala Nya Tidning.* May 13.

2004. Odén, B. and K. Havnevik "Jeffrey Sachs och Milleniemålen" (in Swedish). In Omvärlden, Sida, Stockholm. April.

2004. "Lärdomar av Nordens samarbete med Tanzania – Analys av 40 års utvecklingssamarbete" (in Swedish). In Habari 4/2004, Swedish-Tanzanian Association SVETAN, Stockholm, pp. 20–22.

2002. Havnevik, K., M. Hårsmar and E. Sandström, *Rural Development and the Private Sector in Sub-Saharan Africa*. Stockholm: Sida/UTV: 2002–2003. 104 pages.

2002. "Sub-Saharan Africa, the World Bank and Poverty." In Hallencreutz, E. (ed), *Gender, Poverty and Church Involvement*. MISSION No. 20, pp. 101–112. Uppsala: Swedish Institute of Mission Research.

2001. "Villagisation in Tanzania and possible lessons for Rwanda." (in Norwegian). Festskrift for Rune Skarstein. *Vardöger*, Nr. 26, Trondheim, pp. 175–195.

2001. "Sustainability and local dynamics in a global perspective; rural development in Sweden." In *Proceedings from international rural development conference,* Worriken, Belgium.

2001. Havnevik, K., Y. Gunnarsdotter, A. Setterwall, A. Tivell et al. *Methods for rural development – is that sufficient?* (in Swedish) Research-based assessment of the Method leader programme in Northern Sweden. Umeå: Centre for Development Research, SLU and Centre for Evaluation Research, University of Umeå, 177 pages and annexes.

2001. "Multi-functionality – A new trend with opportunities for everyone?" in *Forest, Trees and People Newsletter,* No. 44, April, pp. 74–76. Uppsala: SLU.

2001 Havnevik, K., J. Myrdal, R. Gustavsson and Y. Gunnarsdotter, "Ämnesområdet Landsbygdsutveckling vid SLU" (in Swedish). Uppsala: JLT Faculty, SLU.

2001 Havnevik, K., G. Monela, E. Röskaft et al., *Mid-Term Review of the Natural Resource Management Programme, Tanzania.* Norwegian International Development Agency, NORAD. 140 pages plus annexes.

2001. "Se Jorden. Ett samtal kring rymden, vetenskapen och människan." (in Swedish). In Not 1, Sigtunastiftelsen, pp. 13–15.

2000. Havnevik, K., T. Halvorsen et. al, *Assessment of 6 Norwegian Masters' Programmes.* Study conducted for the Senter for Internasjonale Studier, SIU, University of Bergen.

2000. Havnevik, K., M. Rwebangira and A. Tivell *Formative Evaluation of the Land Management Programme in Tanzania.* Stockholm: Sida Evaluation 00/4, Department of Natural Resources and the Environment. 43 pages and annexes.

2000. Havnevik, K. and E. Sandström (eds) *Institutional Context of Poverty Eradication in Rural Africa.* Proceedings from a seminar in tribute of the 20th Anniversary of the International Fund for Agricultural Development, IFAD, Rome. Uppsala: Nordic Africa Institute. 80 pages.

2000. "Introduction." In Havnevik and Sandström (eds), Nordic Africa Institute, pp. 7–15.

2000. "The Institutional Heart of Rural Africa – An Issue Overlooked." In Havnevik and Sandström (eds), Nordic Africa Institute, pp. 38–50.

2000. "Agricultural production and rural development – some necessary reflections." (in Swedish). In *Forskningsnytt,* nr. 7–8, pp. 14–15. Centrum för Uthålligt Lantbruk.

2000. "Agricultural Production and Rural Development." (in Swedish). In *Landsbygd i Västerbotten,* nr. 6, pp. 28–30. Hushållningssällskapet i Västerbotten, Umeå.

1999. Havnevik, K. and M. Hårsmar, *Diversified Future – An Institutional Approach to Rural Development in Tanzania.* Expert Group on Development Studies, EGDI, Swedish Ministry for Foreign Affairs, Stockholm. 120 pages.

1999. Havnevik, K. and P. Malmer, *Nordic Rural Development Research.* Tema Nord 1999:593, Nordic Council of Ministers, Copenhagen, 63 pages.

1997. "The Land Question in Sub-Saharan Africa." In *IRD Currents,* No. 15, December, pp. 4–10. SLU.

1997. Havnevik, K. and R. Skarstein, "Tradition, Land-Tenure, State-Peasant Relations and Productivity in Tanzanian Agriculture." In Bhaduri, A. and R. Skarstein (eds) *Agricultural Productivity and Economic Development*. London: Edwin Elgar, pp. 183–215.

1997. Alting, L., K. Havnevik and P. J. Schei, "Evaluation of the Centre for Environment and Development, the Norwegian University of Technology and Natural Science." NTNU, Trondheim, April.

1997. Gibbon, D., K. Havnevik and J. Jiggins, "Science, Society and Survival". *Inaugural Lecture*. Uppsala: Department of Rural Development Studies, SLU, 24 p.

1996. "Africa at a cross-road." In *Development Today*, Oslo, No. 19.

1996. "Tanzania with Outlooks to Kenya and Uganda." Project 2015, Long Term Development Prospects and Sida's Aid Management. Stockholm: Sida, Department for East and West Africa, 33 pages.

1996. Havnevik, K. and B. Van Arkadie (eds) *Domination or Dialogue? Experiences and Prospects for African Development Cooperation*. Uppsala: Nordic Africa Institute, 130 pages.

1996. Denninger, M., K. Havnevik and M. Brdarski, *Food Security in East and Southern Africa*. Stockholm: Sida 257 pages.

1995. "Pressing Land Tenure Issues in Tanzania in Light of Experiences from Other Sub-Saharan African Countries." In *Forum for Development Studies,* No. 2. Oslo: Norwegian Institute of International Affairs, NUPI, and the Norwegian Association for Development Research, pp. 267–285.

1995. "Knowledge for Development." In Rudebeck, L. and T. Negash (eds) *Dimensions of Development with emphasis on Africa*. Uppsala: Nordic Africa Institute, March.

1995. "Forskning med Relevans for Norsk Bistand: Rammebetingelser, Aktuelle Tema og Utövere" (in Norwegian) in *Norsk Nord/Sör –politikk, bistanden og de kunnskapsmessige utfordringene*. Oslo: The Norwegian Research Council.

1994. "The new framework for developing countries – consequences for trade, development assistance, environment and development" (in Norwegian). Study for the Program Division, the Norwegian Foreign Ministry. 55 pages.

1994. "Structural Adjustment in a blind alley." (in Swedish). In Nilsson, H. (ed.) *Kris och Marknad i södra Afrika*. Afrikagruppernas Årskrönika 1994, pp. 31–41. Stockholm: Afrikagrupperna,.

1993. Gibbon, P., K. Havnevik and K. Hermele, *A blighted Harvest. The World Bank and African Agriculture in the 1980s*. Oxford: James Currey, and Red Sea Press.

1993. *Tanzania – the Limits to Development from Above*. Uppsala: The Nordic Africa Institute in cooperation with Mkuki na Nyota Publishers, Dar es Salaam. 343 pages.

1993. Havnevik, K., J. Hultin and T. Negash, "Evaluation of the Programme Peasant Production and Development in Ethiopia, PPDE". The Centre for Environment and Development, the University of Trondheim. 60 pages.

1993. "Assessment of Third World Forum's, TWF, research programme." Report presented to the Research Office. Oslo: the Norwegian Foreign Ministry, 19 pages.

1993. "Tanzania 1998–1993. Experiences from Nordic development assistance -based on conducted evaluations and in light of historic and actual development trends." (in Norwegian). Report presented to the Evaluation Office. Oslo: the Norwegian Foreign Ministry. 53 pages.

1992. "Aid cooperation: What kind of partnership? Experiences with technical assistance to Tanzania and East Africa." In *Forum for Utviklingsstudier* (Forum for Development Studies), nr. 2. Oslo: NUPI, pp. 163–180.

1992. "The failure of two decades of structural adjustment in Zambia." In *Nytt från Nordiska Afrikainstitutet*, nr. 29. Uppsala: Nordic Africa Institute, pp. 23–41.

1991. "Some perspectives on economic and democratic reforms in Tanzania" (in Norwegian) in *Nytt från Nordiska Afrikainstitutet*, nr. 28. Uppsala: Nordic Africa Institute, pp. 27–36.

1991. "Tanzania's path" (in Norwegian) in Fredskorpsforum nr. 1. Oslo: Norsk Fredskorpssamband, pp. 4–9.

1990. Havnevik, K., B. Odén and R. Skarstein (eds) *Nordic Commodity Import Support to Tanzania: Experiences and Issues*. Uppsala: Nordic Africa Institute, 64 pages.

1990. Havnevik, K., B. Odén, R. Skarstein and S. Wangwe "Nordic commodity import support to Tanzania: A follow-up study." In Havnevik et al. (eds), 1990, pp. 40–59.

1990. "The Strategy of the World Bank for Sub-Saharan Africa: Is it sustainable?"(in Norwegian) In *Vardöger*, June, pp. 121–127. Trondheim.

1989. "Norwegian development assistance to Tanzania in growth and crisis: Experiences from the 1970s and 1980s." (in Norwegian). In *Forum for Utviklingsstudier*, No. 1 pp. 65–89. Oslo: Norwegian Institute of International Affairs, NUPI.

1989. Mothander, B., F. Kjärby and K. Havnevik *Farm Implements for small-scale farmers in Tanzania*. Uppsala: Nordic Africa Institute, 214 pages.

1988. *State Intervention and Peasant Response in Tanzania – mechanisms of government surplus appropriation, their effects on agricultural and non-agricultural production in the Rufiji Valley, Tanzania and their implications for the proposed Stiegler's Gorge multipurpose dam.* PhD dissertation, Postgraduate School of Studies in Planning, University of Bradford, UK, 343 pages and references.

1988.   Havnevik, K., F. Kjärby, R. Meena, R. Skarstein and U. Vuorela *Tanzania Country Study and Norwegian Aid Review* (in English and Norwegian). Background studies by Hofstad, O., B. J. Ndulu, S. Wangwe, I. Shivji, B. Mbwana, B. Odén, T. L. Eriksen and B. Bjorvatn. Center for Development Studies, University of Bergen, 366 pages.

1988.   Skarstein, R., K. Havnevik and W. D. S. Mmbaga, *Norwegian Commodity Import Support to Tanzania – Background, Design and Implications.* NTH-Trykk, Trondheim. 329 pages.

1988.   Skarstein, R., K. Havnevik and W. D. S. Mmbaga, *Norwegian Commodity Import Support to Tanzania: Summary Report and Recommendations.* Evaluation Report no. 4.88. Oslo: Royal Ministry of Foreign Affairs, 93 pages.

1988.   "Pengefondet og Verdensbanken i Afrika" (in Norwegian) in *Samtiden*, nr. 2, pp. 52–58. Oslo.

1987.   Havnevik, K. (ed.) *The IMF and the World Bank in Africa. Conditionality, impact and alternatives.* Seminar Proceeding No. 18. Uppsala: Nordic Africa Institute.

1987.   "Introduction" in Havnevik (ed.), pp. 9–25.

1986.   Boesen, J., K. Havnevik, J. Koponen and R. Odgaard (eds) *Tanzania – Crisis and Struggle for Survival. Uppsala:* Nordic Africa Institute, 325 pages.

1986.   "A resource overlooked – crafts and small-scale industries" in Boesen et al. (eds), pp. 269–293.

1985.   Havnevik, K, R. Skarstein and S. Wangwe, *Small Scale Industrial Sector Study: Review of Experiences and Recommendations for the Future.* Dar es Salaam: The Ministry of Industries and Trade, 313 pages.

1985.   "Some observations on the empirical foundation of theories of underdevelopment with particular reference to Tanzania." In *The Journal of Social Studies* No. 29, Dacca, Bangladesh, pp. 55–67.

1985.   Havnevik, K. and R. Skarstein, "Agricultural decline and foreign aid in Tanzania." DERAP Working Papers, A 341, CMI, Bergen, 28 pp.

1985.   Havnevik, K. and R. Skarstein, "Tilbakegangen i det tanzanianske jordbruket" (in Norwegian) in *Landsbruksökonomisk Forum,* 3:3, pp. 64–69.

1983.   Havnevik, K. and R. Skarstein, "Some notes on agricultural backwardness in Tanzania" in Parkinson, J. R. (ed.) *Poverty and Aid.* Oxford: Basil Blackwell, pp. 151–163.

1983.   "Analysis of rural production and incomes, Rufiji District, Tanzania." Institute of Resource Assessment. IRA research paper No. 3, April.

1983.   Havnevik, K. and J. M. J. Mwene-Milao "Programme for assistance to crafts and small scale industries, Rufiji District – Tanzania: Main Report". Study conducted for the Small Industries Development Organization (SIDO), Tanzania. Bergen: DERAP Publication No. 174, CMI.

1983. Havnevik, K. and A. Ofstad, "Norwegian industrial establishments in developing countries – contributions to a development theoretical perspective." (in Norwegian). In Havnevik, K. and A. Ofstad (eds) *The internationalization of Norwegian industry directed towards developing countries.* Bergen: DERAP Publication no. 149, CMI, pp. 43–56.

1982. "Need for a comprehensive assessment of Tanzanian development" (in Norwegian) in *Nörkontakt*, nr. 6. Oslo: NORAD, pp. 9–11.

1982. Havnevik, K. (ed.) *Development problems in Tanzania.* Bergen: DERAP Working Paper, A 250, CMI, 86 pages.

1982. "Agricultural development in Tanzania." In Havnevik (ed.) 1982, pp. 49–60.

1980. *Economy and Organization in Rufiji District: The case of crafts and extractive activities.* Research Paper no. 65, Bureau of Resource Assessment and Land Use Planning, BRALUP, the University of Dar es Salaam, Tanzania, xii, 207 pages.

1980. "Tanzania in the 1970s: Agriculture, industry, external economy, state and economic crisis." (in Norwegian). In *Forum for Utviklingsstudier* No. 9–10, pp. 20–53. Oslo: Norwegian Institute for International Affairs, NUPI.

1979. *Charcoal and cashewnut production in Rufiji; conflicting production objectives.* Service Paper no. 79/13. Bureau of Resource Assessment and Land Use Planning, BRALUP, the University of Dar es Salaam, Tanzania, 19 pp.

1978. *The Stiegler's Gorge Multipurpose Project: 1961–1978.* DERAP Working Paper, A 131. CMI, Bergen/Dar es Salaam, 41 pp.

1978. "Industrial strategies in Latin America: Experiences." In Worm, K. (ed.) *Industrialization, development and the demands for a new International Economic Order.* Köbenhavns Universitets Institutt for Samfundsfag, pp. 133–154.

1977. *Samir Amin's Theory for Underdevelopment.* Bergen: DERAP Publication nr. 68, CMI, pp. 42–50.

1975. *An Assessment of Norconsult's Stiegler's Gorge Report* (in Norwegian). Bergen: DERAP Working Paper, A 71, CMI.

www.ingramcontent.com/pod-product-compliance
Lightning Source LLC
Chambersburg PA
CBHW061227270326
41928CB00025B/3415